Secrets of the Undergroundtrader

Advanced Methods for Short-Term and Swing Trading Any Market

Jea Yu
Russell Lockhart, Ph.D.

McGraw-Hill

New York   Chicago   San Francisco
Lisbon   London   Madrid   Mexico City
Milan   New Delhi   San Juan   Seoul
Singapore   Sydney   Toronto

The *McGraw·Hill* Companies

1 2 3 4 5 6 7 8 9 0   AGM/AGM   0 9 8 7 6 5 4 3

ISBN #0-07-141737-0

This publication is designed to provide accurate and authoritative information in regard to the subject matter covered. It is sold with the understanding that neither the author nor the publisher is
engaged in rendering legal, accounting, futures/securities trading, or other professional service. If
legal advice or other expert assistance is required, the services of a competent professional person
should be sought.

> —*From a Declaration of Principles jointly adopted by a Committee*
> *of the American Bar Association and a Committee of Publishers*

McGraw-Hill books are available at special quantity discounts to use as premiums and sales promotions, or for use in corporate training programs. For more information, please write to the Director
of Special Sales, Professional Publishing, McGraw-Hill, Two Penn Plaza, New York, NY 10121-
2298. Or contact your local bookstore.

Library of Congress Cataloging-in-Publication Data
Yu, Jea.
   Secrets of the undergroundtrader : advanced methods for short-term and swing trading any mar-
ket / by Jea Yu, Russell Lockhart.
      p. cm.
   ISBN 0-07-141737-0 (alk. paper)
   1. Electronic trading of securities. 2. Day trading (Securities) 3.
Speculation. 4. Stocks. 5. Investments. I. Lockhart, Russell. II.
Title.
 HG4515.95.Y92 2003
  332.64--dc21   2003001408

Contents

Chapter 3

Chapter 4

Chapter 5

Chapter 10

Chapter 11

PART 2. SYSTEMATIC METHODS

Chapter 12

Chapter 13

Chapter 14

Chapter 15

Appendix A

Appendix B

Preface

THE NEW MARKET PARADIGMS: WHAT HAS CHANGED SINCE BOOK ONE

The equities markets have gone through the bursting of a bubble since *Undergroundtrader.com Guide to Electronic Trading* was published in July 2000. The fiery *bull* market got doused by the ice-cold bear in the steep Nasdaq descent, shaving over $7 trillion in market capitalization. The bear market brought a dose of reality to the markets and filtered out any trader who wasn't flexible and adaptable enough to play both the long and the short side. Depressed stock prices, lighter volume, and decimalization have worked to shrink the volatility and momentum in the markets. We have gone from one extreme to the other. Traders were either forced to adapt or forced out of the markets altogether. There will always be three types of money in the market: smart money, big money, and sheep.

What is clear is that the buy-and-hold philosophy purveyed by Wall Street is *not* a safe harbor; if anything, it is an idea that not only is undermining investors' awareness of risk, but, more important, fails utterly to engender the awareness of the absolute necessity for the investor to be responsible for her or his investment decisions.

"Investing for the long term" teaches the investor to simply ignore losses of value—even losses of value approaching the risk of ruin. Should not a loss in value of nearly 85 percent be a risk to be avoided? The investor has been led to believe that investing for the long term is the only sure and certain road to growth in the financial markets. As with any other belief, one wonders whether there are *any* circumstances that would lead Wall Street to abandon this proffered faith. But belief and faith are never *willingly* tested for veracity. Only when reality overwhelms the capacity to ignore disparity is belief broken, so that the former believer is able to look at reality with fresh eyes.

Perhaps the chief lesson of the great bear market of 2000 is that the individual investor (and trader) must become responsible for his or her own money at risk. The *good* side of not being able to believe corporate leaders, of seeing the hypocrisy of market analysts, of the revelations of collusion among esteemed brokerages, admired companies, and respected investment banks in grand schemes to defraud investors—the *good* side of this would be not for heavy-handed government to try to make the markets "safe" for investors, but for *every investor* to realize that trying to make money grow will always and forever be a perilous and risky activity and that the primary responsibility for the fate of any investment must always be in the hands of the investor. This is an unpopular view, perhaps even a dreamy idealism. Investors have no time, no knowledge, no *way* to be responsible. And so responsibility is handed over to others almost without thought. Probably in no other area of life would the "average public investor" be so thoughtless, trusting, gullible, unknowing, and irresponsible— a/k/a sheep.

In the process of adapting to these markets, we have also had to adjust, refine, add to, and modify the methods we use to stay on top of changing conditions. In the end, we feel that we have the best tools that have been proven through every type of market, from the macro bull and bear to the micro oscillation and trend, and in the heavy-, moderate-, and light-volume markets. The methods have been tested daily in the trenches at undergroundtrader.com and have proved to be consistently effective. In addition to the methods, more emphasis needs to be placed on money management and share allocation. Decimalization has brought a new element to the markets, providing backfills and coil overshoots that can allow traders to maximize gains and minimize losses.

If there is a bright side to the market plunge, it is that it has severely tested both the methods and the traders out there that are still around. It has truly separated the real traders from the hobby players and the gamblers. The line has been drawn. Someone who made a small fortune buying and holding an Internet stock through a short squeeze in the old days got slaughtered on the way down. The market is cruel and uncaring, and in the end, it will take back what it may have temporarily loaned to those who did not have the discipline or the desire to adapt.

It can easily be maintained that anyone who can trade a thin bear market can survive and thrive in any market. This truth has made itself apparent, as cruel as it may seem. The markets are a machine. As we have always maintained, stock market analysts either are ignorant or have ulterior motives. This has been brought to the forefront, and the false rug of comfort that the average investor stood upon was pulled out from underneath him or her by accounting scandals and fraud. We never subscribed to that belief, especially when we witnessed market makers selling into the upgrades and vice versa.

The only thing that matters is *price* reaction. Now more than ever, a trader must focus strictly on *reaction* and put aside fundamental beliefs. The public is under the impression that news moves the markets. This is the farthest thing from the truth. The reality is that markets move as they wish to move, and the public looks for an excuse after the fact in the form of news. It is human nature to search for an explanation for a phenomenon. A trader needs to let go of this basic instinct and learn to live with the fact that markets will do what they do, and that trying to explain why is an exercise in futility.

The ultimate inside information is order flow. This is something that we cannot have. However, we also know that dinosaurs can't walk on the sand without leaving footprints. These dinosaurs are the big money, and they move the markets, for better or worse. Their actions cause volatility. Tracking their footprints is the basis of technical analysis. The public and the media are always looking for explanations as to why the markets moved in a certain direction each day. These are nothing more than excuses after the fact. We don't concern ourselves with why the markets moved; we are concerned only with when and how they moved. This is the basis of reaction. Trading is war. However, it is a very different type of war. It is a war in which victory comes from successful adapting. In this war, if the enemy is stronger than you, then you join that side.

In the several years since *Undergroundtrader.com Guide to Electronic Trading*, we have had the opportunity to work with and train hundreds of traders and to derive more insight into what is the most effective way to improve the largest number of traders in the shortest duration of time. This book is a sequel giving these improved and adapted methods along with an application of our training methods with new and experienced traders to help them reach the next level. There are three steps that need to be taken systematically to cross that learning curve. *Step one is learning the methods first and foremost. Step two is implementing the methods. Step three is managing the methods psychologically and physically.*

This is a game of probability. The goal is to enter a trade at a time when the scales are tipped in your favor. As much of a cliché as that sounds, it is the truth. What most traders lack is knowledge of what elements of a trade will tip the scale. We have a way to methodically read the scale.

Understand that the game is very simple. The goal is to find the transparency and take action *before* it becomes too transparent and the window of profitability closes. This is the bottom-line fundamental goal of the game. Every market day is like a big slab of stone, and as time wears on, that slab of stone gets chiseled and takes shape, finally forming a completed sculpture by 4:01 p.m. Eastern time. On a micro level, you can use the same analogy with any stock out there. Your goal is to allow yourself enough time to see the silhouette and the shape take some form, but to take action before the form is completed.

Trading is not meant to be excruciatingly difficult and painstaking. Although you can't control the markets, you can control your actions. When the market gets choppy, tight, and noisy, it's like a pond filled with piranhas and snakeheads—you wouldn't dive right in, would you? Trading is simple in the right environment and much tougher in the wrong environment. These environments change intraday within minutes to hours. A trader needs tools to let him or her know when the environment is ripe for opportunity and when it is crawling with traps.

We have seen traders evolve and grow, and we have seen traders crumble and fail. The toughest aspect of trading is acquiring the ability to step outside of oneself and simply watch with focus.

The saddest thing that happens to most traders is that they blow through their capital before they realize what they should be doing. Usually, traders will enter this game motivated and hungry, only to trip over their own feet after a few initial victories. They discover that hard work and desire alone are not enough. From there, the real death spiral begins as desperation sets in and eventually crushes the trader and his or her capital.

The missing element, naturally, is a trading system that works. Through thousands of hours and years of implementation every day from the trenches, we have developed a system that works, one composed of our methods. By explaining the system to our traders, we save them numerous hours on the learning curve. However, that is only the beginning. Knowing the methods and implementing them are two different things. As the saying goes, the flaw doesn't lie in the game plan, it lies in the execution. This is a game of probabilities, so one must remain disciplined, yet flexible.

The very basic premise of trading is *to find the transparency before it becomes too transparent* and to react in a timely enough manner before the window of opportunity closes. This theme will be played out many times throughout the book. There are two more premises that should always be in your mind. The second premise is that *what works in one time frame can work in all time frames* and that *markets as well as methods are linear*. The final premise is that *slower is better*. This applies both to trends in the market and, most importantly, to the progression of your trading.

This book is divided into two sections to expand on the newly revised methods of Jay Yu and Russ Lockhart. Yu's methods, aptly entitled "Discretionary Methods," require active management on the part of the trader. These methods utilize a beautiful combination of multiple time frame analysis with stochastics and moving averages to determine trades. This is a very discretionary style of trading, as the trader must be aware of and constantly manage the time frames. This style appeals greatly to shorter time frame intraday traders. This style also works well with e-minis futures trading. We include an appendix that demonstrates methods for trading the e-minis.

From there, Lockhart delves into the systematic methods, utilizing a completely different set of tools—one that stresses price/time analysis, complete with target and time projections utilizing a plethora of methods, including wave theory, Fibonacci calculations, market structures, harmonics, Gann angles, and candlestick formation triggers. This style appeals greatly to longer time frame intraday and multiday traders across various different markets. John Allen demonstrates this in Appendix B when he uses these methods to trade in the soybean market. Lockhart's section also focuses on the psychological aspects of the markets to allow the reader better understanding of the underlying forces that cause the moves.

While the methods are starkly different in style, you will find that they work together and complement each other. They are two roads that lead to the same target. The ultimate goal of this book is to expose the reader to two different yet complementary styles of trading in an effort to allow the reader to pick a style that suits her or him the best, or even a hybrid style that combines both methods. The underlying theme is to nurture the total embodiment of the complete trader and to help the reader in his or her journey to become a consistently profitable trader.

PART ONE

DISCRETIONARY METHODS

Deriving the Tools

This chapter provides a soup-to-nuts approach to the evolution of the trading methods discussed in this book, described through the eyes of a trader.

The key to building a solid foundation as a trader is to equip yourself with the tools you will need and a system in which these tools will work synergistically to provide guidance and foresight; we call this the *methods*. This collection of tools has been a product of years of real time–tested experience at undergroundtrader.com.

If there is one characteristic that many traders lack, it is focus. In the bubble era of the Nasdaq, it was easy to hop on the momentum train and jump from stock to stock without knowing any particular stock well. Those days are over, and failure to acknowledge and adapt to this has led to the downfall of many traders. Impulse trading is a surefire way to buy at the top and short at the bottom, resulting in strings of frustrating stop losses. For this reason, we absolutely stress that traders should start with *one* basket stock and do nothing but follow that stock day in and day out, observing how the stock reacts on light volume, heavy volume, uptrending days, downtrending days, oscillation periods, flat-line ranging periods, and the usual Prozac moments.

The more you watch, the more you will start to realize that stocks have personalities, just as people do. Some days the follow-through is fluent and generous, and some days there is barely any spread movement and noise. Familiarity breeds confidence.

Remember, a trader is up against all the market makers and other traders who have been watching the stock and are intimately fluent with its rhythm. Market makers who do nothing but make a market in that stock are waiting in the shadows, armed with order flow, unlimited capital, and access to all ECN order books and watching every tick of the futures. Imagine what chance a newbie trader jumping in impulsively has against these sharks. In a nutshell, such a trader will get shaken, wiggled, rattled, chewed up, and spit out because this is a zero-sum game: Either you will take their money or they will take yours. To sum up trading in a nutshell, all the work goes into the preparation of waiting (as in fishing) for the right setup, pulling the trigger, letting the market react, and managing the profits or stops. Let the cards fall where they will once that trigger is pulled. Therefore, the most important thing a trader needs to accomplish in the beginning is to learn the methods in order to be able to properly identify the setups. This is where we start.

The first step is to pick a basket stock and watch, watch, watch. Basket stocks are tier 1 stocks with enough volume and movement that correlates with the futures. For example, MSFT happens to be a great basket stock to trade, as it tends to move in lockstep with the Nasdaq and S&P 500 e-minis futures. (We tend to favor the e-minis because they trade around the clock, with the exception of the 4:15 to 4:45 p.m. EST period, when they close and reopen.) Your basket stocks are your bread and butter. Day in and day out, these are the stocks you specialize in, knowing them intimately through good and bad times. Focus is key.

It is also very important that you establish whether you are a scalper, a range/swing trader, or a combination of both. A *scalper* is a trader who looks for the short-term movements in a stock based on the 1-minute and 3-minute moving averages and stochastics charts. Scalpers will take their money off the table early because the longer they are in a position, the more risk they incur. Scalpers like immediate gratification with only a moderate amount of wiggle. A *range/swing trader* is one who is comfortable with a longer time frame and the wider wiggles that accompany such a time frame. A range/swing trader will primarily use 13-minute and 60-minute moving averages and stochastics charts. By allocating fewer shares, this player tempers the risk associated with the longer-time-duration trades. A *combination trader* is one who will be proficient at taking gains fast on larger numbers of shares, as a scalper does, yet will use paring to trim down the number of shares in order to be able to swing if the 13-minute and 60-minute charts warrant it. Be aware that choppy oscillating markets tend to favor the scalper and tighter-range leaning-trend markets favor the range/swing trader.

One of the most important facts that a trader absolutely must acknowledge is that the market has two very distinct environments throughout the day. These environments will determine how effective a trader will be. This is probably the element of the market that is most misunderstood by traders. A good scalper will thrive in a wide-channel, heavy-volume market. This same scalper will get wiggled and stopped constantly in a tight-channel, light-volume market. Have you ever made good profits in the first hour, only to give them back for the next 3 hours? It is not your trading that is the problem. It is that you are trading in an environment in which your style is ineffective. A range player will thrive in a tight-channel, light-volume, and trending market. A scalper will thrive in a wide-channel, heavy-volume, trending or oscillating market. A combination trader will thrive in both. We will discuss how styles make fights in more detail later in the book.

A TRADER'S DISCOVERY PROCESS—FIND THE NEED AND APPLY THE FIX

What we're going to do here is take an imaginary trader by the name of Mark and go through the steps he would take to build a solid foundation. This will be a good illustration and will provide a true-to-life saga that you may identify with. The *best* way to truly appreciate a tool is to first find a need for it. Although it may seem as if we are working backwards, it is important to illustrate how the need for a tool to help fill a particular gap will arise. One must want to fill that gap in information in order to truly appreciate and use the tool. Deprivation is a wonderful teacher. It identifies what is missing. Hunger tells you what you need. When one is deprived of food, one hungers for it more and more. When the food is eventually given, one truly appreciates the essence of the food. In the same vein, a trader must initially be able to identify what is needed and want to eliminate that need in order to understand and appreciate the tools that help fill the information gap. So we begin with a story of a typical trader in his quest to fill the gap of knowledge and experience as he hungers for a trader's staple of food.

Mark is a trader who has been frustrated with his performance and is at the end of his rope trying to figure out how to consistently trade the equities markets. Yet, despite all his frustration, Mark remains hungry. In fact, Mark's poor performance and frustration has only stimulated his hunger to find something to grasp onto that will let him make sense of this chaos.

For a while, Mark was making decent money just trading news plays, but now it seems that stock movements on news and analyst research are ambiguous. He is stumped. Why do stocks react so ambiguously and unpredictably to news? One day, a voice spoke into Mark's ear; it said, "Pick a basket stock and just watch it all day; don't trade it." So Mark obliged and proceeded to watch MSFT on Nasdaq Level 2. MSFT moved up and down and up and up and down and down and up down up down. Mark tried to find a pattern to the moves, but nothing he saw made much sense. Sometimes when MSFT's bid was showing some heavy size—30,000 shares— MSFT would make a nice bounce up, which made sense. But other times, when MSFT showed 30,000 shares on the bid, it would start to bounce, only to sell right back down. Other times, MSFT would hold the bid level with just a few 100-share-size bids, then reverse and go back up.

Mark was even more confused than before. At least before, he had had some news to lean on. But Mark continued to watch MSFT all day every day. He figured that no one was watching, so a few times he snuck into some trades on MSFT based on Nasdaq Level 2. He took some longs when the bids looked strong, only to see them evaporate and panic him into taking a stop, and vice versa on the shorts. He couldn't help but shake his head. Mark was thinking to himself, "MSFT sure does make some nice moves, if only there were a way for me to figure out when it will pop or drop. But almost every time I think it's going to pop and I get in, it wiggles me right out. Damn!"

A few days later, the voice spoke to him again: "One-minute stochastics." Taking the advice of the voice, Mark set up MSFT on a 1-minute stochastics chart and saw how the 1-minute stochastics chart gave some nice signals. When MSFT's stochastics oscillators dipped under the 20 band, it was oversold, and when the oscillators bounced through the 80 band, it was overbought. Mark witnessed how MSFT would bounce nicely in price in an almost textbook fashion when the 1-minute stochastics chart bounced back up through the 20 band. Mark also was amazed at how MSFT would drop in price as the 1-minute stochastics fell under the 80 band.

It started to click. Mark was finally getting a foothold on figuring out this chaos. He watched religiously throughout the day, seeing how MSFT would oscillate up and down between the 20 band and the 80 band. He told himself, "Now this makes sense! I'll just buy MSFT when the stochastics crosses up through the 20 band and short MSFT when it falls under the 80 band." Mark had good early success just using the 1-minute stochastics chart. He felt that he was finally grasping the idea of making profits consistently in the stock market.

1. The *need*: A way to spot entry and exit signals based on an overbought and oversold indicator

2. The *fix*: The 1-minute stochastics oscillator chart

The next day Mark proceeded to buy MSFT at 48.75 just as it started to cross the 20 band. He expected MSFT to bounce and move higher, but an interesting thing happened: MSFT continued to drop! The 1-minute stochastics bounced just above the 20 band, and MSFT sold off. Mark sat frozen, staring at the screen, for another 5 minutes, not believing what he was seeing. MSFT did not cross back up through the 20 band until 15 minutes later, after it had dropped $0.75 in fast selling. Mark was in shock. What the heck had happened this time? Why didn't MSFT rise after it initially crossed the 1-minute stochastics 20 band? Why wasn't there any follow-through? He was starting to doubt the validity of the 1-minute stochastics chart after this nasty incident. Then the voice spoke to him again and said, "Three-minute moving averages chart."

Mark set up the 3-minute simple moving averages chart to gauge the trend. This chart is composed of a 5-period simple moving average and a 15-period simple moving average. It shows the trend of the stock. An uptrend is indicated by a chart that shows higher highs (5-period moving average) and higher lows (15-period moving average). In a downtrend, the chart shows lower lows (5-period moving average) and lower highs (15-period moving average). A consolidation is taking place when the 5- and 15-period moving averages are going sideways, indicating no trend.

When Mark went back and reanalyzed his MSFT trade, he noticed that the 3-minute moving averages were trending down. He also noticed that at the time of his MSFT trade, the 5-period moving average downtrend resistance was 48.80 and the 15-period moving average downtrend resistance was 49.05. He remembered buying MSFT at 48.75 and seeing it make a quick uptick to 48.80 and then fall back down fast. Hmmm. Mark thought to himself, "I suppose the stochastics is effective only if I am playing with the trend. In fact, all those times that I saw MSFT bounce up through the 20 band and move higher, it was usually bouncing off the 5-period or the 15-period moving average as it was uptrending. When MSFT slipped under the 80-band stochastics on the 3-minute uptrend, it fell down to the 15-period moving average before it bounced again."

The wheels were turning. Mark realized that the 1-minute stochastics was still an excellent tool; however, he had to make sure that he was not playing against the 3-minute trend. Upon further observation, he also realized that there were times where he would see MSFT make a large panic move down, sometimes to 0.50 lower than the 5-period moving average, then get a 0.20 to 0.40 bounce on the 1-minute stochastics 20-band cross back up. When the stock bounced, he would usually see it stick to the 5-period resistance. If the 5-period resistance broke, however, he would often see it continue higher, to the 15-period resistance.

Mark was truly taking it all in. It was almost miraculous how well the stochastics and the moving averages explained the movements in MSFT. Finally it was starting to make sense. He also understood that when the moving averages were in a consolidation, he shouldn't pay too much attention to the Nasdaq Level 2 movements because they were noise for the most part. The beauty of moving averages is that they filter out the miscellaneous noise to give a true reading of the trend and support/resistance levels. Mark started to focus more and more on the charts instead of watching the choppy action on Level 2.

1. The *need*: A way to determine the overall *trend* of a stock and its support and resistance levels

2. The *fix*: The 3-minute simple moving averages chart

On his 3-minute moving average charts on MSFT, Mark would often see the stock try to break out of a consolidation, only to revert to the consolidation levels. Then, when Mark least expected it, MSFT would break out, and the 3-minute uptrend would be triggered before he could take an action. So Mark asked himself, "How can I tell when a real breakout is happening instead of a wiggle before it's too far into the uptrend? Is there some kind of leading indicator that I can use that will perhaps foreshadow the breakout?" He pondered these questions. Although the stochastics and the 3-minute moving averages charts were good, they seemed to be lacking enough foresight to allow him to get in early on the breakouts and, more importantly, to distinguish between a real and a fake breakout attempt. He waited and waited for the voice to speak to him. The more he watched, the more he prayed for some indicator that would give him an edge by letting him know when a breakout was for real and foreshadowing the breakout.

A week later, the voice spoke again: "Noodles and 3 shift." Huh? "Nasdaq 100 e-minis futures and 3-period exponential moving average shifted –3." OK, that's better. The Nasdaq 100 futures act as the *lead* indicator for all the tier 1 stocks. When the futures move higher, stocks tend to follow. The 3 shift is a 3-period exponential moving average that acts as a confirmation break indicator. "So if the futures move first, then, theoretically, I should watch their stochastics and moving averages to get a heads up on what MSFT will do," Mark said to himself. So Mark set up the 3-minute moving averages on the futures along with a 3-minute stochastics chart and a 1-minute stochastics chart. He also added the 3-shift indicator to his 3-minute moving averages chart for MSFT.

Mark noticed that when MSFT finally broke out from consolidation, the 3 shift would actually cross the 5-period moving average first, giving him a 1- to 3-minute heads up before the full brunt of the volume came in. Wow! It worked like a charm. What looked like a simple consolidation one day would turn into a strong breakout move that was foreshadowed by the 3 shift crossing up through the 5-period moving average on the 3-minute chart on MSFT. Mark felt that he had found the missing link that he was looking for. He continued to watch MSFT during the consolidations for the 3 shift to lead a cross either through the 5-period moving average to break out into an uptrend or under the 15-period moving average to break down into a downtrend. Every single time there was a breakout, the noodles moved first, so it worked as a great leading indicator.

1. The *need*: A way to get *foresight* on a potential move of a stock—a leading indicator that will move first, giving enough time to react before the stock mirrors it

2. The *fix*: Nasdaq 100 futures e-minis, also referred to as the noodles

1. The *need*: A way to *confirm* a breakout or a breakdown with time to spare
2. The *fix*: 3-shift exponential moving average

The next day, the noodles made a nice breakout move higher on the 3-minute moving averages chart, as the 3 shift crossing through the 5-period simple moving average had foreshadowed. However, Mark noticed that MSFT was not moving up very strongly. In fact, it seemed to be selling lower into the noodles upticks. This is called a sell-side fade, where a stock will diverge with the futures. Mark had seen these before, and he knew it was advantageous to take a short position if he could get a higher-band 1-minute stochastics slip. His main hesitancy was that the noodles were steadily climbing higher and higher, and he was nervous about taking a short in case MSFT's sell-side fade actually turned into a market laggard, which could trigger a short squeeze.

One day, around 1 p.m. EST, MSFT seemed to be locked in a 0.30 range between 48.90 and 49.20 on very light volume. Mark thought nothing of it, as the 3-minute moving averages chart had pretty tight 5- and 15-period moving averages. MSFT looked harmless, as it was neither coming nor going other than the usual fast spread moves that gave the illusion of volume. Anyone could take a look at the 3-minute volume bars and see that there was no volume, which is what Mark told himself after he got wiggled out.

On several occasions, Mark tried to enter what looked like a possible 3-shift break up at 49.20, only to see the bid drop and MSFT slip back to 49, or tried to short at 48.95, only to have MSFT pop back up to 49.15 and stop him out. The 3-minute charts gave many 3-shift crosses up and down but the follow-through was not there, which caused him to take multiple stops. He was getting wiggled, and he finally got fed up with it and took a walk. He returned to the computer 10 minutes later, only to find MSFT selling on a fast panic down to 48.55. He couldn't believe that he had missed the actual breakdown. What had made this breakdown happen when the earlier entries had made the 48.90 area feel like a rubber band that just coiled right back up? Is there a tool that can give *more* foresight than the 3-minute charts, especially during lighter-volume periods?

Suddenly the voice responded, "Thirteen-minute and sixty-minute charts." Mark proceeded to set up the 5- and 15-period moving averages and the stochastics on a 13-minute chart and a 60-minute chart for the noodles and for MSFT. At first glance, they looked similar to the 3-minute charts. However, he noticed that the MSFT 13-minute chart's stochastics was coming down from the 70 band to the 20 band when MSFT fell from 49.10 to 48.55. In fact, when Mark got stopped out of his MSFT short at 49.10, the 13-minute stochastics was already crossing down through the 80 band and the 60-minute stochastics had slipped down under the 40 band. Both of the 13-minute and 60-minute simple moving averages were in clear downtrends. Therefore, on the longer time frames, MSFT was slowly declining, even though the 3-minute charts indicated a consolidation range. The longer time frame charts give a bird's-eye view that enabled him to see the long-term trend.

1. The *need*: A way to get a bird's-eye view of the direction of a stock that is not visible in the shorter time frame, the way a Doppler weather radar detects potential weather changes
2. The *fix*: 13-minute stochastics/moving averages charts and 60-minute stochastics/moving averages charts

The 13- and 60-minute charts looked familiar to Mark because they were just slower versions of his 3-minute charts. This also meant that more wiggle room and wider ranges were involved. Although the 3-minute and 1-minute charts gave the initial moves, the 13-minute and 60-minute charts gave the undercurrents, acting as a lead indicator very much like a Doppler weather radar. This was an amazing tool. He asked the voice if there were any other indicators that he should add to his arsenal. The voice immediately responded, "Add a 200-period simple moving average to the 3-minute and 1-minute charts."

Mark proceeded to add a 200-period simple moving average to his 3-minute and 1-minute charts on MSFT and the noodles.

The first thing he noticed was that the 3-minute 200-period moving average often could be far away from where the stock was currently trading. However, as he watched he noticed that this 200-period simple moving average acted as a significant resistance when stocks were uptrending under it and as a significant support when stochastics was downtrending near it. The 3-minute 200-period moving average was stronger than the 1-minute.

Upon further observation, he noticed that when stocks or futures made a strong breakout move near the 200-period moving average, the average would often pop a little higher and then proceed to wiggle back down to the 5-period moving average. The 200-period simple moving average would break after two tests, and the prices had to slowly grind up to it and slowly break through it. Once the 200-period moving average was broken, it would then become a strong support level. Hmmm. It was almost like magic seeing stocks bounce and pop and hit the 200-period simple moving average looking as if they would break higher, only to reverse and fall back down.

1. The *need*: An indicator to show an absolute support/resistance and a short-term support/resistance
2. The *fix*: A 200-period simple moving average on a 3-minute chart and on a 1-minute chart gives resistance and support levels. Usually stocks will not break these levels on an impulse move. It takes time or volume to break these levels, allowing opportunities to play a countertrend trade on the initial break attempts.

When the 5/15-period moving average channels get tight, stay out. The tighter the moving average channels, the smaller the opportunities to make money, which is why there is no volume. Everyone is sitting on the fence. Ideally, you want to play the wider-channel moves, as there are opportunities on both sides of the trend. Playing with the trend has the best odds, but countertrend moves can reap solid gains.

STOCHASTICS CHARTS

Stochastics can be viewed as the engine that drives momentum. The stochastics chart is the key tool for oscillations that determine overbought and oversold levels. In addition to using the 1-minute stochastics chart, we like to attach a stochastics chart to the bottom of all of our moving averages charts: the 3-minute, 13-minute, and 60-minute charts. The effectiveness is linear through all time frames. Keep in mind, however, that the longer the time frame is, the slower the movement. Wider time frames mean more of a bird's-eye view.

The stochastics chart is composed of two stochastic oscillators. Depending on your trading platform, you will have either five variables (Realtick and Cybertrader) or three variables (qchart, esignal, and atfi). The settings for Realtick and Cybertrader are 15, 5, 2 for %dslow and 15, 3 for %d. With other platforms, you should use a 15, 3, 5 setting for %k and %d, always picking the slow stochastic. This will provide a lead stochastic (%d or %k, depending on your system) and a laggard stochastic (%dslow or %d). The stochastic oscillators are overlaid on a chart composed of bands from 0 to 100. The 20-band level or below is oversold territory, and the 80-band level or above is overbought territory. It is also important to set the number of days data back to 2 days; this will allow a smooth continuation of the stochastics from the opening bell.

The typical buy trigger occurs when the lead and laggard stochastics cross back up through the 20 band. The typical short trigger occurs when the stochastics slip back underneath the 80 band. These are very effective signals that can generate nice, healthy profits on both longs and shorts. What do you do if the stochastics are stuck in a range between the 20 and 80 bands? Usually, you will do nothing. There are cases where a mini pup formation may foreshadow a move (we will address mini pups in Chapter 3). For now, the basic rules are to buy on the 20-band cross and short on the 80-band cross.

However, as our trader Mark noted, there are discrepancies when you use just this one chart. In the MSFT example, using a

1-minute stochastics chart, the stock may give full oscillations from the 20 band to the 80 band with a nice price movement of 0.50 or more on one oscillation, and then it might get choppy and wiggly on the next oscillation, resulting in no net movement. Sometimes the stochastics will make a full oscillation move from the 80 band down to the 10 band with only a 0.10 move in the stock price, and yet an hour later it may make the same full oscillation with a 0.80 move down in the stock price. This is the main reason why many traders have written off the usefulness of the stochastics charts.

Unfortunately for those traders, they don't realize that stochastics absolutely needs to be used within the context of the trend. What they fail to see is that stochastic oscillation moves upward can be thwarted and limited in the context of an active downtrend. However, stochastic oscillation moves down are very effective. The converse is also true; stochastics moves down can seem ineffective in an uptrend, but stochastics moves up are dynamic in terms of price acceleration. This is the key thing to remember when using stochastics charts: The *trend* will set the pace for the stochastics. Therefore, a trader who likes to scalp using the 1-minute stochastics chart will absolutely have to pay attention to the uptrend and use the stochastics for buy signals. Such a trader will have to be very careful about shorting an uptrending stock even with the stochastics, as it is very possible to get squeezed without fast timing. This type of countertrend trading will be discussed later in the book.

So let's move to the tool that helps us to quantitatively determine a trend.

MOVING AVERAGES CHARTS

If the stochastics is the engine that drives momentum, then the moving averages are the road map that determines the destinations. All the moving averages charts are composed of a 5-period and a 15-period simple moving average. Once again, we want to make sure we have a 3-minute, a 13-minute, and a 60-minute chart with data set at 3 days back. We will primarily focus on the 3-minute moving averages charts for the short-term trends. The 5-period moving average is the lead, and the 15-period is the laggard. The combination of the two produces a visual representation of the trend.

The space between the 5- and 15-period moving averages is the *channel*. Channels can be wide or tight, depending on volume. A tighter channel usually represents less volume, making it much less tradable. A wider channel represents more volume, allowing for more opportunities to trade oscillations within the trend.

The beauty of moving averages charts is that they allow the trader to view the actual trend without having to pay attention to the noise and choppiness in price action. The moving averages by nature filter out noise and streamline all the price action into a viewable illustration of the trend.

200-Period Simple Moving Average

We also add a 200-period simple moving average to each of our charts, as this can represent a very strong support or resistance level. If the 200-period moving average is above the current stock price, then it is considered a resistance, and if it is above, it is considered a support. Many times the 200-period moving average will be rather far away from the stock price. In these instances, we note its existence and where it sits and keep it in the back of our minds. It is like trying to predict in July when the next 20-degree day will occur. It is fruitless to try to predict the exact date. However, when it happens, we know we need to turn up the heat. Therefore, if a stock's price approaches the 200-period moving average, then we prepare to react on a break or a reversal.

The rule of thumb is that the 200-period moving average usually cannot break without heavy volume or a longer duration of time. Thus, when stocks make a breakout move, the 200-period moving average acts as a tough resistance, and vice versa on breakdowns. Stocks may overshoot (briefly trade higher) through the 200-period moving average resistance, but it is most important to watch and see if the candles can close above that level. Most of the time stocks will peak and retrace right back under that resistance. Scalpers usually like to short off the 200-period moving average resistance on lighter volume with the understanding that there is some meat on the retracements back to the 5-period moving average support.

3-Period Shifted Exponential Moving Average

Traders who use the 3-minute moving averages chart often have complaints about getting head-faked on what at first looked like a breakout. Have you ever stepped in early on an initial pop through the 5-period moving average, only to get wiggled right back out when it retraces? After enough head fakes, you give up and decide to just sit out the pops, only to shake your head in dismay when the very next pop turns into a strong breakout move higher. Have you ever wished for an indicator that would be able to not only confirm a breakout but give you an early heads up before it happens? Your wish has been answered. We call it the 3 shift.

This is a powerful new indicator that we use to get early confirmations of trend breakouts and breakdowns. This indicator is placed on the 3-minute, 13-minute, and 60-minute charts (see Figure 1-1). To set it up, just add a 3-period exponential moving average and set the lead/lag or adjustment to −3.

The basic premise is to wait for the 3-shift moving average to cross the 5-period moving average before going long and the 15-period moving average before going short. In fact, whenever the 3 shift breaks through a moving average level, the move is confirmed to be a break. This is especially useful when the 3 shift crosses through the 3-minute 200-period moving average resistance or support. There is one caveat here: Always let the 3 shift cross through before entering the trade. The 3 shift can give you a lead time of up to 6 minutes before the rest of the world realizes that the uptrend or downtrend has been formed. The reason you wait is that many times the 3 shift will touch the moving average and appear to be trying to cross, only to reverse. So the key is to wait for the crossover at all times. You will have plenty of time to enter the trade once the 3 shift crosses.

This is a moving averages stochastics chart.

This is the main chart you will need to understand. It is split into two parts.

The top part is the "road map" portion, composed of the 5-period simple moving average (the lead) and the 15-period simple moving average (the laggard), which visually depicts the trend. The 3-shift moving average is added to confirm when a moving average or pivot has broken. We include a 200-period moving average, which acts as a support/resistance level, and, finally, the pivot points, which also act as support/resistance levels.

The bottom portion of the chart is composed of the stochastics oscillators, which act as the driving engine. The lead indicator is the %d (15, 3), and the laggard is the % d slow (15, 5, 2). When they fall under the 20 band, they create an oversold condition, with a buy signal triggering on the 20-band cross up. When they rise above the 80 band, they trigger a sell/short signal when they cross and slip back under the 80 band.

Once again, this is your main tool. Everything else after this is just a matter of adjusting the settings to different time frames.

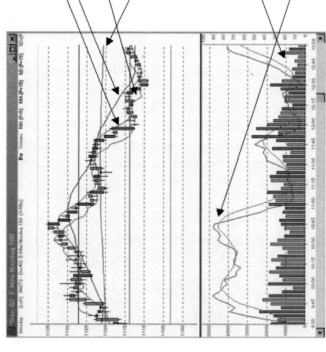

Figure 1–1 Main weapon: moving averages stochastics chart.

1-MINUTE STOCHASTICS DIVERGENT SITUATIONS AND WIDE-CHANNEL CONSOLIDATIONS

As mentioned earlier, you will encounter often situations in which the 1-minute stochastics on your stock will make a full oscillation from the 20 band to the 80 band, resulting in a 0.70 range from low to high on the movement. You also will see times when the identical 1-minute stochastics full oscillation from the 20 band to the 80 band on the *same* stock results in a 0.10 move from low to high. The reason for the difference is the tightness of the channel on the 3-minute moving averages chart. The channel consists of the space between the 5-period and 15-period simple moving averages. The second scenario was probably one in which the stock's 3-minute moving average chart was indicating a consolidation, whereas the first scenario indicated an active trend, allowing for a wider 5/15-period simple moving average and more movement. So the bottom line here is that you should look to play a stock only when there is a wider channel or a trend in process. Sometimes, you will get a wide-channel consolidation on your stock, which will allow for optimal scalping opportunities. Wide-channel consolidations do not tend to stay wide; they occur when a stock has had panic in one direction and then back the other way or a series of back-and-forth panics in a wide range. These will eventually tighten, so it's important to recognize this and not go to the well too many times trying to scalp each oscillation.

NASDAQ 100 E-MINIS CHARTS (NOODLES)

The market is basically pulled by a set of strings known as the *futures*. As futures rise, stocks are bid higher. As futures fall, stocks are bid lower. This makes the futures a solid leading indicator for trading stocks. We use the Nasdaq 100 e-minis, also called noodles, as our lead indicator. The reason we use the e-minis instead of the full contract is that the e-minis are active around the clock, with the exception of a 30-minute halt from 4:15 to 4:45 p.m. EST. You must make sure that your noodles feed is set to all sessions, meaning a full-fledged around-the-clock data feed. This is extremely important, as the 60-minute noodles chart can give very strong foreshadowing signals in the premarket, often indicating what the rest of the day may do.

We chart the noodles on a 1-minute stochastics chart, a 3-minute moving averages and stochastics chart, a 13-minute moving averages and stochastics chart, and a 60-minute moving averages and stochastics chart. Every single trade is affected by the noodles, making this your core indicator. An appropriate football analogy with the time frames would be that the 3-minute noodles chart represents the first-down marker, the 13-minute noodles chart gives guidance to the midfield, and the 60-minute noodles chart gives guidance to the end zone. The longer the time frame, the stronger the underlying trend will be.

For example, suppose the noodles show a rising 60-minute stochastics in a moving averages uptrend with a falling 13-minute stochastics in a moving averages consolidation. This means that although the noodles are in a greater uptrend, they will show a pullback in the nearer term. Therefore, shorting the nearer term will give some decent profit potential until the 13-minute stochastics moves back up to join the 60-minute trend. It is very important to be able to spot the different currents in the time frames, especially when these currents are in the same direction. We will discuss the 13-minute and 60-minute time frames further in Chapter 3.

Market makers and specialists are always hedging with the futures. When the noodles are rising, market makers bid up stocks, and when the noodles are slipping, they bid stocks down. This is the dance. It also explains why stocks can move without any volume or institutional orders. Many new traders are under the assumption that if MSFT is rising, then a combination of mom-and-pop buyers and institutional buyers must be driving up the price of the stock. Nothing could be further from reality. MSFT can move higher without a single share being bought by a retail player or an institutional buyer. Market makers will hedge and trade back and forth among themselves parallel to the movement of the futures. This is what moves stocks! It is not news or analyst recommendations. It is all the futures, which are the puppet strings that pull the market.

PIVOT POINTS

Pivot points are additional support and resistance levels on stocks and futures. Pivot points are synonymous for all time frames, as they are based on the prior day's high, low, close, and open prices. Realtick and Cybertrader have pivot studies already included. These lines represent additional support and resistance levels and should receive as much emphasis as the 3-minute 200-period moving average. These are speed bumps that take time or volume to break. The following is the formula for calculating pivots if your platform does not already include them. Often one can enter a countertrend play for a fast reversal on impulse panic bounces or drops near a pivot.

The study uses the previous day's high, low, close, and open price to generate a pivot, two support levels, and resistance levels. Today's pivots are a function of yesterday's high, low, and close for a specific contract.

H = yesterday's high

L = yesterday's low

C = yesterday's close

The five equations for the pivot lines are
Red line:

$$P = (H + L + C)/3$$

Blue line:

$$R_1 = 2 \times P - L$$

Green line:

$$S_1 = 2 \times P - H$$

Yellow line:

$$R_2 = P + (R_1 - S_1)$$

Yellow line:

$$S_2 = P - (R_1 - S_1)$$

SOX.X INDEX AND VIX.X

We add these charts as confirmation tools. The sox.x is the semi-conductor index, which tends to move directly with the noodles and stocks. When there is a divergence between your basket stock and the sox.x, then the spider senses have to be tingling. Any 3-minute moves should be confirmed with the sox.x oscillations. Naturally, there will be exceptions to the rules, but to get the best probability on your trades, it's wise to make sure that the sox.x is confirming the move.

The vix.x is the volatility index, which measures the put/call ratio. Usually, when the vix.x rises, the equity markets fall, and vice versa. We keep this on the 13-minute moving averages and stochastics chart to spot pups or mini pups. The reason we keep it only on the 13-minute chart is to get a bird's-eye view of the trend. There is an inverse relationship between the vix.x and the noodles. This means that if the 13-minute vix.x forms a stochastics mini pup, then we anticipate that the equities markets will fall and the 13-minute noodles will probably show us a breakdown, usually in the form of a mini inverse pup.

THE COMPLETE LAYOUT

We have now gone over all the charts you will need. To sum up the complete layout, you will need to have one of each of the following:

Nasdaq Level 2 screen with time of sales for the stock (linked to stock charts)

1-minute stochastics chart for the stock (moving averages optional)

3-minute moving averages and stochastics chart for the stock

13-minute moving averages and stochastics chart for the stock

60-minute moving averages and stochastics chart for the stock

1-minute stochastics chart for Nasdaq 100 e-minis

3-minute moving averages and stochastics chart for Nasdaq 100 e-minis

13-minute moving averages and stochastics chart for Nasdaq 100 e-minis

60-minute moving averages and stochastics chart for Nasdaq 100 e-minis

3-minute moving averages and stochastics charts for sox.x chart

13-minute vix.x moving averages and stochastics chart

Also note the following points:

Each moving averages chart also has a 200-period simple moving average and a 3 shift.

Pivot point lines also can be included in the 3-minute and 1-minute charts.

The 13- and 60-minute charts need to be set to data for 13 days back in order to get an accurate 200-period simple moving average.

The 1- and 3-minute charts need to be set to data for 3 days back in order to get an accurate 200-period simple moving average.

Figure 1-2 shows you the layout of these charts on your screen.

The Complete Layout Page (Single Monitor)

Nasdaq Level 2 and
Time of Sales

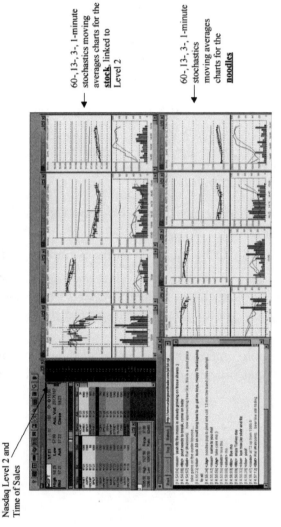

60-, 13-, 3-, 1-minute
stochastics moving
averages charts for the
stock, linked to
Level 2

60-, 13-, 3-, 1-minute
stochastics
moving averages
charts for the
noodles

This is the basic layout page for a single monitor. It is composed of the Nasdaq Level 2 and Time of Sales linked to the four charts next to it, which are the 60-, 13-, 3- and 1-minute stochastics and moving averages charts. At the bottom is the chat room (optional), the four charts next to it measure the noodles on 60-, 13-, 3- and 1-minute stochastics and moving averages charts. This is the page that allows us to track the dinosaurs. Remember, the moving averages and pivots make up the road map; the stochastics is the engine.

Figure 1-2   Basic layout page.

CHAPTER 2

Trend Channels and Breakouts

This chapter gives a definitive explanation of trends and how they develop and emerge.

Now that we have gone over all the tools and charts, let's delve into their utilization. There are only two things a stock can do in the market: It can either trend or consolidate. That's it. Nothing more. Stocks can only trend or consolidate. As for oscillations, they tend to move within the trend channel until the channel tightens back into a consolidation.

CONSOLIDATIONS

A consolidation can be seen on the moving averages charts, indicated by the 5-period and 15-period moving averages going sideways. A consolidation is basically a sideways range and is usually accompanied by light volume. The volume is light because neither side is really pushing or showing its strength. Consolidations often occur after a breakout or a breakdown. They give the stock some time to breathe after a large move, allowing it to form the base for another move or a reversal.

A consolidation is basically a neutral period in which one side (the bulls or the bears) is stronger but is not showing its intentions just yet. Keep in mind that the market tries as hard as possible to avoid transparency, and consolidations are usually how this is done. A wide-channel consolidation can usually be played for some oscillation scalps initially, but scalpers have to be careful not to go to the well too many times, as wide-channel consolidations usually get tighter. A tightening consolidation occurs when the 5- and 15-period moving averages start to get closer. This leaves very little room for scalping opportunities but also starts to foreshadow an oncoming trend. As a rule, scalpers should not be trading consolidations and tight 5- and 15-period moving average channels on the 3-minute charts.

One of the biggest mistakes that traders make is to overtrade consolidations. Rather than watch the moving averages charts, traders tend to overstress Nasdaq Level 2 and tape reading, and they get wiggled out constantly without noticing that the moving averages chart is just moving sideways in a consolidation. *Do not overtrade consolidations. This applies most to scalpers.* Consolidations are a signal to step back and simply watch. Since everyone else is also doing this, it is again an impetus for lighter volume. It is best to watch for the 3 shift to cross for a breakout or breakdown move to enter a trade.

UPTRENDS AND DOWNTRENDS

An *active* uptrend is defined as higher highs (the 5-period moving average) and higher lows (the 15-period moving average), usually with elevated volume. An *active* downtrend is defined as lower lows (the 5-period moving average) and lower highs (the 15-period moving average) with elevated volume. Consolidations are periods when both the 5- and 15-period moving averages are going sideways with very little volume. Please note the word *active*. It implies that, like a volcano that is already exploding and sending out deadly lava, the stock is already moving on volume. Can a stock be in an uptrend and not be active? Absolutely. An inactive uptrend is one in which the 5-period moving average is no longer making new highs, yet the 15-period moving average is still rising. How is this possible? Very simply. Remember once again that it takes time or volume to move the indicators. MSFT can break out from 46.25 to a 47.10 peak on volume and retrace to 46.75, then sit in a range from 46.80 to 47 for the next 15 minutes. At first glance, a trader may say that MSFT has peaked out and isn't moving. A trader who has been watching the 3-minute moving averages will see that MSFT has peaked and retraced back to the 5-period moving average at 47, but that the 15-period moving average is still rising and catching up. This is a very dangerous situation for anyone who is shorting MSFT. Remember, the 15-period moving average is the trend support, and the longer MSFT sits at a higher range, the more steadily it will rise until it goes into a pup breakout or a consolidation.

PUPS AND MINI PUPS

We have discovered a powerful formation that shows up on the moving averages charts and the stochastics charts that results in strong short squeezes on breakouts and rapid collapses on breakdowns. *Pups* is short for power uptick breaks. A pup is a formation that is triggered during an inactive uptrend as the 5-period moving average flattens out while the 15-period moving average continues to rise. During this time, the bears are preventing the stock from rising any higher by shorting the 5-period moving average level. The bulls are represented by the 15-period moving average, which continues to rise slowly. Eventually the channel tightens until a make-or-break situation arises. The unstoppable force meets the immovable object. When the stock moves above the 5-period moving average (confirmed by the 3-shift cross through the 5-period moving average), it immediately causes a chain reaction, triggering shorts to panic cover as buyers come off the fence, driving the stock higher on large volume.

The effects of a pup breakout are immediate and dramatic and have follow-through after the initial spike. This allows scalpers as well as swingers to take part in the action. Often you will have to wait out the first reaction on the 5-period overshoots. The bears like to short the initial pups to shake the trees to the 15-period moving average, where hammers will often form (candle formations detailed in Chapter 9). This shakeout draws in more shorts, and then the hammer off the 15-period moving average is what causes the short to squeeze and break hard back through the 5-period moving average and trigger the pup on the backs of the shorts.

The same formation in reverse triggers an inverse pup breakdown. This occurs when a stock is in an inactive downtrend composed of a flattening 5-period moving average and a falling 15-period moving average. The bulls are trying to establish a bottom and are stepping in to buy at the 5-period moving average to stop the bleeding. The bears are steadily selling down with the 15-period moving average until the channel tightens, and once again a make-or-break situation arises. When the stock moves below the 5-period moving average (once again using the 3 shift crossing the 15-period moving average as a trigger), the chain reaction is triggered, causing the bulls to immediately panic sell and bringing in more bears and sellers to short and dump the stock in dramatic fashion, causing a fast, voluminous collapse.

A mini pup is the same as a pup, but it is found on the stochastics chart, using the %d where the 5-period moving average would be and the %dslow where the 15-period moving average would be. When the stochastics attempts a mini pup, look for breakouts in the moving averages chart. When the stochastics attempts a mini inverse pup, look for breakdowns in the moving averages chart. You will see a dueling situation in which the mini pup may set up against a moving averages inverse pup formation (see Figure 2-1). In these instances, wait for the reaction and break for the true follow-through.

Finally, remember that pups and mini pups need volume to be effective. The volume should instantly rise as the pups trigger. When

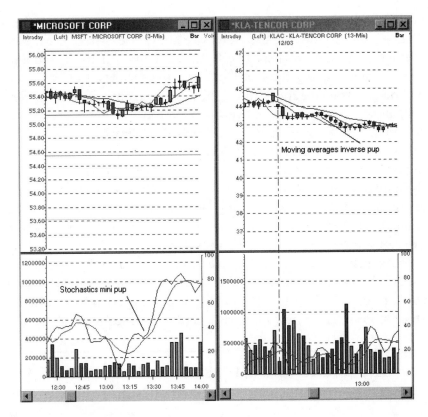

Figure 2–1 Mini pups and pups.

they do not lift the volume, it is important to watch to see if they fade. A fading of a mini pup or pup can turn into a strong reversal, and in make-or-break situations, they can mean the opposite pup effect (e.g., mini pup versus moving averages inverse pup).

ANATOMY OF A LIVING TREND

When stocks break out, they go from a consolidation into an uptrend formation as volume rises. This causes the 5- and 15-period moving average channels to widen, meaning that the 5-period moving average will rise faster than the 15-period moving average, leaving more distance between the two moving averages. Traders will usually see the stock rise above the 5-period moving average and move higher. The bulls will come off the fence and start buying, forcing the bears to cover their shorts. Initially there will be an explosive move in the stock price from the short covering, allowing it to jump above the 5-period moving average and continue higher. Eventually the stock will climax at the stock's pivot or a moving average or when the noodles hit a pivot or moving average resistance. Once the stock climaxes, it will retrace to the 5-period moving average and either coil off that level or overshoot to the 15-period moving average and tighten the range again, probably moving back into another consolidation before a breakout or breakdown (see Figures 2-2 and 2-3).

As just discussed, an active uptrend is one in which the 5-period moving average is rising and making new highs. A rising stock price will drag up the moving averages. Therefore, when a stock stops making new highs, it will often retrace to the 5-period

---

The Trend and Breakout/Breakdowns

- A trend is a force in one direction that forms from a break. As with inertia, an object in motion tends to stay in motion until it meets an equal and opposing motion. There are parts to a trend; once the part hits, it returns to part 1.

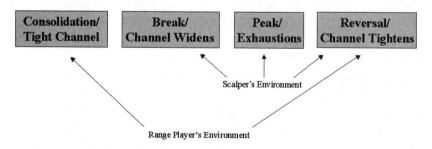

Figure 2–2 The four important parts of a trend.

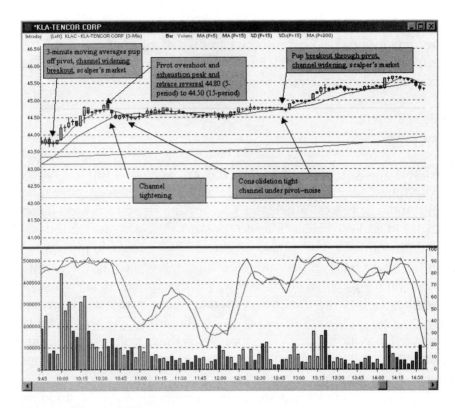

Figure 2–3 The four parts of a trend.

moving average, which is the momentum support. Keep in mind that the longer a stock stays above its 5-period momentum support, the higher the support will rise. This is a very important factor to keep in mind, as it may appear that the stock has made a strong bounce and is now just sitting around, but in reality it is pulling up the moving-averages for a potential move higher. This is very common on the market opening from 9:30 to 9:45 a.m.

If the 5-period uptrend momentum support breaks, then a move to 15-period moving-average trend support is possible. This is usually signaled by a stochastics 80-band slip, which is the Achilles' heel of all short squeezes in all time frames. It is also followed by a 3-shift cross through the 5-period moving average.

Once the stock reaches the 15-period moving average, the trend is no longer active. This is where careful watching of the 3 shift is important. If the 3 shift crosses through the 15-period moving average support, then the trend reverses.

FADES

Market makers adjust their bid and ask spreads proportionately with the noodles. When the noodles rise, market makers raise their bid and ask prices. When the noodles fall, market makers drop their bid and ask prices. This is why stocks oscillate during the day with the noodles. This is also why stocks can change in price without a single retail or institutional order. However, there are times when an institutional order may be so large that there is a sense of urgency to buy or sell stock. A market maker who has a large sell order from an institution needs to find liquidity. The best liquidity is to sell into the buyers. Therefore, when the noodles rise, the market maker will short into the rise. Sometimes this selling becomes very obvious in the form of a fade.

A fade occurs when stocks move inversely with the noodles. An example of a sell fade is KLAC's selling off into a noodles rise. An example of a buy fade is KLAC's price rising into a noodles selloff. These fades can foreshadow a larger move when the noodles reverse direction. If the seller is too obvious in the efforts to sell shares, the other market makers will smell blood and step in front to short the stock, causing a faster breakdown when the noodles support gives way. So if KLAC is sell-fading as the noodles peak out on the rise, then your first instinct should be to look to time a short on KLAC as the noodles move back down. Fades can be distinguished by comparing the 1-minute and 3-minute stochastics/moving averages charts of the stock to those of the noodles. Fades can also many times be noticed on Nasdaq Level 2, as a particular ECN or market maker will hold a price level, preventing parallel movement of the stock with the noodles.

There is a caveat about fades. Fades are most useful in moderate to heavy volume and least useful in light volume. Light volume can make a stock look as if it is fading when in reality the light liquidity is making market makers more cautious about upticking unless the noodles make a stronger move. In other words, light volume can cause a delayed reaction in stock movements. Many times you may see KLAC appear to fade with the noodles as it doesn't uptick, only to uptick minutes later when the noodles move a little higher. Often you won't see stocks react until the 3-minute noodles stochastics get to a higher band, such as the 80 band, and then you will see a fast dynamic push up in the stocks. In contrast, stocks may appear to buy-fade as the 3-minute noodles oscillate down, only to get a dynamic panic after the 3-minute noodles slip under the 20 band. The traders who misread a buy fade in light volume will be buying the stock only to stop out in a fast panic when the stock finally reacts to the more extreme noodles' leandown. This is a situation that you do not want to get trapped in.

A trader has to be very careful about looking for fades in light volume. This is another pitfall of light volume. The delayed reaction on the part of market makers and their failure to adjust spreads instantly with the noodles can head-fake many traders. Therefore, the rule with fades is to use them only in moderate to heavy volume time periods and to remember to slow down on trying to read fades with light volume.

3.5-STRIKE TREND REVERSALS

A trend is a force that will continue to be pushed until an opposing force stops it, just as an object in motion tends to stay in motion. The force behind a trending move can be met with either dynamic volume or erosion through time. The 3.5-strike reversal takes a methodical approach to breaking down the indicators of the opposing force.

A trend reversal is simply an uptrend that reverses into a downtrend or a downtrend that reverses into an uptrend. Despite what many may think, trend reversals do not sneak up out of the blue. Any time a trend reverses, it will go through 3.5 steps, or strikes, as we like to call them. As you know from our discussion on trends, an active trend is one in which the 5-period moving average is continuing to move higher or lower, with the 15-period moving average following. The first step of a reversal is for the 5-period moving average to stop making forward progress and to stall. This leaves the 15-period moving average to continue to progress. The second step is for the 15-period moving average to stop making progress. Technically, this is a consolidation, as both the 5- and the 15-period moving averages are stalled. The 2.5 step is a fade on the retracement. The final 3.5 strike occurs when the retracement coils back and crosses the 3 shift through the 5-period moving average, causing a breakout and reversing the trend.

Let's take an example with MSFT. MSFT is in a 3-minute moving averages active downtrend. This means that the 5-period moving average is making new lows and the 15-period moving average is following lower. Let's say that MSFT's price dropped to 47.40 and coiled back to the 47.50–47.60 range. MSFT's 3-minute 5-period moving average price is 47.50, and the 15-period moving average value is 47.75. Strike 1 happens when MSFT's 5-period moving average stalls as MSFT ticks back up through 47.50 and sits in a range between 47.50 and 47.60. Meanwhile, the 3-minute noodles stochastics rises through the 40 band and the 1-minute noodles stochastics makes an oscillation to the 85 band. This will stall the 5-period moving average and flatten it out. The 15-period moving average, however, is still progressing lower, thereby setting up a potential inverse pup breakdown.

Ten minutes later, MSFT continues to trade around 47.55–47.60 and the 15-period moving average has now dropped to 47.60 and has stopped falling, thereby tightening the channel and forming a consolidation. This is strike 2; we now have a 3-minute moving average consolidation with a 47.50 to 47.60 channel. The 1-minute noodles now peak out at the 90 band and slip back under the 80 band as they oscillate to the 20 band. The 3-minute noodles stochastics stalls at the 60 band. MSFT takes a bounce through 47.60–47.70 and then retraces to 47.60 as the 1-minute noodles fully oscillate under the 20 band. What we are seeing here is a buy fade as the 1-minute stochastics on MSFT and the noodles have made a full oscillation down, but MSFT is actually holding steady on the consolidation. This is strike 2.5. As the 1-minute noodles cross back up through the 20 band, the 3-minute noodles trigger a mini pup from the stall. MSFT holds that 15-period moving average support at 47.60, and as soon as the 1-minute noodles coil back up through the 20 band, the MSFT 3 shift crosses the 15-period moving average up as MSFT makes a fast thrust to 47.80. This is strike 3.5.

MSFT has now reversed into an uptrend, with the 5- and 15-period moving averages actively moving higher. MSFT went from a downtrend to a consolidation to an uptrend. This is how all trend reversals act. Naturally, volume will dictate how fast and how dynamic the reversal will be. Some trend reversals can take an hour (usually on light volume with a long consolidation period), whereas some can take a matter of minutes (on heavy volume with a short consolidation period).

If you are aware of the 3.5-strike reversal, then you should rarely have stocks take you by surprise on the reversals. If you are short MSFT in a downtrend, you are aware by strike 2.5 that a stop and possible reversal of your trade to the long side should be implemented. Once you are in a trade, a downtrend that turns into a consolidation will naturally mean that your premise is no longer intact. Knowing that a stock can never reverse without first breaking the 5-period moving average, many traders use that 5-period moving average as a trailing profit stop. The final trailing stops are always implemented when the 3 shift crosses through the 15-period moving average. It is unfortunate that most traders have no idea about the dynamics of a trend reversal.

SHORT SQUEEZES

All breakouts start off as short squeezes. As previously explained, market makers uptick and downtick their spreads proportionately to the noodles' movements. Therefore, when stocks reach overbought levels, the majority of the market makers are hedging shorts into the buyers. This is how liquidity is provided. The short positions at the high-band stochastics are covered when the stochastics peaks and oscillates back down. This is a natural progression of oscillations and range-bound movement. This is also the pattern in a consolidation.

What happens when a stock breaks through the 1-minute stochastics 90 band and stays up there? This forces market makers to panic, as they have been shorting on the way up. The extended time above the 80 band makes traders very nervous and forces them to start covering their shorts and even hedging back to the long side. The short covering comes in the form of buying and drives the stock higher in price, forcing other market makers to cover their shorts. This in turn triggers a breakout and continued follow-through, bringing in buyers. Short squeezes are extreme, since they rely on the stock's staying above the 80 band, the rational overbought level, on the stochastics for an extended period of time. Usually we cite examples of 1-minute stochastics short squeezes; however, short squeezes can occur in all time frames. It is not a matter of whether a short squeeze will eventually end. The question is when it will end.

There are many instances of the noodles 3-minute stochastics holding above the 80 band for hours, squeezing the market to new highs like a rocket. These are the extreme days; they occur less than 5 percent of the time. The most important thing to remember about short squeezes is that they are active uptrending breakouts. In an active uptrend, the 5-period moving average is the most important support level for continuing the momentum. This 5-period moving average can be quite a distance below where the stock is actually trading, since short squeezes are so violent and fast. The Achilles' heel for a squeeze will be an 80-band stochastics cross back down. Remember the word *cross*! Many times, the stochastics will head-fake to test the 80 band, only to coil back up off the 80 band, causing premature shorts to continue getting squeezed higher. It does not pay to be early shorting against a squeeze.

When the 80-band stochastics finally crosses back down, the stock will usually move back to test the 5-period moving average momentum support. This is usually where a countertrend trader will be covering or paring out shorts. If that 5-period moving average momentum support breaks, then a further retracement to the 15-period moving average support level is possible. This is considered a home run on the retracement, as a potential 3.5-strike reversal also may play out.

It is always important to remember that you are fighting an uptrend and therefore have to restrain your greed. Overstaying your trade on a short squeeze can lead to a short-term profit on the 5-period moving average retracement but getting killed as the stock violently coils and continues to break higher through the 5-period moving average. This is not a place where you want to be sitting too long. If the stock triggers a 3.5-strike reversal breakdown, then new shorts can always be added. It is foolish to give up the natural gains on the retracement in the hope of a home run reversal. Most of the time, traders will catch one leg of the retracement without taking profits, only to get squeezed hard when the stock bounces off its 15-period moving average and breaks out higher. The stupidity is that they will give up a full 1-minute stochastics oscillation to the 20 band in the hope of a bigger move. If you pay attention to the trends and respect the power of a trend, then you will not be one of the many victims of a squeeze.

OVERSHOOTS AND BACKFILLS

Decimalization has brought an interesting phenomenon to the dynamics of stock price movement. Because of the penny increments, stocks tend to overshoot certain price levels. Traders simply panic in order to find liquidity, and the overshooting is a form of spillage that comes from this panicking. It is too tedious and time-consuming to constantly try to match the penny-for-penny bid as a stock is falling rapidly. Just as a trader has keyed in the inside bid to exit MSFT, it can downtick, forcing him to repeatedly cancel and reenter his sell order. All this time, he is missing the inside bid while losing value in his stock. Instead, traders will tend to place an order 0.10 under the inside bid to sweep the ECNs and find liquidity by sacrificing a little in price. For example, when a trader desperately wants to sell shares of MSFT at 49 as the price is declining, but the inside bid and ask are sitting at 49.01 and 49.02, she will often place an order at 48.90 in order to find liquidity on this exit at any price down to 48.90. It is human nature to panic-sell when the bids evaporate as the ask swells with size to sell and vice versa. Therefore, if the crowd goes one way, an experienced trader will find liquidity in that panic.

Stocks tend to overshoot 0.10 above and below 0.50 increments. For example, when MSFT gets to 48, a trader knows right off the bat that 47.90 is an overshoot support level and 48.10 is an overshoot resistance level. Understanding this, an experienced trader who has shorted MSFT at 48.10 will watch the panics overshoot through the 48 level and place his buy order to cover his shares near 47.90, since that's where many longs placed their sweep limit orders to exit. Like a baseball catcher who prepares for the fastball to land in his mitt, an experienced trader reacts in this way to overshoots. Panics provide the best liquidity. On the flip side, if a trader is long MSFT from 47.90 and it overshoots 48, she already anticipates that 48.10 is the overshoot resistance and places her sell order into the buyers up to 48.10.

What happens after an overshoot support or resistance level is hit? The stock will usually backfill. A backfill is a retracement from an overshoot support or resistance level. For example, MSFT may overshoot 48 and hit the 48.10 overshoot resistance, then backfill to under 48 (but usually above 47.90) before reestablishing upward momentum. Backfills once again come from panic. Since these are fast movements, traders will panic into a rising stock and then panic out of the stock once the momentum reverses.

Backfills are useful for taking stop losses. For example, if you shorted MSFT at 47.95 and it overshoots through 48, you should be aware that 48.10 is the overshoot resistance and the spot where a backfill is most likely to take place. Once MSFT hits 48.10, it will often backfill right back under 48, allowing an astute trader to take a stop on the short on the panic overshoots. In this example, you would have reduced your trailing stop to an even stop by waiting for the backfill as opposed to a -0.15 stop by panicking out at 48.10.

This is why overshoots and backfills exist in the market. The de facto rule of thumb is to always look to lock in profits on overshoots and use backfills for stop losses. Taking advantage of overshoots and backfills will help you to maximize your gains and minimize your losses. In short, remember that the levels are 0.40 and 0.60, and 0.90 and 1.10, which are the levels 0.10 above and below the 0.50 increments.

PING-PONG RANGE

The prior examples of overshoots and backfills naturally lead us to the situations in which stocks tend to just hover at the 0.50 increment level and bounce back and forth between 0.10 below and 0.10 above. Constant overshoots to 1.10 or 0.60 and then backfills to 0.90 or 0.40 is a Ping-Pong range. This tends to be a common phenomenon on lighter volume, especially during consolidations. Experienced traders will take advantage of these levels, using the 1-minute stochastics for long and short entries, provided that the noodles are in a consolidation range. By buying under the 0.50 level at the overshoot support and selling the oscillation bounce into the overshoot resistance for 0.15 to 0.20 scalps, traders can methodically profit from the Ping-Pong range.

The caveat here is that eventually the consolidation will break out or break down, and therefore traders should not go to the well too many times. The longer the Ping-Pong range phenomenon continues, the more likely it is that the range will eventually break. By keeping a close eye on the 3 shift, you can avoid getting nailed when the range eventually breaks.

2.5 DE FACTO LEVELS

Every stock has a de facto support level and a de facto resistance level that can be assigned regardless of the charts. This is the 2.50

incremental price level. The 2.50 levels start from 0 and move up in 2.50 increments. For example, a series of 2.50 levels is 15, 17.50, 20, 22.50, 25, 27.50, and so on. This can be attributed to the fact that options are priced in 2.50 increments. Just like a 3-minute 200-period moving average support or resistance or a pivot support or resistance, these levels are sturdy, usually taking strong volume or longer time to break.

We also take into account the 0.10 overshoots on both sides. This means that 2.40 and 2.60 are the overshoot support and resistance, respectively. Does this sound familiar? Overshoots and backfills are very common at the 2.50 levels. Therefore, if MSFT is pulling back from 48, the de facto support would be 47.50, with a 0.10 overshoot support at 47.40. Upon first glance, at any price, a stock will have de facto 2.50 range support and resistance levels. If KLAC is at 32, we can immediately assign a support at 30 and a resistance at 32.50 using the 2.50 de facto level rule.

STICKY 5s LEVELS

Extrapolating from the 2.50 de facto levels, the sticky 5s levels are increments of 5, as in 25, 30, 35, 40, 45, 50, and so on. The ranges are 0.60 above and below the 5s level. For example, MSFT at 45 has a range of 44.40 to 45.60. These levels are deemed "sticky" because a great deal of volume or time is needed to break the range. These ranges rarely break the first time they are tested. A stock's price can be contained within this range for hours, if not days, at a time. Understanding this, a trader can use the low end of the sticky 5s range to enter longs or cover shorts and the high end to exit longs or enter shorts. If a trader is short MSFT at 44.90 and it panics through 44.50, he should be immediately aware that 44.40 is the overshoot support and, most importantly, the sticky 5s low-range support. With this understanding, he will look to lock in his profits as the 44.50 overshoots to 44.40. If a trader is long MSFT from 45.20 and it rises on volume through 45.50, she should be aware that 45.60 is the sticky 5s high-range resistance as well as the overshoot resistance, and she will most definitely anticipate locking in her profits by selling into the buyers through the 44.50–44.60 level. On the flip side, a trader will look to enter the long side on the sticky 5s overshoot support and to short at the sticky 5s overshoot resistance.

Sticky 5s levels can break. They just take a very long time to do so. It is never wise to short the sticky 5s support or to chase the sticky 5s resistance long unless the stock has already broken through those levels first. Therefore, one would want to wait for MSFT to fall to under 54.40 and stay under 54.40 before considering shorting it. Just as you wouldn't touch a cable that fell off a telephone pole, as it could be a live wire, you want to give a stock enough time to securely break the overshoot levels before entering it. By *securely*, we mean that we want to make sure that we are once again in a "safe" neighborhood, with at least the 13-minute and 3-minute moving averages stochastics charts on the stock and the noodles moving in the same direction as the overshoot-level break. Add in a moving average pup and/or a mini pup and it's an even safer entry.

OVERLAPPING SUPPORT AND RESISTANCE LEVELS

Trying to pay attention to all the support and resistance levels on the different time frames in addition to the 2.50 and sticky 5s levels and the pivot points can seem overwhelming. Stocks never move straight up or straight down. These support and resistance levels act as speed bumps. When one level breaks, then it's time to focus on the next level incrementally. The rule of thumb is to focus on the immediate near-term levels closest to the stock. If and when the stock gets closer to another level, you need to once again pay attention to the respective level. We can't predict when a stock will test a support or resistance level, but when it gets close, then we react accordingly.

There will probably be instances of overlap. This is expected and makes things even simpler. When you get two support levels, like a 3-minute 200-period moving average support at a pivot support, it adds more emphasis to the strength of the support. Therefore, overlapping support and resistance levels have double the strength. This means that you will need a very heavy amount of volume or an extended period of time to break those levels. As a trader, you can opt to play with the overlapping levels by playing the long side on overlapping supports and playing the short side on overlapping resistance levels. Never get overconfident about an overlapping support or resistance level. The overlap does not mean that the level cannot break. It just means that it is very difficult to break, thereby buying you time. If a stock has been coiling off an overlapping support level with the stochastics and the noodles, then you can continue to play the long side, with the understanding that eventually it may break down.

To reiterate, throughout the day, both stocks and futures simply move up and down between speed bumps. Either *time* or *volume* will move stock prices over these speed bumps. When volume is lacking, time will take precedence. This is a very linear concept to keep in mind, and it applies to all charts in all time frames. During consolidations, stocks may not appear to have much movement and may have even less volume. However, time is something that is continuing to move. Time along with subtle stock movements can create a trend or a breakout situation. You should be able to pull up the charts on any given stock at any point in the day and immediately point out the speed bumps in the road. Once again, we do not predict whether these speed bumps will be broken. We simply get ready to react once these speed bumps are near. Understanding this makes you stronger than most traders out there.

Overlapping supports also mean that you get many chances to play longs off those levels, especially to counter panic situations. Similarly, overlapping resistances allow you to play multiple shorts off those levels. Does this mean that the supports or resistances cannot break? Absolutely not. They usually cannot break on one push, but several pushes or time erosion will eventually break even overlapping support and resistance levels. The more times you play the overlapping-level premises, the more cautious you have to be and the more aware of the possibility of a break.

Nuances of the Longer Time Frames

This chapter provides an explanation of the advantages and nuances of 13- and 60-minute charts.

Just as a TV meteorologist will use a wide-range Doppler radar to spot oncoming storm fronts, a trader needs to use the wider-range charts, which foreshadow potential moves that the immediate charts are not showing. The 13-minute and 60-minute intraday charts help to foreshadow potential moves in the market. The relationship here can be a little tricky. Although the longer time frames naturally appear to be laggard compared to the 3-minute and 1-minute time frames, they have the ability to show the underlying currents in the market in greater depth. For example, if the TV meteorologist says that there is a strong thunderstorm headed in your direction, wouldn't it be wise to seek precautionary shelter even if it is only drizzling right now? As farfetched as it sounds, the scenario just posed is the equivalent of a 13-minute stochastics 60-band slip and a 3-minute noodles 80-band peak and cross down. In this scenario, you see the 13-minute stochastics coming down, but the 3-minute stochastics is rising. Once the 3-minute stochastics peaks out and falls back down, it moves in line with the 13-minute stochastics, which is still coming down.

The 13-minute stochastics eventually will take precedence; therefore, thunderstorms will abound.

The nice thing is that we no longer need to make a decision as to whether to use the 1- and 3-minute charts or the 13- and 60-minute charts. Instead, we use all of them. By having four time frames, in effect, we get a complete picture of both the local weather and the regional weather. This allows us not only to react to the immediate and present action but to prepare for the upcoming action.

Linearity is a key factor with charts and their time frames. A trader must understand the premise that a stock can be in multiple opposing trends depending on the time frame the trader is playing. For example, MSFT can be in a 3-minute and 13-minute uptrend at the same time that it is in a 60-minute and daily downtrend. It is all a matter of perspective. Range/swing traders will favor fully playing the 13- and 60-minute charts. Scalpers should use the 13-minute and 60-minute charts only as a backdrop for their shorter time frame trades.

NUANCES OF THE 13-MINUTE CHARTS

The 13-minute moving averages and stochastics chart should be considered a midrange time frame. In the game of American football, it can be considered the midfield. This chart will have near-term effects on the 3-minute moving averages chart. If the 13-minute stochastics chart is rising, then this helps to strengthen a 3-minute stochastics rise. The rule of thumb is that *you don't want to fight the direction of the 13-minute stochastics for any extended duration of time, even in the shorter time frames.* This means that if the 13-minute stochastics on MSFT is coming down through the 70 band, then you want to be clear that going long is a countertrend play, and therefore you want to keep it to as short a time duration as possible. The better trade is to utilize the 3-minute and 1-minute triggers to find an entry on the short side to coincide with the 13-minute stochastics oscillation down.

This is not to say that going against the 13-minute charts is ineffective. There are instances in which the 3-minute and the 60-minute charts are pointing in the same direction but in the opposite direction from the 13-minute charts. In these cases, the 60-minute chart will eventually take the lead direction, but *not* without a wiggle or reversal attempt on the 3-minute chart. A short-term trader like a scalper will probably get wiggled out long before the 60-minute chart can have its effect. Therefore, it is very important that scalpers learn to accept their style and enter trades only when the background longer time frames are aligned with their shorter time frames for the best safety.

The noodles are the puppet strings that pull the rest of the market. This is why we stress watching the 13-minute noodles charts carefully intraday. We mostly want to note when the 13-minute stochastics is making a 20-band cross up or an 80-band cross down, in addition to the trend of the moving averages. This information helps us to plan out our basket stock trades, using the movement of the noodles as a lead indicator.

Please always remember this rule: *If the 13-minute noodles are in an uptrend and the stochastics crosses down through the 80 band, then we can expect a pullback to test the 15-period moving average.* For example, if the noodles are uptrending on the 13-minute moving averages chart with a 5-period moving average momentum support at 965 and a 15-period moving average support at 955, then we can expect a pullback to 955 when the stochastics crosses back down through the 80 band. Usually, this will happen when the momentum support at the 965 level breaks down. A trader can use the 3-minute moving averages chart for entry on the short side with this backdrop, entering the short when the 3 shift crosses through the 965 level.

If the 13-minute noodles are in a downtrend and the stochastics crosses up through the 20 band, then we can anticipate a move to test the 15-period moving average. For example, if the noodles are downtrending on the 13-minute moving averages chart with a 5-period moving average momentum resistance at 955 and a 15-period moving average resistance at 965, then we can expect a bounce to 965 when the stochastics crosses back up through the 20 band.

In most cases, the 15-period moving average on the 13-minute chart will often overlap with the 5-period moving average on the 60-minute moving averages chart (see Figure 3-1). Therefore, it is very important that traders understand that while these trades may appear to be breakdowns on the 3-minute chart, they are merely retracements on the 13-minute and 60-minute trend charts. With this understanding, traders will look to take their profits on those tests of the 15-period moving average. If the 3.5-strike rule can apply and a trend reversal occurs, then we can simply reenter on the long side with more safety.

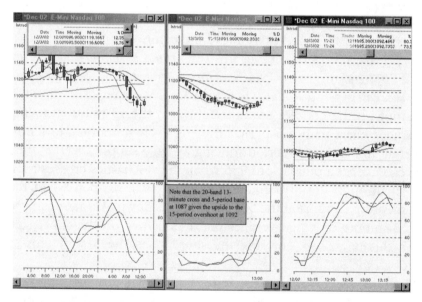

The 60-minute chart on the right is a downtrend and stochastics full oscillation slip. The 3-minute noodles show a hammer just near the pivot and 20-band cross up and a mini pup at the 40 band. Notice how the 13-minute noodles make a 20-band cross on the 5-period base at the 1087 break, allowing an upside to the overlapping 13-minute, 15-minute, and 60-minute 5-period resistances at 1192.50.

Figure 3–1 Wider time frame channel tightening.

MINI PUPS AND PUPS ON THE 13-MINUTE CHARTS

The greatest foreshadowing setups on the 13-minute charts are the stochastics mini pups or moving average pups. This is an absolutely amazing phenomenon that all traders need to be aware of. *If the 13-minute stochastics on the noodles or your stock forms a mini pup, always take this as a sign that you should watch the 3-minute moving averages for a potential pup breakout.* This pattern has been a consistent moneymaker. The wider time frames will give mini pups or pups first and then deliver them to astute traders in the form of a 3-minute moving average pup (see Figure 3-2).

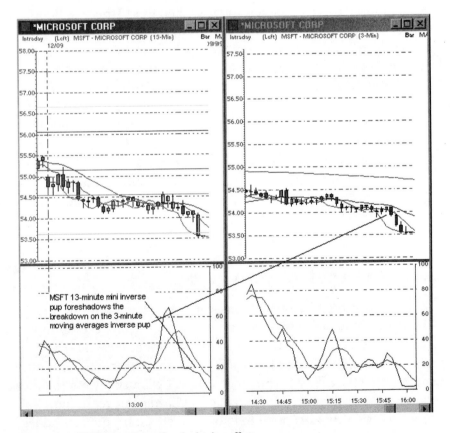

Figure 3–2 Wider time frame foreshadowing effect.

The beauty of this formation cannot be understated. In normal circumstances, we would have to wait for a 3-shift crossover through the 5-period moving average to trigger a moving average pup breakout on the 3-minute chart. Although we know that a potential pup may be triggered from a flat 5-period moving average with a rising diagonal 15-period moving average, we wait for the confirmation before taking the breakout entry. With a 13-minute mini pup, we don't have to wait for confirmations. The mini pup already tells us to lean on the pup being triggered on the 3-minute charts. This allows us to make early entries and to reap larger gains when the pup triggers.

This is great when the pup triggers on your basket stock. However, when it triggers on the noodles, its effects can be felt throughout the whole market. In fact, when the 13-minute noodles trigger a mini pup, all traders need to watch the 3-minute noodles moving averages for a pup breakout setup and then watch their own basket stocks, which usually will mirror the noodles. A noodles-based 3-minute moving averages pup can cause stocks to explode to the upside dramatically, as the noodles will pull them higher. This is where strong basket traders will hit a number of tier 1 stocks long side for the breakout in the noodles. The opposite would naturally apply with mini inverse pups on the 13-minute noodles. In that case, we would be watching for 3-minute moving averages inverse pup breakdowns on the noodles and across the board on basket stocks.

NUANCES OF THE MINI PUPS

By now, you should be pretty familiar with what a mini pup looks like. A mini pup is a pup on a stochastics chart. You need to understand that every mini pup on a 3-minute stochastics chart is usually composed of at least two oscillation attempts on the 1-minute stochastics chart. This means that scalpers will usually enter either the first leg or the second leg of the stochastics move. In light volume, the first-leg movement may be very small. It's the second leg, once the 3-minute mini pup is triggered, that is the biggest move.

This makes perfect sense. The 1-minute stochastics will always move higher first and peak out first. When the 1-minute stochastics peaks out, the sellers and shorts come in. The 3-minute stochastics may be rising, but it will never rise faster than the 1-minute stochastics. A scalper will usually exit on the 80-band overshoots into the peak. Once that stochastics slips, the 3-minute stochastics should stall, thereby setting up a potential mini pup on a 1-minute stochastics cross back up, which represents the second leg of the 3-minute stochastics oscillation.

If you think through what a mini pup represents, this should make complete sense. The shorts that come in to sell on the 1-minute stochastics peak and oscillation back down will stall out the 3-minute stochastics oscillation move up. Once that 1-minute stochastics crosses back up, the 3-minute stochastics continues higher, thereby squeezing out the shorts and driving the price higher.

The converse naturally holds true on mini inverse pup formations. The 3-minute stochastics will oscillate back down while the 1-minute stochastics has already oscillated back down and is crossing back up. The crossing up of the 1-minute stochastics stalls out the %d on the 3-minute stochastics to set up a mini inverse pup attempt. When the sellers come in and overwhelm the buyers off the low band, the 1-minute stochastics will peak early in the oscillation and then sell off again, thereby kicking off the second leg of the 3-minute stochastics oscillation down by triggering the mini inverse pup.

NUANCES OF THE 60-MINUTE CHARTS

The purpose of the 60-minute charts is to get the ultimate bird's-eye view of the intraday trend. The 60-minute charts are the equivalent of the end zone on the other side of the field in the game of American football. A 60-minute moving averages trend will often have a wide channel and last from less than a day to several days. This is the swing trader's main weapon of choice. It is also the toughest chart for a scalper to play, since its range is usually so wide. The range on a 60-minute chart may be 5 to 10 times what a scalper may expect on a normal 3-minute chart wiggle. This reiterates the point that scalpers need to use these wider time frame charts, especially the 60-minute chart, only as a backdrop to gauge the environment. Trend support and resistance levels on the 60-minute charts are very strong, and they need to be known and respected even by short-time-frame players. They will often overlap with existing support and resistance levels on the shorter time frames.

The key is to know what those overlapping levels are. It is also very important for traders to know that a 60-minute moving averages support or resistance level doesn't simply break by overshooting that level or even getting a 3-shift cross on the 3-minute chart. For example, even through MSFT's 60-minute 15-period moving average uptrend support may be 46.50, a trader should not assume that MSFT has broken its 60-minute 15-period moving average until the 3 shift crosses through it. In fact, MSFT may show a 3-minute moving averages breakdown through 46.50, causing MSFT to trade down to 46.25 momentarily on panics. It is foolish to step right in and assume a 60-minute breakdown because MSFT can bounce right back on the 60-minute chart even from as low as 45.90 without breaking the uptrend. This is how lenient a 60-minute chart can be.

MINI PUPS AND PUPS ON THE 60-MINUTE CHARTS

As with the 13-minute charts, the best foreshadowing effect of the 60-minute charts comes in the form of stochastics mini pups or moving average pups and inverse pups. When the 60-minute charts show a mini pup, this bullish pattern can last all day. The effects will often not be very transparent in any of the other charts. This is good. We can't make money in complete transparency. *When you spot a 60-minute mini pup on your stock, you must immediately watch for the 13-minute noodles to align in the same direction and then look for the 3-minute moving averages pup setups.* If you spot this pattern on the noodles, it's a wake-up call to prepare for a strong rally in the markets. You cannot pass up 60-minute stochastics mini pups on the noodles or pups on the moving averages. In these cases, assume that the largest domino has been tipped over and that a chain reaction will be triggered when the 13-minute noodles stochastics crosses back up.

Low-band mini pups on the 60-minute charts and high-band mini inverse pups are very strong breakout and breakdown formations, respectively. Once again, you do not need to play them for the full wiggle and move; rather, you should spot them and use the shorter time frames for the trigger entry. In Chapter 4, we will show you a pattern called the Perfect Storm that is a prime setup triggered primarily by the 60-minute mini pup. Remember, the 60-minute noodles are the major domino out there. If they break or fall, then it's just a matter of time before the rest of the dominos fall over.

There is another inherent benefit of the 60-minute pups and inverse pups. This applies to gaps on stocks. Many times, stocks may gap up or down far enough to trigger a moving average pup or inverse pup on the opening. If the gaps down are large (through the 5-period moving average), many times we can assume the inverse pup on the open and take premarket shorts that are confirmed by the 3 shift shortly after the opening bell. The opposite applies on gaps up, where we see a 60-minute moving average pup breakout on the opening ticks.

One caveat to note: If they lean down a 13-minute mini pup or especially a 60-minute mini pup, it means that the sellers are *very* strong, and this should be noted. It takes a lot of strength to lean a mini pup down or a mini inverse pup up. This is what accounts for the nice follow-through that we usually get as a result. Also keep in mind that pups and mini pups need volume to be effective. This volume comes from the squeezing action or the panics triggered by leandowns. When volume is light, it is important that you give the mini pups and pups some time to play out.

DEVELOPING THE MINDSET FOR THE LONGER TIME FRAMES

Scalpers should use the longer time frames only as a backdrop upon which to base their short-term trades. For example, seeing a 13-minute mini inverse pup slip and a 3-minute stochastics 80-band slip sets up a nice short for an oscillation down on the 3-minute stochastics. To actually maximize gains from the longer time frames, it takes a swing trader's mentality to be able to calmly sit through the shorter time frame wiggles that may ultimately trigger reversals.

This mindset is not something that can easily be adopted immediately. Taking the previous example, a true 13-minute player would not only ride the 3-minute stochastics oscillation down, but also stay short through a 3-minute stochastics oscillation back up. To a short-term trader, this is sloppy and indicative of someone who is not paying attention to the trend. However, both traders are right. A 3-minute trend player is following his rules, whereas a 13-minute player is paying attention only to the wider trend, which allows for wider ranges. In fact, the ranges are so wide that a 3-minute uptrend and downtrend can be established within the ranges of the 13-minute trend. You should be able to see that it is not so much a matter of mental toughness as of assessing which time frame you prefer to give priority to.

To develop this comfort zone takes experience. It is not easy, as you will have to actively control your reactions on the shorter time frame moves. This will go against what you are conditioned to. The experience can be obtained by starting off with fewer shares, paring on shorter time frame moves with the 13-minute time frame, and riding the resulting smaller position only as long as the wider time frames maintain the original premise of the trade. Always keep in mind that since you allocated fewer shares, the dollar difference will remain the same. This is the key factor that will allow you to fend off the gag reflex.

In addition, the moving averages in the longer time frames are used in the same way as those in the shorter time frames. This means that if the stochastics is oscillating down and the stock is in a downtrend, then the 5-period moving average is the active downtrend resistance and the 15-period moving average is the resistance. Knowing these quantitative values helps to alleviate the stress and confusion because you are aware and prepared to react.

A 13-minute time frame may mean that you will have to sit through triple the wiggle range you expect with a 3-minute time frame. A 60-minute time frame may mean a wiggle range of up to 5 to 10 times the scalp range, and this range can last hours to several days. For this reason, the best way to play is to allocate specifically to the time frame and stick to those premises. *Range/swing traders are best adapted to play the 13- and 60-minute charts. Scalpers should use the 13-minute and 60-minute charts only as a backdrop and should use the shorter time frame (3-minute and 1-minute) charts for the actual trades. Combination traders will use the short-term triggers to pare profits and trim shares to the smaller numbers of shares typical of the range/swing trade style for the 13-minute and 60-minute charts.* This will ensure the least amount of discomfort and provide the securest method of capturing profits.

In professional boxing, styles make fights. The same applies in trading. There will be days when the scalpers will get very little action because of the tight-range trending action, which the range/swing traders will enjoy. There will be days when there are a lot of oscillations with little net trending movement, where the scalpers will reap the most benefit and range/swing traders get very little. Ideally, you want to build yourself up to be a combination trader, able to switch time frames fluently to take advantage of most market conditions. We will go over developing into a combination trader in Chapter 6.

THE BEST METHOD FOR WIDER TIME FRAMES

Adjusting to the wider time frames is tough when you have the shorter time frames in front of you. The solution is to create a second layout page, calling it the range page, and just have the 13-minute, 60-minute, and daily time frame charts set up for the futures, stock, $vix.x, and $sox.x. By not having the 1- and 3-minute time frames and Nasdaq Level 2, you distance yourself from the shorter-term wiggles and noise. Remember that ranging a trade using the 13- and 60-minute time frames requires wider wiggle room for a larger gain; therefore, make sure you have a compelling trend to play. The nice thing about range trading is that it can be less stressful as long as you are adjusted to the time frames and aware of the wider ranges.

Prime and Fractured Trade Setups

This chapter provides an explanation of the best setups to enter and exit trades, with illustrations.

The market will always try to hide transparency. The majority of a market trading day will be filled with noise, consolidations, and lighter volume. This is all part of an effort to wiggle and shake you out and take your money. This should be a given going into every single trading day.

What most traders do not realize is that most trades are made fractured time frame setups. A *fractured* setup is one in which the 3-minute, 13-minute, and 60-minute moving averages and stochastics are divergent. For example, there is a 3-minute downtrend on MSFT but a 13-minute rising stochastics uptrend and a 60-minute falling stochastics in a consolidation. These fractured setups are the most common, and they can lead traders to overtrade and take a lot of stop losses. This is a bad environment to step into, especially for new traders.

How does a person reduce the odds of getting mugged? He stays out of rough neighborhoods. This same thinking applies to trading. You want to make sure you are in a friendly and safer environment when you make trades. This "safe" neighborhood is one in which at least the 13-minute time frame and the 3-minute time frame on your stock and futures charts are pointing in the same direction.

PRIME SETUPS

Every trader needs to start off with a prime setup. Prime setups are the highest-probability trade setups, which also means that they will not be common. Usually one will find at least two prime setups during a trading day. Some trading days will have more than others.

In addition to being elusive, prime setups have a small window of opportunity for traders to enter before the setup becomes too transparent and the risk rises. Timing is everything. Most traders can't tell the difference between a prime setup and a fractured setup, and that is a crying shame. This is why most traders fail at this game. When traders fall into a slump, they need to have something to fall back on. This would be reverting to playing only prime setups. So let's go over them.

Three-Lane Highway

This formation occurs when the 60-minute, 13-minute, and 3-minute moving averages and stochastics charts are moving in the same direction. The nice thing about a three-lane highway is that it is very forgiving. If the 3-minute moving averages chart reverses and forms a breakout, there will be many overlapping resistance levels stemming from the 13-minute and 60-minute charts. Ideally, traders want to gauge the 13-minute and 60-minute charts and use the 3-minute chart as the entry point and trigger.

From this point, the scalpers will use the foreshadowing effects of the wider time frame 13- and 60-minute charts to scalp the panics on the 3-minute breaks. Range/swing traders will continue to ride the 13- and 60-minute time frames. Combination players will use the 3-minute trigger with trailing profit stops to pare 70 percent of their profits and range trade the remaining shares with the 13-minute and 60-minute premises. This setup has something for every style of trader.

Once again, the optimal time to spot a three-lane highway is often right before the 3-minute time frame triggers it. The 13- and 60-minute time frames are obviously the tougher time frames that need to be aligned. Once the 13-minute and 60-minute time frames are aligned, it is just a matter of the 3-minute direction reversing. It's like a three-number combination to a lock. Once that third number is clicked, the lock opens. Always try to position yourself as the last time frame starts to turn. This will allow you to reap the most from the setup. *The rule of thumb is to start by noting any time the 13-minute and 60-minute time frames are moving in the same direction in terms of trend and stochastics.* Once this is set up, it's just a matter of time before the 3-minute time frame triggers the trade. So remember, watch the 60-minute, gauge the 13-minute, and time your entry with the 3-minute.

Perfect Storm

This formation is the same as a three-lane highway, but with the addition of mini pups (or inverse pups) or moving average pups on the 13-minute and 60-minute charts with a trigger on the 3-minute moving averages chart (see Figure 4-1). This will usually be set up with a 60-minute mini inverse pup and a 13-minute mini inverse pup that will foreshadow a 3-minute mini inverse pup. When this formation triggers, you need to jump all over it.

The beauty of this setup is that everyone can win. On a perfect storm short setup, the scalper can benefit from the 3-minute breakdown on the immediate panics. The range/swing trader can benefit from the extended selling presented by the 13-minute mini inverse pup and the 60-minute mini inverse pup. This setup basically covers the first down, midfield, and end zone. The beauty of it is that there shouldn't be much room for wiggles, since there are three layers of resistance that overhang, presenting enough opportunities to profit from the breakdowns across the board (see Figure 4-2).

Once again, always make sure that you are aware of your time frames. If you are a scalper, you will feel confidence in the 13- and 60-minute mini inverse pups, but you will take profits on the

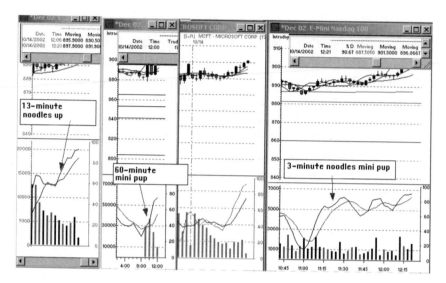

Figure 4–1 Perfect storm setup.

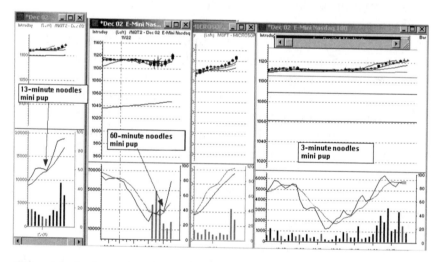

Figure 4–2 Another perfect storm.

breakdown panics nonetheless. The range players will also pare profits on panics and set stops based on the 13- or 60-minute moving averages. The 5-period moving average will be the profit stop on the 3-shift cross, and the 15-period moving average can be the final stop on a 3-shift crossover.

It is important that traders do not get overconfident and sit in the position without taking profits in the allocated time frames. Eventually, all perfect storms will develop into fractured setups. Naturally, the 3-minute charts will eventually bottom or reverse and go back up. This alone negates the perfect storm, and there is now a fractured setup with two opposing charts. Treat it as such! The 13-minute charts will provide the next key resistances. If those resistances break, then the 60-minute charts provide the last layer of resistance.

If the 13-minute and 60-minute charts continue to hold resistances and break the 3-minute chart back down, then traders can look to reenter on the 3-minute trigger. See how that works? However, if the 3-minute charts break into an uptrend (3-shift crossover confirmation) and the 13-minute charts break into an uptrend, then traders can opt to go long on the 3-minute trigger, as two charts are bullish against one chart that is not (the 60-minute). The best long-side play will be to wait for all three charts to reverse and go back up and then use the 3-minute charts for a new trigger on the long side. Always remember that transparency does not last in the market. Therefore, when it's there, you must take advantage of it and be cashing in your chips.

Scalper's Perfect Storm

The mini inverse pup or inverse pup across three time frames (usually the 3-minute, 13-minute, and 60-minute) is a traditional perfect storm. There is another smaller version of a perfect storm that is best suited for scalpers. This formation is composed of a 3-minute mini inverse pup, a 3-minute moving averages inverse pup, and a 1-minute mini inverse pup trigger. This is not a very common pattern, but when you get it, you should jump all over it for the scalp.

The nice thing about this pattern is that the 1-minute stochastics triggers the actual entry for a mini inverse pup oscillation down. The 3-minute mini inverse pup and moving averages inverse pup make the pattern safe against immediate wiggles, as the trend is also triggering a powerful breakdown signal. Normally, you would get a 3-minute moving averages inverse pup dueling with a 3-minute mini pup for a make-or-break situation triggered by the response from the 1-minute stochastics. In this case, you get no resistance from the 3-minute stochastics because it's in a mini inverse pup pattern also. This is a license to take all the money you can from the bank vault within a short period of time!

The caveat here is not to get too comfortable because this is primarily a scalper's perfect storm. If you overstay your welcome, the trade can move against you. This is why it's important to prioritize the 1-minute time frames, using the 3-minute moving averages and stochastics to watch your back.

Fractured Setups

The majority of the setups during the day will be fractured setups. These are setups in which the 3-minute, 13-minute, and 60-minute time frames diverge. This means that one or all of the charts may show different moving averages trends or stochastics directions. This divergence is what prevents the setup from being a three-lane highway and makes it a fractured setup. These types of setups are only for traders who have already nailed consistency in playing prime setups.

When it comes to fractured setups, traders need to make sure that at least two of the charts are in the same direction. The more time frames are in the same direction as your trade, the better the odds. Allocation is also very important. The shorter the time frame, the larger the number of shares that can be used. By the same token, the longer the time frames, the smaller the number of shares that can be used. For scalpers, the best fractured setups will be those using the 13-minute stochastics and moving averages with the 3-minute stochastics and moving averages. In fact, *a good rule of thumb is to avoid fighting the 13-minute stochastics.* This means that if the 13-minute stochastics is rising on the noodles and your stock's chart, then it is not wise to be shorting. It's even less wise if the 13-minute moving averages are in an uptrend.

The time to short uptrending 13-minute moving averages is when the 13-minute stochastics peaks and crosses the 80 band down and the 5-period moving average support breaks down. This will allow shorts to reap a potential oscillation on the stochastics to the 15-period moving average support. The 3-minute and 1-minute stochastics charts will often give you a good signal to enter on the short side. Although the 3-minute moving averages chart may be in an immediate downtrend, it is important to remember that the 13-minute chart is still in an uptrend, although the uptrend is no longer active. Once again, this provides a nice way to benefit from the 5-period momentum support breakdown, which will often panic the futures and the stocks to test their 15-period moving average supports.

The most important thing to remember about playing fractured setups is that there is a time frame looming that is going against your trade. If you play the 13-minute and 3-minute time frames, then you must understand that the 60-minute time frame is still looming against your trade. It is important to know where the support and resistance levels lie on that 60-minute chart in order to properly gauge the extent of the moves before the conflicting time frame gets tested. The 60-minute 5-period moving average often sits on the 13-minute 15-period moving average in trends.

In many cases, a fractured setup may get you into the trade for a nice pared profit gain and then turn into a three-lane highway for continued gains. Quite simply, if the 13-minute and 3-minute charts are weak enough, they may be able to turn the 60-minute charts into a breakdown also. Therefore, that 15-period moving average support on the 13-minute uptrend may actually turn into a breakdown that is strong enough to drive the noodles and your stock to test and break the 15-period moving average supports on the 60-minute chart.

This is naturally the best-case scenario, as you have pulled off a beautiful 3.5-strike complete reversal and breakdown on every time frame. This is considered the home run result of playing a fractured setup. However, this is not the result to be expected every time. What happens when you try to swing for a home run every time? You strike out a heck of a lot more. Home runs are a gift and the result of good luck. You strive for base hits and get rewarded every once in a while with a home run. You should never be looking for home runs on every trade.

In the last scenario, the trade with the least resistance would naturally be to wait out a 3-minute stochastics and moving averages downtrend to enter on the long side, since the 13-minute and 60-minute charts are indicating an uptrend and the stochastics are rising. You check the 5- and 15-period moving averages supports on the 13-minute and 60-minute noodles and your stock charts and wait for those to test. If they hold, the 3-minute charts will be the trigger on the 3-shift cross back up to enter on the long side. What formation did this just set up? Exactly. It set up a three-lane highway, since the 13- and 60-minute charts are uptrending. You simply waited for the 3-minute downtrend to reverse and took the long side with the uptrend. You now have 3-, 13-, and 60-minute uptrending charts—a full three-lane highway from a fractured mode. See how that works?

Threading the Noodles

When we make a shorter time frame countertrend play like a 1-minute or 3-minute against the opposite direction of the 13- and 60-minute charts, we call it *threading the noodles*. It's like surfing on the edge before the wave comes crashing down. This type of trading is naturally dangerous in that you have only one lane in your favor, the shorter time frame chart.

Why would you make this dangerous play? In light-volume markets, there is less fluidity, which allows the shorter time frames, especially the 1-minute, to oscillate without moving the wider time frames immediately. In fact, the 13- and 60-minute charts will still be in a stage of trying to find a direction. This allows a short-term scalper to capitalize on quick scalps, naturally being careful not to overstay her welcome. In light-volume markets, the only liquidity available will be at the tail end of pops and drops. This means that you can't really go long because if you get filled, it's probably going to be at the peak. You also can't go short because when the stock drops, you're likely to be filled near the bottom. Therefore, the only way to play is to short the pops on 1-minute stochastics high-band peaks near pivot resistances and to go long near pivot and overlapping supports with a 1-minute stochastics 20-band bounce. In these instances, it is also wise to get the support of the 3-minute stochastics in the same direction as your 1-minute stochastics. This type of trading works well in those Ping-Pong ranges with overlapping support/resistance levels and coils.

This type of trading should be limited to only two trades a day. What tends to happen many times is that traders get overconfident after two or three good trades, completely ignore the 13-minute and 60-minute charts when they trigger, and get squeezed out of all of their earlier profits. Know when to say when.

Mini Pup versus Pup Make or Break

Right before a moment of impact, you will often get a make-or-break scenario in which the 3-minute moving average will show a pup setup with flat-line 5-period and rising 15-period moving averages and the 3-minute stochastics will show a mini inverse pup setup. As the name says, either the 3-minute moving averages will form a pup breakout and cross the stochastics back up or the 3-minute stochastics will form a mini inverse pup and the 3 shift will cross the 15-period moving average to break down. Whenever you see this setup, get ready to react.

Let's quickly review the dynamics of what sets up a make-or-break situation. The stock will make a move like a breakout squeeze, then peak out and retrace to the 5-period moving average momentum support. Meanwhile, the 3-minute stochastics also makes an oscillation up through the 80 band. The bulls are in control here. After the initial peak, which will probably be near a pivot resistance, the stock will retrace through the 5-period moving average and often wiggle to the 15-period moving average. When this wiggle happens, the 3-minute stochastics also peaks and slips back under the 80 band with the 1-minute stochastics. The bulls are taking a breather on profit taking, and the bears have stepped in to short. The bears know that the 15-period moving average is where the stock is likely to attempt a 1-minute stochastics bounce, so they cover on the 1-minute stochastics low bands. At this point, the 3-minute stochastics is slipping to the 70 band as the 1-minute noodles near the 20 band and cross back up, and the stock is bouncing off its 15-period moving average support on the 3-minute chart. The 1-minute stochastics coil and bounce is expected and tries to oscillate back up. This is where the make-or-break scenario will play out.

If the 1-minute noodles bounce hard enough to cross the 3-minute stochastics back up, thereby nullifying the mini inverse pup, then the 3-minute moving averages will trigger a pup break-out to the long side. If the 1-minute stochastics bounces and then peaks and slips again, then the 3-minute mini inverse pup triggers and will nullify the 3-minute moving averages pup into a consoli-dation breakdown. The 1-minute stochastics holds the key to which scenario is going to play out. Ideally, you want to watch for mini pups on the 1-minute stochastics chart for a stronger signal. So if the 1-minute stochastics bottoms and coils back up to the 40 band, then stalls and forms a mini pup, you can take the long side for a pup breakout on the 3-minute moving averages chart. If the 1-minute stochastics bottoms and crosses back up through the 20 band, then stalls and triggers a mini inverse pup slip, you can short the stock using the 3-minute mini inverse pup as the lead premise. The 3 shift on the 3-minute moving averages chart will be your confirming indicator (see Figure 4-3).

Is there a way to perhaps get a foreshadowing heads up as to which will trigger? Absolutely. The 13-minute stochastics will fore-shadow the 3-minute moving averages pup if there is a mini pup and a 3-minute moving averages inverse pup if there is a mini inverse pup. As discussed earlier, this is the beauty of the 13-minute charts: They can foreshadow which way the underlying current is flowing.

The Lead and the Trigger

You should not confuse the role of the 13- and 60-minute charts with that of the 1-minute stochastics chart. The 1-minute stochas-tics chart will be the trigger. The 13- and 60-minute charts act as

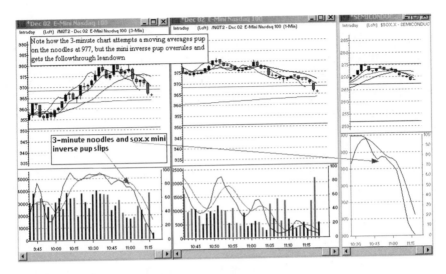

Figure 4–3 Make or break: mini inverse pup versus moving averages pup.

a Doppler radar; they do the job of foreshadowing and thereby take the role of a lead tool.

When a make-or-break situation arises, a trader should always note whether the 13-minute stochastics, especially on the noodles, is trying to foreshadow a mini pup or a mini inverse pup. If there is a mini pup, then a trader should naturally be predisposed to looking for a 3-minute moving averages pup breakout and waiting for the 1-minute stochastics to give the trigger on a mini pup or a crossover back up. If there is a 13-minute mini inverse pup forming, then the trader should be looking to play the 3-minute moving averages inverse pup breakdown, using the 1-minute stochastics as the trigger on a mini inverse pup or a crossover back down. The wider time frame charts act as a lead, and the 1-minute stochastics is the trigger.

Tightening the Lanes

Anytime you get yourself into a slump or a series of drawdowns, you have to go back to the basics and tighten the lanes. That means reverting to the three-lane highways. If you are scalping, then make sure you are in an environment where the channels on the 3-minute moving averages are wider on your stock and the noodles. Look for three-lane movements using the 1-minute stochastics, the 3-minute stochastics and moving averages, and the 13-minute stochastics and moving averages. If the channels are tight, you must revert to the 13-minute, 60-minute, and daily charts for range mode. The wider the time frames you are using, the less you are concerned with what is happening now as opposed to what will be happening in the future. The wider time frames have a great ability to foreshadow.

LIMITING RED TRADES

It's not a matter of making green trades in this game, it's a matter of keeping the red trades to a minimum. By following five basic rules, you can probably reduce your percentage of red trades by at least 50 percent. There are exceptions to the rules at times, but in the long run, the rules will play out and will be statistically significant. Especially in the beginning, traders must follow these rules:

Rule 1: Don't Fight the 13-Minute Stochastics and the Trend

The 13-minute stochastics will usually win 80 percent of the time, so don't bother fighting it. Either trade with the 13-minute stochastics in the immediate term or wait for it to reverse.

Rule 2: Don't Play in Light Volume

Light volume makes for lots of noise. What may appear to be a mini pup can turn into a crossover and back. When there is no volume, there are head fakes galore, especially for scalpers.

Rule 3: Don't Play Tight Channels

Tight channels are usually consolidations, so wait for the confirmed breaks. If the tight channel is in a trend, that trend can reverse fast. With only a few candles, it's better to wait for the breakout expansion into a wider channel to play.

Rule 4: Don't Chase Extreme Stochastics Bands

This means that you should stay away from going long above the 80 band on the 3- and 1-minute stochastics charts and shorting under the 20 band on the 3- and 1-minute stochastics charts.

Rule 5: Don't Fight the Pivots or Overlapping Support or Resistance Levels

When pivots first test, they act as a support when stocks fall or a resistance when stocks bounce. An overlapping pivot and moving averages level is even tougher to break on the first attempt. About 80 percent of the time, you will get an overshoot and then a reversal. Therefore, it's wiser to go against the immediate moves on the pivot overshoots for retracements. It's better to wait for the pivot and overlapping level to slowly break first.

DERIVING PREMISES

When you are deriving premises, you have to understand that the moving averages are a road map and the stochastics is the engine. In order for a stock to get from point A to point B (moving averages and pivots), there must be a force that drives it (stochastics). By using both of these together, you will be able to develop premises. For example, you may look at an MSFT chart and note that if the MSFT 3-minute chart forms a mini pup with the 3-minute noodles, then the next upside resistance sits at 51.25. MSFT is currently trading at 50.80 with rising 13-minute noodles and 13-minute stochastics charts. The 1-minute stochastics just retraced to the 30 band, and the noodles are just shy of the 955 pivot support as MSFT slips back to the 15-period moving average support at 50.80. From here, you can derive the premises, using the 1-minute stochastics as a trigger for an entry into an uptrending 13-minute noodles and 3-minute noodles mini pup for a 3-minute moving averages pup breakout on the 5-period break at 50.90 on MSFT.

To help you derive premises even better, we have put together a cheat sheet (Figure 4-4) that allows a trader to determine strong setups.

Traders' Cheat Sheet

- Always analyze by starting with the wider time frames and narrowing down. It's a mistake to go from short-term to longer-term charts– this is the problem with the impulse traders who go backward and start with the shorter time frames before looking at wider time frames.

- **Premises for Long Trades and *Short Trades (in italics)*:**
  - 1-minute stochastics low-band coil (mini pups even better) or *1-minute stochastics high-band slip for short*
  - 3-minute stochastics low-band coil (mini pups even better) or *3-minute stochastics high-band slip for short*
  - 13-minute noodles stochastics up (mini pups even better) or *13-minute stochastics high-band slip for short*
  - 60-minute noodles stochastics up (mini pups even better) or *60-minute stochastics down for short*
  - 3-minute 200-period moving average support
  - Pivot support
  - Overlapping support (even better)
  - Fibonacci support/resistance level

- **Type of Play**
  - Reentry into the trend off 5- or 15-period moving average or support resistance
  - Exhaustion peak and reversal
  - Channel tightening coil gap fill to 15-period moving average
  - 3.5-strike reversal
  - Three-lane highway
  - Breakout of breakdown
  - Fractured setup scalp threading the noodles
  - Perfect storm!!!

- **Support/Resistances Road Map (Figure Out Support and Then Resistance)**
  - Pivot support on stock and/or noodles
  - 200-period moving average support (3, 8, 13, or 60 minute)
  - Wider time frame 5-15 and period moving averages support/resistance (13-minute, 60-minute, daily, or weekly)
  - 2.50 and sticky 51s level

- **Type of Trade** (pick one)
  - Scalp – low-band stochastics entry for longs, wide channels
    - high-band stochastics entry for shorts, wide channels
  - Range – lighter shares on range break (cast a net) – use 8- , 13- , and 60-minute charts

Figure 4–4   Secret cheat sheet.

CHAPTER 5

The Moody Market Day

In this chapter, we document the best time frames in which to be actively trading during market hours and the morning and evening preparation. In addition, we reveal the special phenomenon known as mood shifts and their time frames. It is in these time frames that the significant market moves are usually made.

Every market day brings new opportunities to make money and to lose money. Those opportunities will not be the same every day. One thing should always be assumed to be a constant, and that is that every day is a clean slate. Each market day should be broken into periods. During these periods, your chances of profitability will increase or decrease. Certain periods, such as the open and mood shifts, are more prone to transparency and more favorable to trade than others, such as the dead zone.

MORNING PREPARATION TO FIND CANDIDATES AND SETUPS

There is a routine you must follow every morning to prepare yourself for the trading day. First and foremost, it is important that you always check the daily stochastics and moving averages support and resistance levels on your stock. Write them down. If there is a mini pup or mini inverse pup on the daily stochastics, this is very significant, as you will watch with a bearish bias. If there is a moving averages pup or inverse pup, this is also very significant, as it will play a big part in your intraday trading and you will be on guard with a bullish bias.

Daily support and resistance levels are strong and need to be respected. For example, if you are long MSFT at 44.20 and the daily 15-period downtrend resistance sits at 44.60, then you will be looking to exit the position into that daily resistance. The possibility that MSFT can break the resistance is not even a factor. The known fact is that the resistance exists at 44.60. The unknown is whether that resistance can break. We do not concern ourselves with the unknown. Since we know that there is a resistance, we assume that resistance until it is broken and take profits. If that resistance can break intraday, then we will look to consider playing the long side.

Gauging Premarket Noodles

We chart stock data only from the opening bell at 9:30 a.m. Eastern time to the closing bell at 4:00 p.m. Eastern time. The futures are a different story. The noodles data are a continuous feed, with only a 30-minute break every trading day from 4:15 to 4:45 p.m. Eastern time. Since trades are made around the clock, it is important that the noodles feed be continuous and set for all sessions. The noodles will continue to trade through the night and the early morning. The liquidity is much lighter, but the trends are nonetheless significant.

When you are getting set up in the morning, you need to check and write down the noodles data. The moving averages and the stochastics for both the 13-minute and the 60-minute charts should be noted from 8:35 a.m. Eastern time forward. This is because most premarket economic reports come out at 8:30 a.m. Eastern time. We want to read the noodles after their knee-jerk reaction to those reports. We don't place much emphasis on the 3-minute and 1-minute stochastics and moving averages charts premarket because of the light volume. Instead, we want to make sure that we are aware of and that we note the 3-minute 200-period moving average support or resistance level.

An example of proper notes would be phrased like this: "13-minute noodles falling stochastics through the 80 band with uptrend supports 900 × 895 for 5- and 15-period moving averages. 60-minute noodles stochastics 60 band rising with uptrend support 893 × 885 for 5- and 15-period moving averages. 3-minute 200-period moving average support at 893." These notes tell us that the 13-minute stochastics is coming down while the 60-minute stochastics is moving up. This immediately limits any plays we may consider to those for a fractured setup. We can also note the multiple overlapping supports sitting at 893, including the 13-minute noodles 15-period moving average, the 3-minute 200-period moving average, and the 60-minute noodles uptrending 5-period moving average. In addition, there is a coil support off the 895 support level. We know that 893 will be an extremely tough level to break, and therefore we are cautious about taking shorts at 893. Instead, we would prefer to lean to the long side with the trend should we get a pullback to the 893 level. This premarket noodles gauge helps us to be aware and ready to react. Being ready is 80 percent of the battle.

Every once in a while, you will get a nice gift premarket. As explained earlier, the 60-minute chart tracks the overnight Globex trading, thereby giving you a complete view of the trend. These overnight data are continuous and absolutely important because they give the complete picture. The most important formation that should grab your attention is a low-band mini pup or a high-band mini inverse pup. We know how powerful these formations are. If the 60-minute chart is giving a 20-band mini pup crossover, then we just need to get a 13-minute or a 3-minute signal for entry into a three-lane highway. Often these 60-minute mini pups will provide a perfect storm scenario. Once that 60-minute chart mini or mini inverse pup triggers, it's an easier battle and there will be shorter wait for the smaller time frames to become parallel and trigger a prime setup.

As powerful as mini pups and mini inverse pups are, they are the most powerful in a 60-minute time frame because they encompass the entire market. The 60-minute mini pup compared to a 3-minute mini pup is like a hurricane compared to a thunderstorm. Hurricanes contain thunderstorms, just as 3-minute mini pups will be set up in the context of the larger 60-minute mini pup. *The rule of thumb is to always be gauging the premarket for situations in which the 60-minute noodles are giving a 20-band mini pup crossover or an 80-band mini inverse pup crossover.* These are golden opportunities to get a foreshadowing of a storm to come.

Economic Reports

Economic reports are usually released at 8:30 a.m. and 10 a.m. Eastern time. They are usually accompanied by a strong knee-jerk reaction in the noodles, which will naturally lead to a knee-jerk reaction in stocks. The 10 a.m. economic reports, such as Michigan sentiment, consumer sentiment, Chicago Purchasing Managers Index, and factory orders, provide the largest knee-jerk element. The CPI and GDP reports at 8:30 a.m. are the most influential reports premarket. For most traders, it is best to stay in cash ahead of the economic reports and gauge the situation after the knee-jerk reaction. As a rule of thumb, you want to wait at least 5 minutes after an economic report before determining the trend. It is important to wait for the 13- and 60-minute stochastics to smooth out as well.

More experienced traders can play the knee-jerk reaction, but they usually play the exhaustion reversal off overlapping noodles and stock supports, not with the panics. We will give more details on exhaustion reversals in Chapter 9.

FOMC Rate Decisions

The Federal Open Market Committee meets every few months to make decisions on interest rates. Most of the FOMC meetings are 1-day meetings, with a rate decision announced that afternoon at 2:15 p.m. Eastern time. However, some meetings are 2-day meetings, with the rate decision announced at 2:15 p.m. Eastern time on the second day of the meeting. This is the granddaddy of economic news and knee jerks. The result is a large panic in either or both directions after the announcement, then a channel tightening, and then a trend. The rule of thumb is to consider the rate decision days as market days that have two market opens, the 9:30 a.m. Eastern time open and the 2:15 p.m. Eastern time open.

When the rate decision is seen as a market open, many of the same rules will apply. You can play the reversal on the panic moves off overlapping supports or resistance levels. Scalps are the key to playing the first 15 to 30 minutes until the channels tighten and a trend forms. By 3 p.m., the trend has kicked in and a range environment will usually set in.

PLAYING THE OPEN

The open is defined as the first hour of trading, starting at 9:30 a.m. The open is the highest-volume part of the day. It is fast and chaotic. This is like the opening round of a boxing match. The first 15 minutes of the day are only for the more experienced traders who are fast scalpers. The noodles will be fast and choppy, and you should watch for fading opposite to the 3-minute noodles movements. If there is a large gap open, that means that the 5- and 15-period moving averages from the prior close need to catch up. This allows for countertrend shorting opportunities on any noodles weakness, ideally a 1-minute 80-band stochastics slip. However, these are only countertrends, and therefore traders should be quick to scalp the panics. *The rule of thumb is to keep trades to only scalps in the first 15 minutes.* This is because the opening action can be extreme and will almost always shake both ways.

There is another very important point that needs to be made about the opening hour. Traders need to strengthen their psychological and emotional aptitude prior to the open in order to bounce back immediately from stops. This is a very important point. We cannot control the market. We can control only our actions. It is very important that a trader be able to take stop losses and get right back into the game. We have seen many traders let one stop loss cause them to be overwhelmed and immobilized by fear and let clear opportunities slide right on by. There is nothing more tragic than a trader who takes a few hours after the opening bell to mentally recover, by which time the action has thinned out into the dead-zone period and the odds of clearer signals are at their worst. When the volume and action are there, we as traders must take our shots, for better or worse. The opening period from 9:30 to 10:30 a.m. is the best time for opportunities and has the clearest signals. Make it a rule of thumb that if you start off with a loss, you brush it right off mentally and continue to stay on your toes to watch for another opportunity. The market open allows traders to make errors and still have an opportunity to make back losses and even be more profitable because the volume and followthrough are there. This is quite opposite during the dead zone where losses taken from stops may not be so easily made back because of the lack of volume and followthrough.

Every stop loss tells us something about either the stock or our management. Either the premises were wrong and turned, or our envelope and allocation were wrong. Analyze the whys on your feet fast and determine whether the envelope or the premises need to be tweaked for a more effective play. If played properly, stops can be used to possibly make greater gains the other way. It is simply a case of losing a dime to make a dollar. This is the mentality that traders need to have going into the market day.

The opening hour is the period that a trader cannot afford to stay out of. Why do bank robbers rob banks? Because that's where the money is. A trader needs to know that the open is where the most opportunity lies. *A stop loss should be seen as simply a pause in the trading to reassess either the premises or the envelope, tighten the premises, and look for another opportunity.*

Every once in a while, you will encounter a fluke trade where there is news that hits and immediately moves a stock against you faster than you can execute a stop loss. This is almost guaranteed. This is also where your mental and intestinal fortitude gets tested. Everyone sometimes has blowouts that he or she can't control. The key is to maintain your composure and fight back from the loss. The reality is that in the long run, these fluke trades are a small fraction of your red trades. Just as you will sometimes hit a home run, sometimes you will strike out hard. The base hits are what keep you alive and in the game. Remember that as a trader, you *must* play the opening hour every day in order to keep the odds in your favor, especially after a fluke trade.

Mini Pup Short Squeeze on the Open

It is very important that you keep an eye on the 13-minute and 60-minute noodles stochastics whenever they open under the 20 band. Most short squeezes tend to happen when the noodles open under the 20 band. The ideal squeeze setup is a 13-minute noodles mini pup and a 60-minute noodles 20-band cross up, even in downtrends. The full effect of the squeeze is usually not seen until the 3-minute stochastics also crosses back up. This naturally sets up a three-lane highway, resulting in a strong market short squeeze. If you take shorts after 9:45 a.m., make sure you are fully aware of where the 13-minute and 60-minute noodles stochastics are positioned. Although Nasdaq Level 2 may appear to indicate a sell fade and show lots of selling on upticks, it is just a matter of time before the 3-minute stochastics turns back up, triggering the short squeeze.

Gap Openings

In the event of a gap up opening where the futures gap above fair value and stocks open higher than the prior day's close, the rule to remember is that the 5- and 15-period moving averages need to catch up. Shorting gaps up is naturally countertrend. This sets up opportunities to place shorts off existing pivots or 200-period moving average resistances at least until the 5-period moving average catches up. Gap openings should be considered to be like short squeezes, so it's important to make sure that the 1-minute stochastics gives 80-band crosses down or mini inverse pup slips through the 80 band before taking shorts. The Achilles heel of a short squeeze is an 80-band stochastics slip on either the 1-minute or the 3-minute chart.

The first 15 minutes of the opening should be traded only by experienced traders, since this period is fast and frenetic. The 13- and 60-minute noodles reading should be done after 9:45 a.m.

If you take a position overnight to play the gap down or up and it gaps against you, it is important to make sure that you give it 10 to 15 minutes after the open and mark the highs and lows of that opening period. If the high in that period breaks, then keep a stop. If the low breaks, then manage to pare and clip the gapper.

In the event of a gap down opening where the futures gap below fair value and stocks open lower than the prior day's close, the same rule concerning the 5- and 15-period moving averages needing to catch down to the gaps applies. This means that the countertrend move to go long off a pivot or 200-period moving average support can be played. The upside on the bounce is the 5-period resistance overshoots for the scalps. Getting a good stochastics 20-band crossover on both your 1-minute stochastics and the futures 1- and 3-minute stochastics is the key to assuring a clearer move.

9:45 A.M. TRANSPARENCY

After the first 15 minutes of the market day, the 13-minute and 60-minute noodles charts will give more accurate readings. Always gauge for stochastics mini pups or mini inverse pups on either formation for a foreshadowing effect on the 3-minute noodles charts. This is where trends will start to develop. Trends that develop after 9:45 a.m. can often have follow-through into the mood-shift period. On the mornings when there is a 10 a.m. economic report, it is very wise to get back into cash ahead of the report. These mornings may also have lighter volume on the open, as everyone is waiting for the report release before getting into the market.

The reactions to these reports are unpredictable, regardless of what the report says. However, there are times when the noodles are at such an extreme band that a knee-jerk reversal can be played. This is only for very experienced scalpers. You may enter near 9:55 a.m. if the noodles are at an extreme 3-minute and 1-minute stochastics band, such as a 10 band or lower (longs) or a 90 band or higher (shorts), for a likely knee-jerk reversal reaction. It is also safer if you are near a pivot or overlapping support level on your stock and the noodles. These trades have a 70 percent success ratio. However, it's best to scalp into the 9:59 a.m. anticipation coils to be safe. Remember, 30 percent of the time the market will turn against your trade. This means that if the noodles are sitting at the 10 band, 30 percent of the time the report may cause a harder leandown panic. This can result in fast losses. In these instances, the extreme reaction can create a great countertrend reversal opportunity, especially going into the mood shift.

One more note about 10 a.m.: It ends the first 30 minutes of the day. It is always wise to mark the high and low of the first 30 minutes. You can do this manually and draw trend lines off the highs and lows, or you can use a 30-minute candle chart to gauge the first candle of the day. The significance is that if we break that 30-minute high, the chances are that we will move higher, and if we break that 30-minute low, the chances are that we will move lower. These levels act as support and resistance. Make sure that you are using the moving averages and stochastics tools to help guide you naturally. For example, if we break that 30-minute high on MSFT with a three-lane highway move up on the noodles, then there is a very highly probable play to the long side with trailing stops at that 30-minute high in addition to the normal trailing stops on the trending 15-period moving average.

FIRST MOOD-SHIFT PERIOD: 10:30 A.M.

Markets tend to reverse a trend or exaggerate a trend near a mood-shift time period. If a trend is very active with volume, then a trend reversal attempt is possible as early as 10:15 a.m. The 3.5-strike rule will apply on any reversal attempt. If the trend is moving on light volume, then a reversal attempt usually happens near 10:30 a.m. These mood shifts are significant periods in which a strong action is taken either with or against the immediate trend.

The best way to gauge a potential mood shift is to watch the 13-minute stochastics and moving averages chart. Mini pup crossovers through the 20 band tend to give a heads up of an impending trend reversal to the upside. Naturally, a 13-minute mini pup will foreshadow the entry of the 3-minute noodles moving averages pup. By the same token, if the 13-minute noodles are showing a mini inverse pup falling under the 80 band, then this will foreshadow a reversal breakdown through the 3-minute noodles moving averages inverse pup. The pups are the best gauge of a trend reversal. It is always important to also gauge the actual trend on the 13-minute moving averages chart. A downtrend that shows a 3-shift cross through the 15-period moving average is a sign of a reversal breakout. An uptrend that shows a 3-shift cross down through the 15-period moving average is a sign of a reversal breakdown.

When the charts *lean* on an existing trend, you will have to be extra careful. What may look like a reversal attempt can peak at the 15-period moving average, only to get pushed back lower. This is where the 60-minute noodles stochastics and moving averages chart comes into play. The wider time frame 60-minute chart gives us a good reading of just how strong the trend is. Any mini pup or mini inverse pup formation will indicate an exaggerated leaning process with the immediate trend. *The basic rule of thumb is to always be aware of a possible reversal near a mood-shift period and use trailing stops if you are in a trade with the immediate trend. If you are not in a trade and you want to take the countertrend trade for the possibility of a reversal, then you must scalp the 5-period overshoots and pare lightly for the full 3.5-strike reversal attempt.* A scalper will use the 13-minute background but trade only the 3-minute charts. A range/swing trader will trade with the 13-minute chart completely. A combination player will pare with the 3-minute chart and stop on the 13-minute chart.

THE DEAD ZONE: 11 A.M. TO 1 P.M.

When we look back at most losing trades, the majority of the time they will have taken place during the 11 a.m. to 1 p.m. Eastern time dead-zone period. This is when the volume thins out and traders go to lunch. During this time, liquidity is very light. This light volume can make for very choppy ranges from spread moves and cranks. Cranks are the large sizes that pop up on the inside bid and ask in an effort to prop up a stock or shake the trees. Nonrefresh or reserve-order games are also played. This is happening when there is a small size on the inside bid or ask that continues to hold as trades hit it on the time of sales. This means that a market maker or trader may be displaying only 200 shares but actually have 10,000 shares to buy or sell.

There are a lot of one large candle pops and drops on the noodles in this time frame. Because the volume is light, it doesn't take too much buying or selling to move the noodles and in essence move stocks. This is a very congested time period that should be avoided most of the time. Traders get head faked and wiggled all the time, leading them to overtrade. This is a good time frame in which to go to lunch or take a walk.

There will obviously be exceptions once in a while where the market will try to squeeze or lean down during this period. Once again, these exceptions are few and far between. If you do play this period, you must play very lightly and make sure that you use only prime setups. It is easy to take two well-timed scalps in the Ping-Pong range from 0.90 to 0.10 for 10-cent clips, only to get overconfident and get squeezed for a 0.50 move against you. In this game, it's most important to neutralize the red column on your profit-and-loss statement. The most fertile environment for red trades occurs during the dead zone. Be forewarned! This is a great time to go to lunch or take a walk and come back later, near the second mood-shift time frame.

SECOND MOOD-SHIFT PERIOD: 1:30 P.M.

As the dead zone comes to a close, the mood shift and potential trend reversal or lean effect come into play. Once again, if volume is active, then the mood shift can come as early at 1:15 p.m. Eastern time. If volume is very light, the mood shift can come as late as 1:45 p.m. Normally, 1:30 p.m. marks the mood-shift attempt.

This mood shift has the same characteristics as the first mood shift. Trends can either reverse or get exaggerated and become even stronger during this period. Always look to the wider time frames—the 13-minute and 60-minute noodles—for a foreshadowing effect. It is easy to step in early and end up waiting for transparency to develop against you. Therefore, when volume is light, play fewer shares. When volume is heavy, you can play the scalp-size number of shares.

All the rules apply here. If the noodles are near a resistance pivot or an overlapping resistance level, then a countertrend can be played, and the opposite is true of the overlapping support pivots. Just as you want to make sure you have a foothold support or resistance, it's best to make sure that you are near pivots and supports whenever you make a trade in this period. In the event that the trade goes against you, these pivots provide a layer of protection, allowing you enough time to exit with relatively little damage.

There is a make-or-break pattern that tends to work itself into the second mood-shift period. This is a dueling pup scenario that starts on the 3-minute noodles chart and has parallel ramifications on most basket stocks. This will be a 3-minute noodles moving averages pup versus a 3-minute mini inverse pup or the opposite, a 3-minute noodles moving averages inverse pup versus a 3-minute stochastics mini pup. In these make-or-break situations, always gauge the 13-minute stochastics for a potential foreshadowing of which one will trigger. In the event that the 13-minute stochastics is sideways, it is best to wait for the trigger before making a trade.

When volume is light, the 3-minute moving averages pup breakout attempt can turn into a consolidation that will test the 15-period moving average coil support, which is −2 points from the actual 15-period reading. Keep this in mind when attempting to take shorts to lock in profits on the 2-point overshoot coil. For example, if the rising 15-period moving average support is 875 and you take a short, make sure to scalp or clip out your stock when the noodles hit the 873 coil support. It is not until that

2-point coil support is broken that the noodles have broken, which in turn will signal breakdowns on your basket stock. Remember to allow for a wiggle to both coil resistances and supports on the 3-minute noodles moving averages before the make-or-break situation is actually triggered. Naturally, if the 13-minute noodles foreshadow a mini pup or a mini inverse pup, then the 3-minute version of the pup should be played.

MINOR MOOD-SHIFT PERIODS

This portion of the day is for the very experienced traders and is very setup-specific. Markets like to attempt minor mood shifts at 11:30 a.m., 12:30 p.m., and 2:30 p.m. Eastern time. These attempts may not occur every day. However, as those time periods get close, it is important to watch for a possible reversal or a continuation leandown on the existing trend. When volume is heavier, these movements are more reliable, but by nature the 11:30 a.m. and 12:30 p.m. minor mood shifts are smack dab in the middle of the dead zone, so volume is light by default. Pay attention if the volume doesn't pick up or if the 13-minute noodles attempt a reversal of the immediate 3-minute trend on the stochastics.

LIGHT-VOLUME PERIODS AND MARKETS

It is a given that 11 a.m. to 1 p.m. Eastern time is a light-volume period that we call the dead zone. We use the 3-minute volume bars on the moving averages chart to gauge volume. When volume gets light, traders always need to slow down their trading. This is the most vulnerable period because of the noise and lack of clarity during this period. This time frame is notorious for sucking traders into overtrading. We like to note that using extreme bollinger bands with the settings of 20 periods and 2 standard deviation on a 3-minute chart is an effective indicator of the oscillation ranges in light volume. This will deter you from chasing false breakouts and false breakdowns.

The rule is not to chase the upper bands on longs or the lower bands on shorts. Experienced traders will actually play the exhaustions to fade the upper and lower bands.

In light-volume periods and markets, a trader needs to understand that he will have to pay for liquidity. The bottom line is, you want to be early exiting trades, selling into panics to exit longs and covering into panics to exit shorts. This will not always get you the best possible price exit, but you are sacrificing price for liquidity. In light-volume markets, a trader may want to get out at a higher price and ignore the opportunity to sell into the cranks and overshoots, only to realize that she overstayed her position and turn around and sell in panic when the momentum shifts. This is extremely common. For example, you take MSFT long at 46.85 and it overshoots 47 to a 47.05 peak. Selling into panic means that you place your sell order as 47 thins out and you get filled easily at 47.02, for a +0.17 profit. A novice will see MSFT tick through 47 and peak out at 47.05, then see it backfill to 46.90 and panic out at 46.89, for a gain of only +0.04. This happens all the time, usually because the trader is not aware of the light-volume situation. The lack of liquidity can make prices swing faster. This is an illusion because it is very hard to get fills at the best prices.

Light-volume periods are dangerous because sudden knee-jerk cranks can occur out of the blue. If there is a word to describe light volume, it is *subtle*. Everything is very slow and subtle for a reason, and that is to take traders by surprise. This is why traders should limit their trades in light volume. The duration and length of stay in a position should have an inverse relationship to the number of shares. Basically, the longer you are in a position in light volume, the fewer shares you should be playing.

Light-volume markets usually occur before holidays, and during the summertime, when most of the professionals go on vacation. These are full-day light-volume markets, and one needs to be extremely careful with them. During normal market conditions, it may take 1 million shares in volume to move the price of a stock by 0.25. In light-volume markets, there are fewer participants, and therefore even 200,000 shares may be able to move the stock 0.50, especially because of the lighter flow of institutional orders. There is a lot of churning and cranking.

Light-volume markets also mean that there is less support and resistance with the futures. While it may normally take 1000 contracts to move the noodles 2 points, in these markets they can easily be moved with 200 contracts. This means that stocks can react violently in relation to the noodles or not react at all if the noodles are in a range. This type of action screws up the equilibrium and magnetizes a trader's compass. The best advice for light-volume markets is to play lightly and less frequently, as anything can and will happen. Do not go to the well too many times, and always prepare for the worst on every trade.

THE LAST HOUR

The last hour of trading is from 3 to 4 p.m. Eastern time. The bond market closes, and volume will usually attempt to seep back into the market. *The rule of thumb is to never play the last hour unless you are already profitable by at least your daily goal.* By this time, most of the action has been played out. We look at the last hour as a time for dessert and nothing more. The last 30 minutes of the day can have high volume. Any overextended low bands on the 13-minute and 3-minute noodles are viable to attempt squeezes on short covering, and the opposite is true for high bands. The last 30 minutes should be reserved for only the most experienced traders.

The last 2 minutes is what we call the crank's game. This means that extra-heavy volume comes into the market to close stocks above or below certain price levels. Usually cranks will favor the long or the short side and will push the noodles and stocks in that direction. Many times, the stocks and noodles will diverge because the market close is so near. Once again, the end-of-day cranks should be played only by experienced traders on extreme panic countertrend reversals. If you are taking longs, take them off overlapping supports, and take shorts off overlapping resistances. The techniques for playing the last hour are the same as those for any other time during the day. Just remember to stick to your premises and usually limit yourself to scalps on heavy volume.

POSTMARKET

The postmarket or after-hours market should be played only if there is some kind of news regarding earnings. Earnings season hits four times a year, and those periods are the only times when traders should even consider watching the postmarket time frames. Since tiers change so often, it would be fruitless to list the tier groups in this book; however, you can log onto the undergroundtrader.com home page and check the intraday updates to get a current list.

Keep in mind that the noodles close at 4:15 p.m. Eastern time and reopen at 4:45 p.m. Liquidity is thin, and this period should be reserved for experienced momentum traders because charts do not register the postmarket. Most traders should only observe the ranges of stocks that release news in the postmarket. Watch the ranges, and then take those ranges into the premarket trading the next morning. Stocks will move according to the 2.50 and sticky 5s support and resistance levels if there is news. It operates on pure momentum rules, and traders need to work scalps only on overshoots. The nice thing about the post- and premarket is the ability to short without an uptick by routing directly to the ECNs. In fact, traders should focus *only* on the ECNs in the pre- and postmarket periods. Market makers cannot be hit and have no obligation to fill prices, even through you may see them move around on Level 2. Never trust where the market makers are bidding or selling; watch only the ECNs.

INTRADAY SCANNING WITH EXCHANGE-TRADED FUNDS

Scanning for opportunities can be done if we have a wide enough basket of stocks and their respective tier partners. We can use exchange-traded funds to gauge the sectors that are showing strength or weakness and look into playing the tier 1 stocks. The tier 1 stocks are usually a good indicator of how a particular sector is performing. This is the reason why we like to work up to multiple tier 1 basket stocks that move well with the futures. There will always be some divergence among the sectors. When the techs are strong, the biotechs are often weak, and vice versa. If the tier 1s are moving, then the momentum will often flow into the lower tiers in the same sector. This makes scanning for opportunities much easier. The biggest problem with scanning is the danger of impulse trades. Many traders will see a stock break a new high and immediately jump in chasing the top, only to realize that it is overbought and get stopped out. Be careful to trade only stocks that you are familiar with.

The following market minder should be on your layout page:

SMH	Semiconductor holders index: KLAC, NVLS, AMAT, and INTC are tier 1s
RTH	Retail holders index: GPS, MIK, WMT, and HD
SWH	Software holders index: MSFT, PSFT, VRTS, INTU, ERTS, and ORCL
PPH	Pharmaceutical holders index: MRK, BMY, and PFE
BBH	Biotech holders index: AMGN, BGEN, and DNA
OIH	Oil holders index: XOM and CVX
HHH	Internet holders index: EBAY, YHOO, and AMZN

We listed just a few of the heavier-weighted tier 1s that are tradable if the overlying ETF is showing strength. This is just one of the many ways to use tiers to scan throughout the day, especially when there is sector rotation and certain sectors are showing a lot of strength. Use these ETFs to gauge where the money flow is going during the day.

COMMERCIAL SCANNING PRODUCTS

There are commercialized scanning programs out there, but while a program can help a good trader be more effective, it cannot help a bad trader. Ralomatic.com provides a great scanner feature for intraday price breaks. We also highly recommend Cyber-trader.com as a full-service platform complete with cyberquant scanner, charts, and direct-access point and click order routing.

News feeds are also good to have, as they can lead you to where the action is. Dow Jones Newswire is usually provided by your brokerage service and should be considered. Briefing.com is also an excellent analyst site that stays on top of news. However, you have to be careful with the noise element. There is a lot of noise in the news. We aren't particularly fond of playing news-related stories, especially analyst recommendations. It's just good to have access to news and to be aware of what may be stimulating an impulse move in a stock.

Once again, do not make impulse trades on news. That may have worked in the bull market of the Internet mania, but it is not something that has traditionally worked. Always pull up the charts and take a few minutes to analyze where the support and resistance levels are in relation to the noodles. You shouldn't make a live trade on scanned stocks until you have had a chance to fully analyze the technicals. This can take a few minutes or more. You want to think out what potential setups may trigger and watch the stock from a distance first.

NIGHTLY RESEARCH

After a long day of trading, doing research may not be at the top of your priority list. The nightly research is just a fast scan of your basket stocks to see how their daily formations closed. This is where the daily time frames come into play to see if you can get any daily setups that trigger pups.

Nightly research is not something that you need to spend much time on. You should take just 15 to 20 minutes looking for pups on the moving averages or mini pups on the daily stochastics. If any are triggered, then jot them down, along with information regarding what the daily stochastics bands are doing and the 5- and 15-period moving averages supports and resistances. These numbers are important, as they will often overlap with pivots or shorter time frame levels the next day. What you don't do at night, you can easily do as part of your morning preparation prior to the market open.

CHAPTER 6

The Basket Trading Approach: Building the Foundation

In this chapter, we go step by step over how to properly learn to trade by selecting a basket stock and applying the methods, stressing focus as the key element to success. By its nature, the basket approach forces one to focus and ensures better success. This is where we get into the implementation of the methods.

WORK BACKWARDS—THE MOST IMPORTANT STEP

We have talked a lot about the tools, the setups, and the premises. This is foundation material that you absolutely need. However, there is a step that most traders never really work on because of their hunger to get to the actual trading, and, unfortunately, failing to do so is often the root of their demise. This is the most important step, even before you begin paper trading. This step is working backwards to be able to interpret the moves. Please do not forget to take this step.

In any trade you consider making, the result is the unknown element. The premises are there. The setup is there. The only unknown is the result of the trade. The absolutely most important thing to do in the beginning is to work *backwards* and explain the *mechanics* of a move. Since you already know the result when you are looking at prior charts, it is easy to go backwards and explain the triggers. Imagine a trader asking you, "What happened to MSFT today?" How would you explain this to a professional trader?

Take a prior day's chart and explain each significant move. What is the cause and effect? In trader language, the effect is the *result* and the cause is the *trigger*. Thus, you are concerned only with the result and the trigger. Speak in terms of the technical indicators and charts only. Leave out news and analyst recommendations because we care only about the reaction. You should be able to explain the result and what triggered it.

For example, you should be able to explain that "MSFT *resulted* in a breakout at 10 a.m. Eastern time on the 3-minute moving averages chart, confirmed by a 3-shift cross through the 15-period. This breakout was *triggered* by the 3-minute noodles moving averages pup breakout through resistance, which was foreshadowed by the 13-minute noodles mini pup and 3-shift cross breakout, which incidentally mirrored MSFT's 13-minute stochastics. The 60-minute stochastics was uptrending and rising through the 50 band, which meant that the market trend was up." This is a clear explanation of what happened to MSFT (the result) and why it happened (the trigger). It is vital that you be able to go backwards in a trade to the moment of impact where the catalyst triggered the move. That moment of impact is what you want to constantly study and familiarize yourself with.

Repetition is very important here. As you watch, you want to be able to explain the moves after they happen. Only after you can completely explain a *past* move can you even consider playing a move that has yet to happen. You can't live the future unless you understand the past. Work backwards to explain the past moves. Only then can you expect to play the present and future moves. Spend time just watching your stock and its charts and explaining the moves *after* they happen. Go back to yesterday's charts and explain the key breakouts and breakdowns and what triggered them. Being able to interpret yesterday's movements consistently brings you a step closer to being able to anticipate and foreshadow today's movements.

SELECTING A BASKET STOCK

Basket stock trading should be your main bread and butter. This means that you select one stock to start off with and stick to that one stock. Basket stocks should be stocks that move well with the noodles and the $sox.x. Your basket stock should have at least 10 million shares a day average volume and should be priced over $25 a share. This will ensure that you get decent channels and oscillations. MSFT makes a great basket stock, since it moves with both the noodles and the sox.x index. KLAC, QLGC, and EBAY are all good, volatile basket stocks. The higher-priced a stock is, the more it is going to fluctuate. Try to pick stocks that are in the upper tiers of the Nasdaq 100 index.

In order to fully know a basket stock, you need to have been watching it every day for many weeks and through multiple different environments. Be familiar with the times when your basket stock is trading in a scalper environment and when it is trading in a range environment. Understand the nuances of your stock: how it trades at the pivots and how it moves more fluidly in a three-lane highway than in a fractured time frame setup. Observe how it flows when the 13-minute stochastics is rising but the 3-minute stochastics is slipping. Observe the days when it fades against the noodles, as these days do occur. Find the common denominator that separates the noise periods from the trending periods. Take your time learning a basket stock, as it will take care of you and your income for a very long time if you learn it well.

PAPER TRADING

Only after you can explain the moves of your basket stock can you start to paper-trade. This is a different mentality because now you are looking for setups *prior* to a reaction. Most traders completely waste their time by paper trading the wrong way. They inundate themselves on paper with risky fractured setups, assuming that their orders are filled instantly at the prices they see. Paper trading is not something one does just to boost one's ego concerning what one "shoulda, coulda" done. The most important thing about trading on paper or using a simulator is that it allows a trader to be completely objective without the money factor getting in the way. The money factor is a major stumbling block for traders. When money is on the line, rationality and objectivity fly out the window.

Therefore, paper trading is a chance to clearly focus on the setups and the premises. You should not paper-trade every single setup or fractured setup. Never paper-trade something that you wouldn't trade with cash. The key is to foster your ability to spot and react to setups and premises objectively, without the emotional fear of losing money getting in the way. With this understanding in mind, we can move forward.

You should strive to hit 70 percent consistency on paper for at least a month before attempting to go to cash. This means a 70 percent win ratio of green trades to red trades. Paper trading is a way to be objective and concentrate more on the trade than on the money.

KEEP A JOURNAL

Keeping a journal is absolutely imperative with paper trading as well as with cash trading. The journal should be rather simple. Just write in your entry price and the number of shares. Your premises prior to the trade should also be written in. The next line should be your exit price, your net gain or loss, and the result of the premises. Here is an example:

> Bought MSFT 48.60 × 1000 shares; premise: 3-minute stochastics mini pup mirroring the 3-minute noodles on a 1-minute stochastics 30-band mini pup trigger, 13-minute stochastics rising through the 30 band and

60-minute stochastics rising through the 60 band on moving average uptrends, a/k/a three-lane highway.

Sold MSFT 48.90 × 1000 shares, out +0.30; premise: 1-minute stochastics peaked out at the 95 band near pivot resistance; sold into the 0.90 overshoots.

At the end of every day, review your trades. The proper way to review trades is to go over each one systematically and grade yourself solely on the premise of the trade. If your premise was based on a 1-minute stochastics chart and it made the full oscillation, where you took a $0.20 scalp, but went higher after a pullback, you give yourself an A for the trade based on the premise. Even if MSFT moves another $0.70 higher, the point is that you prioritized the 1-minute premise and maxed out the gain based on that premise. However, if you were basing the trade on the 3-minute stochastics premise and you took the 1-minute scalp, but the 3-minute stochastics went higher after the wiggle, then naturally you know that you could have pared 700 shares and ranged the other 300 shares with the 3-minute premise.

It is also important that you grade your stops. If the premises were secure, but the trigger reversed, thereby reversing the premises, grade your stop. Did you panic out at the lower possible price on the shake? Were you able to get out early? Did you let the stock wiggle and then use a backfill off a pivot support level to take a minimal stop? These are all part of the grading process. When taking stops, there are the early fast stops that will do the least amount of damage and the stops where you let it wiggle and then exit into the backfill. The stops taken anywhere in the middle are usually where you get the worst exit price, and you give yourself the worst grade for these.

STOPS

We don't believe in placing an absolute dollar amount on a stop loss. As you know, stocks can and do wiggle a lot with the decimals.

Instead, stops should be based solely on premises. If the premises fail, then use a backfill and exit the position. It's as simple as that. Stops tell you something about either the premises or your envelope. Both pieces of information are extremely valuable for your next trade. If the premises break down, then the reverse premises are activated, allowing a trade going in the opposite direction from the trade that you stopped out of. If you see that your stop was triggered but the stock then continued in your direction, then you know that the wiggle is wider and that trading fewer shares with a wider envelope is required. These are crucial pieces of information. If the clarity is not there, then a stop is used primarily to *buy time*.

Stop losses are triggered when the premises break down or the triggers reverse. You must take stops consistently on paper. If you cut yourself, you wouldn't sit there and watch yourself bleed to death, would you? The first and most important thing in being able to implement a stop loss is being aware of the premises. The second thing is being assertive enough to actually pull that trigger and get out.

How you get out is also a key factor. Always use backfills and overshoots to exit from positions. For example, if you took MSFT long at 45 and the 1-minute stochastics coil turns into a mini inverse pup, MSFT will probably drop too fast for you to exit immediately. If you know that 44.90 is a coil support, and that often MSFT will slip to 44.91 and then backfill to just shy of 45, you would stop out into the upticks instead of chasing it down with monster orders on the bid. It is important to remain calm when your premises look as if they are breaking down. Stops are simply a pause in your trading to buy time so that you can get back to cash and look for some clarity. The best thing about stops is that they free you from being stuck to a position. This means that you can reenter or watch as you wish. There is no obligation, and that is true freedom.

CHAPTER 7

The Transition to Cash

In this chapter, we carefully go over the very important next step, making the transition from paper to cash trading. This is where most traders fail. The mental and emotional stumbling blocks are large.

HOW TO MAKE THE TRANSITION FROM PAPER TO CASH

Paper trading or using a simulator is a great way to learn how to find setups without the stress of managing money or dealing with order executions. All that changes once you go to cash trading in a live account. Remember the confidence in the setups and premises that you built when you were trading on paper? That confidence and astute timing need to be carried over smoothly into the live trading situation. There will be slippage involved in the transition. The results on paper assume that you get filled automatically on your trades, and paper trading also takes your emotions out of the equation along with the money aspects. These will be the two main obstacles that you must overcome: executions and the comfort zone.

The most important thing in live trading is to start off small. The comfort zone is a very fragile element. A person who is trading

100 shares is likely to be relatively relaxed and to pay attention to the setups, even if he has to take a stop. The fluctuations don't work on his nerves too much, and he can still think objectively. Take that same person and make him trade 5000 shares, and his nerves will be fried. Emotions will completely overwhelm him with every single tick. His objectivity will be thrown out the window, and every tick and wiggle will scare him. The larger number of shares is outside his comfort zone.

A trader needs to start very small in order to maintain objectivity. A 0.20 stop on 100 shares is nothing. A 0.20 stop on 5000 shares is $1000, and that can cause much anxiety. Thus, the first step is to emulate the paper-trading results in cash trading of only 100 shares. The purpose is not to make money, because commissions will eat up your profits. The purpose is to focus on the trade and not the money. Try to emulate the paper results in cash. A 70 percent consistency ratio is what you are striving for.

If you can achieve that 70 percent ratio for 2 weeks, then you can *slowly* increase the share increments by 200 shares every 2 weeks until you are up to *comfortably* trading 1000 shares. Remember that if your winning percentages slip, then you need to stay at your current level or even decrease the size of your trades. This is very important. You must take it very slowly as you increase the number of shares you trade. Once you break the 1000-share threshold, you are able to become a combination trader because you now have the ability to pare profits and pare into entries. That is a later stage in the game, however. Do not skip a step. You absolutely must follow this game plan if you wish to succeed as a trader. Take it slowly and earn your way to cash from paper. Earn the right to trade more shares by being consistent. Once you are up to the 1000-share level, you can look at branching into becoming a combination player.

ENVIRONMENT DICTATES THE EFFECTIVE STYLE

There is a very basic premise that traders need to understand from the beginning. The market has two distinct environments that cater to two different and distinct styles of traders. The fast, wide-range, voluminous markets with wide 5- and 15-period moving averages channels on the noodles and stocks cater to the scalpers. The tighter-range, lighter-volume, trending markets cater to the range/swing trader. One of the first things a trader needs to accomplish in order to succeed in this game is to be able to identify when these environments are in place. Usually, the market open caters best to the scalpers. The mood shifts and the dead zone tend to cater to the range/swing player.

Make sure that you are able to identify the type of environment that you are in. Remember that if the 3-, 13-, and 60-minute moving averages are in a consolidation or a very tight range, then a scalper will find the market full of head fakes and wiggles. A scalper will be ineffective, but a range player will thrive because she has a wider envelope for stops with smaller numbers of shares. Let's review the types of traders and their respective effective environments.

Scalper

As we stressed earlier, every trader needs to start off as a scalper. A scalper is a trader who expects a move from point A to point B in a relatively straight line. The scalper's aim is to get in and out with the least amount of wiggles and noise. Scalpers will tend to actually be the most risk-averse because their understanding is that the longer one is in a position, the more risk is inherent in the trade. Therefore, a scalper wants to enter and exit in the shortest time possible. The scalper style is most effective in an environment with high volume and wide channels between the 5- and 15-period moving averages on the noodles and stocks. Volume gives the scalper liquidity and the opportunity to exit into the buyers on longs and to buy into the sellers on short covering. Scalpers love to play panics and wider-channel trends and ranges. Scalpers will always get out "early," which is just an indication of their innate ability to exit without disturbing a stock's momentum. Scalpers will mainly use the 1-minute and 3-minute charts, with a background view of the 13-minute charts.

A scalper is an expert at selling into the buyers and buying into the sellers. Excellence of timing and execution is the forte of a good scalper. Scalpers are either taking profits or trimming losses. When supports overshoot, a scalper will be there to take advantage of the overshoots and scalp out her short covers into the sellers without thinking twice. When a pivot resistance overshoots, a scalper will take that opportunity to sell into the buyers without thinking twice because he knows that the pivot is a resistance and that the result is likely to be a backfill and a short-term peak. Scalpers are aware at all times, and this is their strength. They leave little to chance. *This is an absolute foundation that every trader must start off with, for better or worse.*

After being successful with scalping, a trader will eventually realize that he may have left quite a lot of money on the table by getting out on the shorter time frame signals. When the 1-minute stochastics peak, a scalper will take his profits before the inevitable retracement. However, after the retracement, the stock will continue to move with the trend. Eventually, a pure scalper may realize this. He will then try to use his ability to scalp by cashing out the majority of his shares based on a 1-minute chart but keeping a small number of shares to move with the 3-minute trend, with stops in place if the 3-minute premises warrant it. This way, he gets the immediate gain from the scalp and also gets to take advantage of the trend along the way because he has *pared* some shares out to lock in profits but also maintained a smaller position for a longer time frame to take advantage of the trend. This trader is now moving to the stage of being a combination trader, which is a trader who can scalp and pare initial gains while riding a smaller number of shares for a larger gain.

Range/Swing Trader: Casting a Net

For a trader who goes straight into swing or range trading, it may sound good on paper to set targets and stops and let it ride either way. A range player assumes that a stock will not go directly from point A to point B in a straight line. Instead, she expects an indirect path with lots of noise and wiggles within a price range, but eventually breaking out into the direction of her trade. This is a far cry from the sharp entry and exit exhibited by a scalper. The range trader's style works best in a slow, trending market with tight channels and is also most effective using 13- and 60-minute charts.

In reality, novice swingers will too often have a target price that barely gets hit before the stock retraces and breaks down to trigger their stops instead. Novice swing traders are simply sitting targets if they don't have the skill or aptitude to actively take profits with or without targets when premises apply. This is where the foundation of scalping comes into play.

From scalping, traders may eventually want to ride a trend a little more and may discover that they have the patience to follow a wider time frame premise. From this point on, a trader can decide to become a range/swing player. This trader still has that foundation and can take profits or stops if his premises warrant. His premises, however, are now more often based on a wider time frame, be it 13-minute, 60-minute, or even daily.

Once again, linearity comes into play. What a range/swing player realizes is that everything she did when she was scalping also applies to range/swing trading. The only difference is that the time frames are wider. Range/swing playing is a slower, wider-motion version of scalping! Once you realize this, then you can try to range/swing trade. For example, a range trader may use the 3-minute premise to step in on the 13-minute mini inverse pup on the noodles for 500 shares. Just using the 13-minute chart, he will look to pare out profits on the 43.50 overshoots for a $0.50 gain on 500 shares, or a $250 gain. The downside is based on the 13-minute noodles mini inverse pup reversing back up and breaking the pivot, which would have been a −0.20 downside. This means that a range trader risked losing $50 to get a $250 gain. That's not bad either. This is all calculated and premeditated, whichever style you play.

Range trading applies best in a market where the channels on the 5- and 15-period moving averages on the 3-minute and/or 13-minute charts are very tight, and therefore scalps really are not effective because the wiggles are very small, yet sharp enough to wiggle you out with barely enough profits to cover commissions. In these cases, the market environment is a range player's market.

In this environment, you will have to think like a professional fisherman and cast a net into the water by taking a position inside the range with a wide enough stop to let the range or slow accumulation/distribution trend play out. This sounds easy on paper, but in reality, there are psychological blocks that make it tough, especially for someone with a scalping background. Take it slowly and give it time, and make sure that the underlying 13- and 60-minute charts are moving with the trend of the range you are trying to capture.

Combo Player: The Double Threat

Being a combo player is being a double threat and this is the type of trader you should ultimately strive to be. This type of trader can both scalp and premeditate a range/swing trade. The biggest barrier to becoming a combo player is the psychological aspect of holding through wiggles on wider time frames. This requires establishing a comfort zone for the larger time frame charts. A scalper's instinct will be to scalp out the 1-minute stochastics bounces through the 80 band on the longs. It is very difficult for a scalper to accept a retracement back under the 80 band, thereby giving back the green and potentially risking losses. However, a combination player will often lock in a majority of the profits on the 1-minute peaks and sit tight on a smaller number of shares through the anticipated wiggle retracements. A combination player understands this very basic premise: *In order for stocks to move higher, they must pull back; in order for stocks to move lower, they must bounce.* Therefore, a combination player understands that he must sit through a wiggle, provided that a longer time frame premise is intact, in order to get a larger gain.

A combination player will start a trade off as a scalp and then scale out profits on the 1- and 3-minute charts, leaving a smaller position to play the 13- and 60-minute charts. For example, let's say a trader shorts MSFT at 44 on the 1-minute stochastics mini inverse pup slip, knowing that 44.10 is a pivot resistance and 43.75 is the 3-minute 200-period moving average support. The next pivot support sits at 43.50. The 13-minute noodles stochastics is showing a consolidation breakdown, with a 13-minute mini inverse pup on the stochastics slipping through the 60 band. That

13-minute mini inverse pup is the main premise for a stronger move down on MSFT. However, the 1-minute mini inverse pup is giving an immediate oscillation panic as it overshoots through 43.80. This is where the combo player will scalp out 700 shares of MSFT on the short cover at 43.80, for a 0.20 gain on the scalp (0.20 × 700), or $140. MSFT takes a coil off the 0.75 to 0.90 level. The combo player knows that the 300 shares can be ranged with the 13-minute noodles mini inverse pup, and with a looming pivot resistance at 44.10, his downside on 300 shares is only 0.10. His upside on the 300 shares is a 3-minute 200-period moving average breakdown to test the 43.50 pivot support, which is 0.50. Therefore, the combo trader has already cashed in $140 in profits and is risking only a $30 loss for a possible additional $150 gain on the trade warranted by the 13-minute noodles premise. The upside of the trade is $290 profit versus a downside of $110. See how that works? It's a beautiful thing.

There is no point in paring shares if you don't give the premise a chance to play out. There is nothing more pathetic than seeing someone pare 700 shares out at 43.80 with a trailing stop at 43.90 on the remaining shares. That's defeatist because it doesn't take the wiggle backfill possibility on the trade into account. There is no point in paring if you are setting yourself up to take a stop loss on the remaining shares. This means that there is no upside to paring out 700 shares unless you allow the 300 shares to sit short all the way back up to test the pivot resistance. If you are not going to do this, it is best to just take a scalp and walk with the full gain, not a partial gain. Once again remember that although you are taking a majority of your profits on the initial pop if you pare, the remaining shares are given a trailing stop from your entry level in most cases.

THE ART OF PARING

Paring shares means piecing in or piecing out your position. When done correctly, paring can blur the line between a loss and a profit on your statement. It can maximize the green and minimize the red. In a rudimentary sense, it's like dollar cost averaging in and out of a position. Unlike clueless investors, traders will pare strictly on the basis of their premises and setups. Most important, when pared positions turn sour, a trader can pare out just as well. It is very important that traders who employ a paring technique be fully aware of the phenomenon of coils and overshoots because this is where the most liquidity will be.

Both combination players and range/swing players will use paring. However, no one should even attempt to pare shares until she has psychologically and physically mastered the ability to take stop losses. Failing to do this can have very nasty consequences. A trader who can't take stops is asking to get nailed to the cross by paring shares.

Earlier in the chapter, we gave an example of paring out profits. However, paring can also apply when building up a position or be used to neutralize a loss. Let's take an example of paring in to actually downsize the stop loss. Let's assume that trader Patrick shorts MSFT at 45.35, only to see it squeeze higher on a 3-minute moving averages pup breakout. Patrick shorts more shares at 45.65 in hopes that he can get even. MSFT pulls back to 45.50 on a wiggle, and Patrick gives a sigh of relief. This relief is short-lived, as the 13-minute noodles mini pup triggers another 3-minute moving averages pup breakout that squeezes MSFT to 45.90! Patrick is frozen and starts to pray for MSFT to reverse, but it breaks higher to 46.30, where he finally throws in the towel, taking a –0.80 stop loss on double shares—ouch.

The difference between conviction and stubbornness plays a big role in paring. In the same trade, Mary takes MSFT short at 45.35, only to have it squeeze higher to 45.65, where she shorts again (the average price is now 45.50), knowing that 45.60 is a coil resistance in the sticky 5s. However, Mary notices the 13-minute noodles mini pup and the rising 15-period moving average at 45.37 on the 3-minute moving averages chart on MSFT, indicating a possible pup. Mary uses MSFT's overshoots through 45.50 to take an even stop on her pared shares. This is an example of paring shares at a higher price on a trade that moves against you to *neutralize* the damage. Do not ever mistake paring for averaging down a bad position, which is only throwing good money after bad. Paring is a calculated action that is meant to maximize profits while minimizing risk or averaging a bad position at an overextension level for a natural retracement to neutralize damage on the stop loss.

If the premises are defunct, then even pared shares need to be stopped out. Experienced traders will pare shorts higher just to take a smaller net stop loss on the retracement, as illustrated by Mary. This is something that is completely foreign to a trader who can't muster her- or himself to take stop losses.

MAKING THE TRANSITION TO LARGER NUMBERS OF SHARES

The name of the game is to eventually increase the size of your trades so that you can amply pare shares in and out. Eventually you will plateau at a comfort level as far as share size is concerned. The larger your share size is, the more important it is for you to master the art of paring into and out of positions. It is also important that you be able to pare out of positions into buyers and to pare into positions into sellers. This means being able to take advantage of coil overshoots and backfills.

To make the transition to higher share sizes, it takes patience and a lot of redundancy to build up a threshold for wiggles at your existing size level. As the formula goes, if you are hitting 70 percent profitability in your trades, then you can look to add a little more size. As the size grows, you will need to space out the share-size increases to months from weeks.

Understand that when markets are thinner on lighter volume, it is by nature a requirement that you be playing smaller numbers of shares relative to your comfort level. This is a principle that must always be respected. If you are up to 5000 shares on scalps, then you need to trim down relative to that 5000 shares, perhaps to 2000 shares, for range/swing trades. Eventually you will realize that you will tend to play different sizes for different setups. For example, a three-lane highway move with a 1-minute stochastics trigger allows you to take a larger-size scalp on the 3-minute chart move to pare out profits and a smaller number of range/swing shares on the 13-minute and 60-minute chart moves. However, a thread the noodles move with slipping 3-minute, rising 13-minute, and slipping 60-minute charts may warrant the 1-minute trigger to just play the 3-minute move with fewer shares in the event that it wiggles and joins the 13-minute move. The underlying theme here is to pare and allocate shares according to the setup and the time frame. If you understand this, then you should rarely put yourself into an apples-and-oranges situation where you have a small point loss that results in a much larger dollar loss.

STOPS AND MAKE-OR-BREAK SITUATIONS

A make-or-break situation will often occur when you get a moving averages pup and an opposing mini inverse pup on the 3-minute noodles chart. The implications and effects will be marketwide and will probably affect your basket stock also. The big boys like to test the 5-period overshoots and often head fake the 15-period overshoots. If there is a 13-minute mini pup in the noodles, then a long can be taken on the 15-period test, where a hammer is likely to form. However, if there is no heads up on the 13-minute noodles chart in the form of a mini pup, then you need to either wait it out for a 3 shift or use the 1-minute stochastics trigger after the initial slip. If the 1-minute noodles bounce back through the 20 band, you will usually get upticks back through the 5-period moving average for a 3-minute moving averages pup on the noodles, which will lead to a 3-minute moving averages pup on your basket stock. However, let's say you took the long side on the 1-minute stochastics 20-band coil for a 3-minute moving averages pup on the noodles and your stock. The stock will uptick initially with the 1-minute stochastics bounce. However, a few minutes later you realize that the 1-minute stochastics has stalled out at the 60 band

and is crossing back down. On this move, you see the 3-minute stochastics mini pup starting to trigger. What do you do?

Chances are that you know what you *should* do, but can you execute that stop? Many people don't take stop losses, either because they are unaware of what is looming or because they are just not assertive enough to take action. Both are symptoms of failure. Another reason why traders don't take stops is that they are hoping for the play to work out because they don't want to admit a defeat. When you think of stops in that sense, they have a negative connotation—failure, loss, and defeat.

Stops need to be thought of as simply taking a *pause* in your trading and *buying time*. Nothing more. In a make-or-break situation, a stop loss means that the flip-side premise is triggering. In this sense, there is life after death, so to speak, because if the 3-minute moving averages pup fails, that means that the 3-minute mini inverse pup is succeeding. This means that you would take a stop so that you can reenter on the short side and take advantage of the 3-minute mini inverse pup stochastics oscillation down. Who better knows how weak a stock is than a trader who is sitting in a long position?

For this reason, traders should always view stops as an opportunity to play the flip side of the premise on make-or-break situations. This is why make-or-break situations are so wonderful. You don't have to sit around trying to figure out new premises. Either one or the other will follow through. If you pick the wrong one, then take a stop and reenter the other way. It is a matter of giving up a dime to make three to five times that amount. This is opportunity. You free yourself from the shackles of being in an obvious losing position so that you can reenter into a winning position. Some of the best trades come from being on the weak side long enough to jump over to the stronger side. In this game, you simply follow the strength and stay away from weakness. This is a game of war with a twist: There are no permanent sides in this war. When your opponent is stronger than you, you must be quick to join the opposing side, and vice versa.

Making the Trade

This chapter explains what to do once the trade is executed. Proper trade management is the key to the success of any trader. We delve into the mental and physical aspects once a trade is taken on from a fresh, realistic approach.

There are three parts to making a trade. The first part is preparation beforehand, which means setting up the triggers and being aware of the support/resistance levels on the moving averages and the pivots, especially noting overlapping levels. The second part is pulling the trigger to place the trade. Early entries, sweet spots, and late entries are factored into this equation. The third part is managing the trade, using coil overshoots and backfills to properly scalp and pare out of the position.

PREPARATION

By this time, you should be fluent in the setups and triggers because you have spent enough time paper-trading and working backwards to the point of impact. Right? The answer needs to be yes; if it is not, go back and do your work. There are no shortcuts in this game.

Preparation is 80 percent of the work in making a trade. This preparation starts before the opening, as we reviewed in the section on morning preparation in Chapter 5. Familiarity breeds confidence. When you skip the preparation part of making a trade, the trade will usually be an impulse trade, which is likely to result in a red trade. It is said that luck occurs when opportunity meets preparation. We believe this to be the case; however, we wouldn't call it luck. We would call it destiny.

The key things you need to be aware of are the 200-period moving average support and resistance levels for the noodles *and* your stock for the 3-, 13-, and 60-minute charts. Note that we are not interested in the 5- and 15-period moving averages intraday yet. The pivots will run equally on all time frames intraday for both noodles and stocks (on many platforms, the pivots are not updated until a few minutes after the opening, so it is wise to manually reload your charts page shortly after 9:31 a.m. Eastern time). Also manually note the daily 5- and 15-period moving averages support and resistance levels on the noodles and your stock. These numbers, represented visually with moving average lines on your broker platform, should give you a good road map of the speed bumps on the noodles and your stock.

One more very important thing that you need to manually write down is the moving average support and resistance levels that are overlapping with the pivots or the daily 5- and 15-period moving averages. The weekly 5- and 15-period moving averages can also be used, but *only* if the stocks are near that level and these are extremely strong levels. This is your road map; familiarize yourself with it every morning. Each pivot level or 200-period moving average support or resistance level is a spot where volume will show up and a potential play can be made either with or against. Overlapping support or resistance levels should carry even more weight as places where trades are made.

For the most part, the aforementioned levels will remain static or move only slightly during most days. The dynamic support and resistance levels will be the intraday 5- and 15-period moving averages. These need to be watched continuously, since they cover a shorter time frame and are more relevant. Throughout the day, you will find overlapping support or resistance levels for the 5- and 15-period moving averages on the 3-, 13-, and 60-minute charts. For example, the 15-period moving average uptrend support on the 13-minute chart, the 5-period 60-minute moving average support, and a pivot support may all be within 2 points of each other on the futures and within 0.20 of each other on the stock. In a case like this, where you have a triple support level, the preparation would be for a buy long entry coupled with a stochastics bounce on a 1-minute trigger, usually the first or second time it tests for the best retracement bounce. On the flip side, if you are in a short position trade, you will be looking to cover on or ahead of the triple overlapping support. Always be on the lookout for pups or inverse pups on the moving averages charts. These carry a lot of weight and deserve a high priority for setup premises.

The moving averages and the pivots are like the bumpers in a pinball game. The directional momentum of that pinball is determined by the stochastics charts. We analyze these charts on the 3-, 13-, and 60-minute intraday time frames for the noodles and the stock. Once again, this may seem like a lot, but the reality is that your basket stock will move with the noodles in a near-mirror formation, so don't feel overwhelmed. The 1-minute stochastics chart is always useful. It is a key tool for determining the actual trigger and short-term momentum. Scalpers will always use this 1-minute stochastics chart.

When using the stochastics, always watch for a mini pup or mini inverse pup formation on any of the time frames, even the 1-minute time frame. Mini pups, like pups, deserve a high priority for setup premises. Always jot these formations down or make a mental note when they happen. Whenever you get the 13-minute and 60-minute stochastics and moving averages in the same direction, make a note of that. If the 3-minute stochastics and moving averages turn, then a three-lane highway will emerge, which is a prime setup. Spider senses need to be tingling whenever these setups occur.

Let's step outside of ourselves and see what's going on. Notice the mindset here. We are watching and evaluating based on the multiple time frame supports. We are gathering potential setups based on very valid premises. We are standing at a distance and *pointing out ahead of time* where we can make a trade. We are creating an if/then formula for our trade. We know where the upside or downside potential of the trade will be, based on these support and resistance levels. Simply stated, we are *aware*.

That is the most important thing about preparation: It makes you aware ahead of time. Contrast this to situations in which you may have impulse traded by just stepping into any stock on news or knee-jerked in because of the Nasdaq Level 2 screen. Can you see the difference? Premeditated and calculated is what preparation should be. All this time and effort prior to the trade is what will keep you from getting wiggled out or overstaying your position if the premises change. You are seeing what looms above your head. The flaw in not being aware is fixed when preparation is carefully done ahead of time, prior to your trades.

This doesn't mean that you need to stop and prepare for every single trade. There will be times when you may stop out of the long side and immediately go short because you are in a make-or-break situation. The premises reversed, thereby providing you with the opposite trade on the same preparation. However, all this was premeditated and factored into the initial trade based on—you guessed it—preparation.

Deriving High-Probability Setups

Once you have all your preparation information up and running, it's time to watch the real-time action on the 3-minute charts. The 5- and 15-period moving averages and stochastics are the most dynamic movers and require the most attention. However, you naturally shouldn't be taking your eyes off the 13- and 60-minute stochastics and moving averages charts. You may ask, which time frames do I prioritize? It's very simple: Always start with the wider time frames to get a bird's-eye view and then move to the 3-minute time frame. When the action in the 3-minute charts slows down, then peek at the 13- and 60-minute charts. The important thing to remember is to start watching the 13-minute and 60-minute charts only after 9:45 a.m. Eastern time. The first 15 minutes after the market open can be very choppy and misleading, so give yourself that time before you step in and get a reading on the 13- and 60-minute noodles and stock charts.

Every trade you make will be based on one of three underlying themes.

You are playing either breaks (breakouts or breakdowns), continuations (of the trend), or reversals (countertrend). The breakouts or breakdowns will occur at or near pivots and overlapping moving average support or resistance levels. Reversals will occur at the same levels if the breaks do not occur. Continuations will occur ahead of those levels.

At this point, if you aren't familiar with the prime setups in Chapter 4, make sure that you review them. The best setups are three-lane highways, where the 60-, 13-, and 3-minute stochastics are rising on the noodles and your stock if you are playing the long side and are falling if you are playing the short side. Also, remember that stops are just to buy time. You have to always maintain the mentality that stops are not a negative thing. They are positive in that you stop any further bleeding and you buy time to get a better reading and firmer premises.

Always make sure that you are aware of the 13-minute and 60-minute noodles stochastics and moving averages trends. Make it a rule not to fight the 13-minute noodles stochastics, especially if they are rising along with an uptrend in the moving averages. The clearest setups will happen when you play alongside the 13-minute stochastics on the noodles. It is possible to play countertrend only when overlapping resistances are hit, and these are only for retracement scalps unless there is a very strong overlapping resistance, like a daily or weekly 5- and 15-period moving averages resistance on the short side.

Make sure that you are prioritizing the correct time frames on your setups. As you put your premises together based on proper time frames, you must simultaneously allocate the shares properly, once again based on time frames. This means that if you take a perfect storm setup, then you will allocate large-size scalp shares to play the 1- and 3-minute squeeze and pare to clip out the 13- and 60-minute movements. You need to plan ahead and allocate properly. The 3-minute time frame will be the immediate impact, the

13-minute will be the midrange impact, and the 60-minute is the longer time frame intraday impact.

Here are some examples of good setups worth playing:

Setup A: A 13-minute stochastics 20/30 band mini pup + 60-minute noodles 20-band cross up + 3-minute stochastics noodles cross up off the 20/30 bands + overlapping pivot and 200-period moving average supports = take heavier shares long on the three-lane highway squeeze.

Setup B: A 13-minute stochastics retracement that crosses back up after a hammer off the pivot support + 60-minute stochastics still rising above the 50 band + moving averages uptrend overlapping support + 3-minute stochastics mini pup = take the long on the retracement bounce scalp and pare with 13- and 60-minute uptrends and stochastics.

Setup C: A 3-minute mini inverse pup after a 1-minute oscillation + 2.5-strike sell fade + 1-minute stochastics peak and slip + 3-minute noodles mini inverse pup + 13- and 60-minute noodles stochastics down = take the short for a 3-minute moving averages breakdown and 3 lanes stochastics slip composed of the 3-minute, 13-minute, and 60-minute stochastics slips.

Newbie Mistakes

A newbie is someone who is new to the methods described in this book, not necessarily someone who is new to the stock markets. This needs to be clarified. Newbie traders to these methods should not play extreme situations. That means do not short any stocks under the 20 band on the 3-minute or 1-minute stochastics and do not go long any stocks above the 80-band stochastics.

Also, it is important not to play against the pivot the first time it is tested, as a rule. This means that if MSFT's pivot support sits at 46.50 and MSFT panics to overshoot 46.45 to test the pivot the first time, it is not wise to take the short immediately, since it is likely that the 1-minute and 3-minute stochastics are already under the 20 band. Shorting there is likely to lead to your getting squeezed higher on the stochastics pops. Instead, it would be wiser to play the long-side bounce off the pivot. About 80 percent of the time, when a pivot is tested the first and even the second time, it will usually reverse after the overshoot; therefore, it's wiser to play against the panic overshoots for the retracement bounces. This applies even more in light-volume periods. With those odds, would you rather take the 80 percent probability trade or the 20 percent probability trade? The answer should be obvious.

PULLING THE TRIGGER

The time will come when you can work backwards and you have reviewed all the charts you possibly can in an effort to solidify patterns and setups. This is all preparation for the ultimate test, which is using the methods in real time. The difference between real time and history is minutes. However, history in that sense can't make you money. Trading is all about pulling the trigger and letting the premises play out for better or worse. You can't win if you don't play.

Once you have prepared your setups based on premises, you are ready to pull the trigger *when* the chart trigger hits. That trigger will be based on the 1-minute stochastics and/or the 3-minute stochastics. The most important thing to remember when pulling that trigger is that you aren't so much concerned about what the stock is doing now as you are about what the stock will be doing minutes from now. The premises help to foreshadow the probable movement of the stock.

Timing the Entry

There are three types of entries into a position. There is the early entry, which carries with it some wiggle. You risk the wiggle on the early entry in order to achieve a greater gain. The sweet spot is an entry right at the moment of impact, where your position is positive right on the entry and never looks back. With the late entry, you are looking for an extended leandown or a short squeeze and you get in late for the last-ditch push. Late entries are made at exhaustion levels and are risky because they can reverse fast if you are wrong. Therefore, these entries are either for one last extended push or for a ranged play where you already expect a wiggle attempt and a further leandown, fueled perhaps by a perfect storm or three-lane highway pattern.

The early entry is where you will get your best-executed fill because you are literally going against the crowd. The idea behind an early entry is to get in as close as possible to the exhaustion point of a selloff or a peak, just ahead of a reversal move. You would take an early entry long off overlapping supports into the sellers for the stochastics bounce back up. Early long entries should be made into overlapping supports. Early short entries should be made into overlapping resistances.

Early entries will initially move against you, and this is expected. You just want to make sure that your premises are intact and that you have allocated properly and given yourself the wiggle room to let it play out. It's important to allocate properly in these types of trades. Since wiggle will be expected, it is wise to take a slightly smaller number of shares than scalp size on these.

In light-volume markets, good entries will almost always be early. It is nearly impossible to enter at the sweet spot, since spreads will quickly move away. Late entries on light volume are a recipe for disaster. Since everyone is moving away from the spreads so fast, chasing stocks in light volume should be something you make sure you do not make a habit of. The extra added risk of entering early means that entries should be backed by overlapping supports on longs and overlapping resistance on shorts as well as slightly fewer shares. If played right, early entries give you the greatest upside for gains.

Ideally, the sweet spot is the best and least risky entry to take. By the same token, it also has the smallest window of time to get a fill. You have to be on your toes and assertive to grab a sweet-spot move. Many traders opt for the early entry because getting a fill on an execution in the sweet spot can be so elusive.

A three-lane highway setup will present the sweet spot for the longest duration. This is because there is still some overhang from sellers and the shorts. For example, when the 60-minute stochastics is already rising through the 40 band and the 13-minute stochastics makes a 30-band mini pup as the 3-minute stochastics is finishing off its oscillation down move near the 20 band, traders will notice that the immediate effect seems to be a sell side. That would be naive, since the wider time frame charts are indicating an up move. When the 3-minute stochastics crosses back up, many times you will not see an immediate pop. There will still be lots of shorts trying to short the crossover. They will eventually get squeezed. This is why it is important to make sure that you are watching the wider time frames on the charts and not paying too much attention to Nasdaq Level 2.

Early and late entries are usually where most traders' executions are placed because they tend to have the widest open windows to get a fill.

Late entries are like a game of musical chairs. These entries involve going long above the 80 band on the 1-minute stochastics on the stock and noodles or going short under the 20 band on the 1-minute stochastics. The main reason for a late entry is that there is a critical make-or-break scenario that has just triggered, such as a three-lane highway or a perfect storm, and you are expecting either a short squeeze or a leandown selling panic to break a critical level.

The basic rule of thumb is to severely limit your number of late entries. Most of the time, late entries are bad entries that will reverse. You are playing with fire on late entries, as the snapback against you can be vicious. Once again, take late entries only when you have a three-lane highway or a perfect storm setup where a strong support or resistance level is breaking down. Late entries should be played for scalps; this is mainly because they are such extreme levels that they will eventually reverse. By taking the late entry, you are just hoping for the reversal much later, after an immediate panic in the direction of your trade.

To help your odds even more, late entries should be played only when there is a mini pup through the 1-minute 80 band long or a mini inverse pup through the 20 band on the short. The other way to help your odds is a failed coil bounce attempt, such as a mini pup attempt through the 20 band that fails or a mini inverse pup attempt through the 80 band that fails. These have even bet-ter odds for success, since the reversal has already been attempted and showed signs of failure. This means that if a stock tries to mini pup through the 20 band, the longs have stepped in and are push-ing. If that mini pup gets smothered out and slips, then all the longs will look to panic right out, causing a nice panic drop again. The converse also holds true: When a 1-minute mini inverse pup through the 80 band triggers and the shorts come in, only to have it smother and reverse back up, the shorts will panic and buy to cover. These formations are most apparent in three-lane highways.

Once again, the ideal entry will be sweet spots. Early entries should be made only with overlapping supports or resistances. Late entries should be the smallest percentage of your trades and are applicable only with the backing of a three-lane highway for-mation in the noodles.

Proper Allocation of Shares to Setup and Risk/Reward

The most common problem traders tend to have is misallocation of shares. If you mix apples and oranges, the result is a very uneven profit/loss curve. Have you ever had eight winning trades and then two losing trades that wiped out all the profits? This is due to misallocation. Remember this very simple rule: *Do not play the same number of shares on every trade unless every trade is the same setup with the identical premises.*

It's surprising to see traders fail to follow this rule, either out of ignorance or out of laziness. For example, a trader may take 1000 shares long on MSFT at 47.90 on a 3-minute moving aver-ages pup breakout triggered by the 1-minute stochastics 40-band mini pup and by the 3-minute noodles moving averages pup breakout and rising 13-minute stochastics. This is a beautiful setup on MSFT that ensures an initial pop and potentially longer follow-through supported by the noodles and 13-minute charts. How-ever, taking the same 1000 shares long on MSFT when the 3-minute 5-period moving average is flat, the 15-period moving average is falling, and the 13-minute noodles stochastics is flat is too risky. The downside on the second trade is that the 3 shift could cross the 5-period moving average down, triggering a

3-minute inverse pup breakdown on MSFT and the noodles, which will result in a fast breakdown panic.

Let's assume that a trader takes the first MSFT trade and scalps the 3-minute pup breakout on the 48 overshoots ahead of 48.10 coil resistance for a gain of +0.20. Later in the day, the trader takes the second MSFT trade long 1000 shares at 47.90, looking for a 3.5-strike reversal while the 1-minute stochastics is above the 80 band, only to have the 3 shift cross the 5-period moving average down. MSFT panics hard to 47.50 overshoots and the trader panics out at 47.50, out −0.40 on the panic. The trader is upset because he gave back his gains fast.

Although the premise for the entry may have been valid at the time, the trader did not properly allocate for the potential risk of a 3-minute moving averages inverse pup breakdown triggering. The proper way to trade a pattern like this is to take a smaller number of shares because the reversal can be painful. The trader should have taken 300 shares of MSFT long; this would still produce a 0.40 loss, but the dollar loss amount would be only $120 instead of $400. The reason the trader should not have taken 1000 shares on MSFT the second time is that *the setup was different, as were the premises.* The premises were inherently more risky simply because the trader was playing against the downtrend, and therefore that risk needed to be tempered by taking fewer shares of the stock.

The best way to handle this is to preallocate shares according to setups. This should make all the sense in the world. Every trader should have some prime setups that fit her or his style. These setups are the ones to which the most shares will be allocated. For anything less than a prime setup, the number of shares needs to be scaled down. Countertrend trades will be discussed in the next chapter. Make sure that you allocate the proper number of shares based on setups and time frames.

MANAGING THE TRADE

Once you have pulled the trigger and are filled in the position, the next step is the management of your position. Managing takes a bit of foresight in that although the present is important, the future is what you are focusing on. There are three actions that you can take once you are in a trade: ride, pare, or exit. This means that you will need to constantly be making a decision as to whether to take all profits (scalp), pare and range (combination), take a stop, or take a stop and reverse the trade (make-or-break reversal). The root of all action once you are in a trade will be the premises that you have prepared prior to the trade.

Managing the trade consists of continuously watching your premises as they extend. Premises do not last forever, and eventually they will peak. For example, a three-lane highway composed of 3-, 13-, and 60-minute stochastics rises will not stay a three-lane highway forever. It cannot. By the time transparency is fully developed, there will be profit taking, illustrated by a peaking and reversal of the 3-minute stochastics. Therefore, while the transparency is making its way, a trader needs to react and manage based on her allocation.

If you went long on a three-lane highway with scalp-size shares, you will need to coordinate with the 1- and 3-minute stochastics to exit from your position for scalps. Many times, you may enter a long trade based on a 1-minute mini pup and get the 3-minute stochastics to cross up half way through the 1-minute oscillation in addition to the 13- and 60-minute noodles stochastics rising, and serendipitously you have stumbled onto a three-lane highway formation. In cases like this, it is very advantageous to pare the 1-minute oscillation peaks based on the 1-minute stochastics and then range the rest of the shares with the 3-minute stochastics, fully anticipating a 1-minute wiggle. Understand that in order for stocks to move higher, they need a wiggle. This wiggle shakes out the weak hands and invites in the shorts to squeeze back up.

If you decide that the 13- and 60-minute charts are too bullish and you expect more after a wiggle, then you will need to sell a majority of your long position to trim it down to a range/swing position allocation. Be fully aware of the retracement that looms ahead once the 3-minute stochastics peaks and reverses. In addition, you need to have stops in mind should that wiggle turn into a full-blown 3.5-strike trend reversal.

Riding the Trade

Once your trade is executed, you technically are already riding the trade. The fuzzy logic portion will be how long and how far you stay in the trade with your original position. The type of entry you take will determine how long you will be riding the trade. A late entry means that you will be in it for the shortest duration, since you are taking an extreme-band entry, unless you are ranging it. A sweet-spot entry will allow you to ride the trade and pare along the way. An early entry will mean that you will ride the trade for the longest duration, unless your premises break down and stops are triggered.

The rule of thumb when you enter a trend trade is to stay aware of the 5-period moving average active momentum support and the 15-period moving average regular support. When you take a breakout move, ideally you want to keep the 5-period moving average as a trailing profit stop, especially on pup breakouts, where the 5-period moving average is essential.

Your main premise for the trade will determine how long you will be riding the trade. Remember that it is not a matter of what the trade is doing now, but of what it can possibly be doing moments from now. If you take a trade long based on a 1-minute stochastics bounce, then you will be prioritizing the 1-minute stochastics move and scalping into the 80 band or the peak, whichever comes first. If you take a trade long based on a 3-minute stochastics and moving averages, then naturally that will be your key indicator. You may use the 1-minute stochastics to pare profits along the way. Trailing stops on longs will be triggered on the 5-period momentum moving average support and/or the 15-period moving average support. This applies to both uptrends and downtrends. The 1-minute stochastics exhaustions will usually cause a stock to retrace to 5-period momentum support, where it should continue to bounce off and make new highs if the trend is strong.

A special note here about countertrend trades: The first priority anytime you play a countertrend is to scalp/pare the 5-period moving average overshoots and the 15-period moving average overshoots. For more information on countertrends, refer to Chapter 9.

Paring the Trade

Paring a trade means partially scaling either out of or into your position. Paring applies to taking profits, and you can also pare an exhaustion level as the stock price moves against your position in hopes of a retracement that will minimize your loss and even possibly turn it into a profit. The basis for paring out of a trade is that the immediate trigger or premise is starting to be exhausted, and therefore you want to capture the majority of the profits before complete exhaustion and reversal. However, a wider time frame premise may still be intact, allowing you more upside once the shorter time frame premise completes its wiggle. For example, taking a 1-minute mini pup and 3-minute stochastics through a 30-band oscillation up on MSFT means that you will probably pare out 70 percent of your longs as the 1-minute stochastics reaches its peak near the 90 band. It is completely accepted and anticipated that the 1-minute stochastics will peak and reverse. However, since the 3-minute stochastics is still rising, there is still *a greater probability that MSFT will move higher after it wiggles back down* on the 1-minute stochastics retracement. Therefore, you would lock in profits on the majority of the shares based on the 1-minute stochastics and then give a trailing stop *below your entry point* to allow for a wiggle followed by resumption of the 3-minute stochastics trend to higher highs.

When you pare out of a trade, you need to understand that there must be a premise on a wider time frame that justifies your staying in the trade; without it, you may as well just take the full profit. Your trailing stop should always be below your initial entry point near a 15-period moving average support. Most traders who pare use too tight a stop and therefore end up stopping out of the position with less profits. If you don't give yourself enough wiggle room on the pared shares for the exhaustion retracement, there is no sense in paring.

For example, if you took MSFT long at 48.75 and scalped 70 percent out as the 1-minute stochastics 90 band overshoots through 49.05, you would leave the 300 shares long with a trailing stop closer to the 48.55 level. This gives the trade a chance to play out on the 3-minute oscillation. Many traders will exit at 49.05 and then give a 0.10 trailing stop, which in most cases gets hit just on the basis of a spread wiggle to the 48.90 coil support. Therefore, a trailing stop to anything higher than the 48.75 entry is just wasting the trade, since the stock needs to "catch its breath." This takes a little getting used to, but it works in the long run.

More advanced traders will be able to use paring in order to cut down on losses. You often hear traders being told to take stops and be deliberate about them. This is true for the most part. However, in reality there are times when stocks will move very irrationally, especially during squeezes and panics. Stocks may move so fast and so hard to a near exhaustion point that it may be more beneficial to pare in more shares of the short for an exhaustion reversal play in order to bring the breakeven price higher so that it meets the wiggle retracement level to exit. These scenarios are more common in the opening hours and the dead zone.

We have to caution, though, that these strategies are risky and should be attempted only by experienced traders who have a cushion of green on the day. The only time to be paring into a counterplay is when the wider time frames give you a definitive premise for doing so—for example, a 13-minute mini inverse pup that sets up while the 3-minute moving averages squeeze to pivot overlapping 200-period moving average resistance levels. In a case like this, you may have taken a short early, and the stock may have moved 0.20 against you toward the overlapping resistance level. Since the 13-minute chart is indicating a mini inverse pup, paring in the short at the overshoots would be wise, since it is likely that a shooting star candle may trigger to signal the peak of this move at the overlapping resistance. The premise behind the additional paring of the short is to capture the 13-minute mini inverse pup foreshadowing a 3-minute moving averages breakdown.

The flip side of this trade is that the stock holds above the pivot long enough to turn the 13-minute stochastics around. Normally, you wouldn't wait that long to find out. Once the 1-minute stochastics peaks and makes its retrace, you are already paring back out the short position near the 5-period moving average momentum support overshoots. If you decide to ride the short more, then you would do so with 13-minute-size shares allocated for the mini inverse pup breakdown. Once again, you see how allocation is the key to limiting your losses and maximizing the opportunity for gains. The theory is that every wide-channel 5- and 15-period moving averages trend will eventually have to compress from profit taking. This compressing stage is where traders will look to pare in shorts on uptrends and longs on downtrends. Chapter 9 will go into more detail about the exhaustion reversal plays.

Exiting the Trade

Exiting means completely getting out of your position, either through a stop or through profit taking. Stops, as mentioned, are based on premises. If your main premise starts to break down, then stops need to be implemented. Be assertive. Understand that by not taking stops, you not only continue to bleed but also miss the opportunity to possibly reverse the trade! This doesn't mean chasing any bid down to get out at any price. Depending on the range, you will in most cases get a backfill opportunity to exit a position with a smaller loss if you are patient and assertive enough. Remember that if you are in a make-or-break situation and all of a sudden you see that the premise is starting to slip, you can use the 1-minute stochastics coils to backfill out and even reverse the position.

The other reason to exit a trade on a stop is to buy time and some clarity. In these cases, the premises could go either way, and it is the calm before the storm. Usually, ranges get tight in a consolidation period. In such a period, spreads may be moving extremely fast or extremely slowly, and it is just as easy to say that the action is choppy in a range. However, the most significant breaks can occur in these periods, when most traders are writing them off as noise. Remember, you are not so much concerned with what is happening now as with what may happen moments from now. The ability to take a small stop now to buy time for the real move is a wonderful weapon. This is an ace up your sleeve that you will always have. Too many traders forget that they have this beautiful weapon, the stop. Stops are an action. Stops buy you time and clarity, and therefore, in essence, stops buy you opportunities. Don't ever take them for granted.

Complete exits on profits will come in the form of scalping completely out of a position or taking a profit stop on a pared position. When you are riding a trend, there are two supports. The 5-period moving average is the momentum support of an active uptrend. This 5-period moving average can be used as a trailing profit stop on pared longs. The final stop will occur when the 15-period moving average is broken, usually in the 2.5th strike of a 3.5-strike reversal, as the trend is looking to reverse at this time.

PROZAC MOMENTS AND NOISE

The majority of the trading day will be composed of noise and more noise. There will be spread movements back and forth within the ranges. It is imperative that you understand the noise factor in the game. You will get the most noise when the 5- and 15-period moving averages are in consolidation, as the bulls and bears will appear to be jockeying for a move but going nowhere in the process.

There will be times when your basket stock will have such fast spread movements within a 0.20 range that it's virtually impossible to make head or tail of it, since the trend itself is nonexistent. These are the times to stay out of the market and assume that what you are seeing is noise. Noise is what makes traders overtrade. Another point to keep in mind is that every stock out there will have moments and even days when it is just sporadically moving all over the place with fast spreads and cranks. These moments should be avoided. Take a walk, grab some lunch, or go play some video games. The fast spreads are simply there to entice you to make trades in an effort by market makers to rack up volume. Don't fall for it.

MARKET LAGGARDS

We want to address the laggards for a moment. We discussed tier synergy in the first book. Since then, tiers have changed, because as stocks drop in price, they drop below the radar of tier synergy. The tiers will continue to change as time goes on. Therefore it is fruitless to list tiers in this book, since they may well be outdated in a matter of months. For a better list of tiers, check undergroundtrader.com regularly for the tier lists.

The saying "A rising tide lifts all boats" applies very much to the tiers. When a sector or even the market is very strong, the money flow will naturally flow to the tier 1 generals. However, once the tier 1s are exhausted, the money flow will tend to drive into the lower tiers. Stocks above $10 are considered laggards. Stocks under $10 are considered turds, for lack of a better word. Once a stock breaches that $10 limit and falls below it, that stock will no longer be affected by the tiers unless there is incredible strength in the markets or the sector. You should keep a list of the under $10 turds for those days when the market is just trending higher and higher for laggard money flow. Managing this takes some experience, since turds tend to move with a much different rhythm.

The other type of market laggard is a stock that is fading relative to the market or sector trend, but the market is continuing to get stronger and stronger, and therefore the sell fading subsides as the money flow sees value in the stock, giving it a delayed bounce. These types of plays should always be watched out for when the market is trending strong in an uptrend or a downtrend. It's good to check the new highs and new lows list throughout the day to see which stocks are making new lows as the market is making new highs and vice versa. Naturally, the way to play the laggards is to use the 3.5-strike trend reversal and countertrend playing method to get in on exhaustions or trend reversals.

These laggards can come in all forms—even your basket stock. For example, if MSFT is selling near its lows for the day while the noodles are in an uptrend toward new highs for the day with 13- and 60-minute low-band stochastics coils and consolidation breaks, this means that you are waiting for MSFT to make a 3-minute stochastics crossover. When the sellers finally step back, the stock will make a delayed bounce to bring its price back into alignment with the market. This happens all the time, especially on stocks that have news or analyst upgrades and downgrades.

CHAPTER 9

Playing the Countertrend Reversal

This type of trading is more risky but just as rewarding. Countertrend trading means going against the crowd in multiple time frames in order to move on a trend before it reverses itself. It is most useful when a trader misses out on the upmove and is looking to make more on the reversal down and vice versa.

The old cliché is that "the trend is your friend." This is one of those vague and general statements that won't help you a lick with your trading. The reality is that trends that move in three time frame directions, such as three-lane highways, are not worth playing the countertrend to. However, in fractured setups, we can thread the noodles and take advantage of immediate shorter time frame moves against a wider time frame move. It all boils down to your reference time period. The elusive trend actually relates only to the time frame you are trading. If you trade a 3-minute uptrend but the 60-minute and 13-minute charts are in a downtrend, then one can say that the trend is still down, which is true. The rule of thumb is that the wider time frames act as the overriding trend until proven otherwise.

While this may be true, the oscillation range days far outnumber the strong trending days—literally by 5 to 1. This means that if played correctly, countertrend reversals can mean very nice steady profits. However, when playing against the immediate trend, one has to be aware that the danger of a hard move against you is always out there.

Newer traders should not jump right into countertrend reversals. To be able to play these reversals, a trader needs to have a solid foundation in playing overshoots and backfills as well as the assertive ability to take profits and stops on a dime. The lack of any of these skills means that you can and probably will get hurt more often than you profit.

Playing countertrends can be extremely profitable, yet on the flip side they can be extremely dangerous if they are not implemented correctly. Countertrend trading is such a science that we are dedicating a full chapter to its intricacies. Every trader will get his share of overstaying a countertrend trade, which will often result in getting short squeezed or sitting through a panic selloff. The key is to be able to know what situations will allow you to give yourself as much buffer protection as possible while still allowing you to capture the green.

Remember that a trend is a moving force in one direction. This is very much like the theory of inertia, which states that an object in motion tends to stay in motion until it meets an opposing force. The 3.5-strike reversal helps to provide an exact blueprint of what will cause an opposing force to break down and reverse the immediate trend. We discussed the 3.5-strike reversal earlier, but to summarize, the first strike is the exhaustion level, where the stock will peak and retrace to the 5-period moving average momentum support. This will cause the 5-period momentum support to slow down the momentum and move sideways. The second strike occurs when the stock tests the 15-period moving average coils and holds under the 5-period moving average, thereby making the 15-period moving average go sideways. This is technically the consolidation stage. The 2.5 strike is when the futures bounce but the stock sell fades into the buying, and the last strike occurs when the futures peak out and reverse and the stock breaks down, causing the 3 shift to cross back through the 15-period moving average and a new downtrend to emerge.

Using the 3.5-strike reversal model, there are two types of countertrend trades that you can make.

EARLY EXHAUSTION REVERSAL PLAY

The trade in which we tackle the strike 1 and strike 2 portion is the exhaustion reversal trade. In the exhaustion reversal trade, you are taking an early entry into the resistance or support overshoots. The theory is that the stock will need to take a breather, since it has run too fast and too hard in too short a time. Every market trading day is a 20-mile marathon, and the markets can never maintain a 50-yard-dash pace. On the charts, this means that all wide channels in the noodles (referring to the 3-minute moving averages) and your stocks will eventually have to tighten and compress before there can be another large run.

With this understanding in mind, the underlying theme is that all big breakouts or breakdowns will eventually have to retrace and tighten the 5- and 15-period moving averages channels. This tightening comes from profit taking on uptrends and short covering on downtrends. Exhaustion reversal trades look only to scalp and pare retracements to the 5-period momentum support and the maximum of the 15-period supports on the retracements. The trader has no choice in the matter. Only the stock's movement will determine where the last of the profits will be taken or stopped. This is really just strike 1 and at most strike 2 of a 3.5-strike reversal.

The early entries can be a little scary, and therefore it's very important to make sure that you have overlapping resistances when you short or overlapping supports when you go long against the trend. When the bulls are squeezing the market or a stock up, thereby widening the 5- and 15-period moving averages channels, an opportunity will emerge. The premise is that the channels will eventually tighten—they have to. The market cannot run at a 50-yard-dash pace for the whole day. Either the 5-period moving average will pull back or the 15-period moving average will rise, and eventually either a pup breakout or a consolidation will occur.

With this understanding, we assume that a stock will eventually peak and then retrace at least to the 5-period moving average on an uptrend. That peak is the exhaustion level and the area that we are looking to short. Exhaustion reversals are meant only to take advantage of the immediate pullbacks to the 5-period moving average. Overstaying an exhaustion reversal short can lead to getting squeezed once the pup breakout triggers. The spot to place the short is going to be near an overlapping resistance level on your stock and also on the noodles. If the noodles are showing a 3-minute 200-period moving average resistance and a pivot resistance that is overlapping, this is usually a good premise to use for the exhaustion reversal short. If your stock is also showing the same resistances, then the premise for the exhaustion reversal is that much stronger.

Remember that these are very fast plays that can result in fast gains of 0.10 to 0.30, depending on the stock's price. Naturally the higher-priced stocks will give more of a gain. Always measure the 5-period moving average, then time the entry with a 1-minute stochastics peak. Even better is a 1-minute stochastics mini inverse pup entry through the 80 band for the retracement. There are certain candlestick formations that give a great signal for the exhaustion shorts, like the shooting star and the doji. We will review those candlestick patterns a little later and explain the rationale for what the candles indicate.

Paring also works well on exhaustion plays; however, if you miscalculate the power of the move, it can easily crush you as the stock is squeezed higher if you are long or is crushed lower if you are short. Therefore, you must make sure that you have enough experience under your belt before you attempt any size paring on exhaustion plays.

Since these exhaustion shorts tend to be early, there is a fine line between giving wiggle room and paring in extra shares on the short and taking a stop. Exhaustion shorts tend to work 70 percent of the time. However, an inexperienced trader's three losses will usually wipe out all the prior gains and then some. Therefore, make sure that the overlapping resistances make themselves apparent first on the noodles and then on the stock. Always be sure to clip or pare fast profits near that 5-period moving average.

Gap market opens tend to be one of the best times for these exhaustion reversal plays. The days where the market gaps up on the open near an overlapping pivot resistance allow us to get into the shorts early and capitalize on the fact that the channels will need to tighten and that the tightening process is where we make our profits.

CONFIRMED TREND REVERSAL PLAY

The second type of reversal play is a trend reversal play that waits for strikes 2.5 and 3.5 to trigger. With the trend reversal play, you take the strike 2.5 trade, where the futures take a bounce but the stock is sell fading, and you short into that sell fade because you see a potential 3-minute mini inverse pup trigger on the 1-minute stochastics peak. You are catching it just as the last of the buyers are trying to push the stock up. Once the 1-minute stochastics slips, the 3-minute mini inverse pup will push it back down through the 15-period moving average and cause the 3 shift to cross down, thereby confirming a true trend reversal in 3.5-strike fashion.

The trend reversal play is more of a confirmed entry and less risky than the exhaustion play, with naturally less immediate reward. However, if it turns out to be a true breakdown, then the upside can be very nice. When taking these confirmed trend reversal plays, make sure that you also are checking the 13-minute and 60-minute time frames for support or resistance as well as pivot levels to plan out your profit taking.

OVERLAPPING SUPPORT AND RESISTANCE LEVELS FOR COUNTERPLAYS

The first line of defense when playing counter to the trend is to always note where the support and resistance levels lie on the 3-minute, 13-minute, and 60-minute noodles and also on the daily and weekly noodles and stock charts. This means knowing where the 5-period and 15-period moving averages, the 200-period moving averages, and the pivots are. The strongest resistances on uptrends will be the overlapping resistances, and naturally the strongest supports on downtrends will be the overlapping supports. An overlapping pivot and moving average support or resistance level is also strong. The rule of thumb here is that *the wider the time frame that is overlapping, the stronger that level is.* This means that a 3-minute 200-period moving average support that overlaps with a pivot is indeed strong. However, a 3-minute 200-period moving average resistance that overlaps with a daily 5-period downtrend resistance is even stronger.

Once again, don't go into a frenzy trying to remember all these levels. First of all, these levels apply only once the noodles or stocks get near them. Second, they should all be visually marked on your charts anyway so that you can see the overlapping effect when the prices get close. The other thing to remember is that a 13-minute 15-period moving average is usually at or near the 60-minute 5-period moving average, meaning that they like to overlap. If there is a resistance on the 13-minute and 60-minute charts and a pivot, then the chances of its breaking on the first attempt are less than 5 percent, which is excellent odds if you short those overshoot levels.

CAUTION!

The reason the countertrend reversal gets its own chapter is that everyone will get squeezed eventually. It's not a matter of whether you get squeezed; it's a matter of how little damage you take in the process. There is a very real edge in the trading game where experience and skill can make the difference between a small stop and a large monster stop. The experienced traders will not get hurt much because they either react fast enough or trim the shares enough to keep damage to a minimum. Unfortunately, the newer trader can have his head handed to him playing against a trend by overstaying his welcome on the reversal and not knowing when he needs to exit, or just freezing and not taking action. Being complacent can cause the exception to wipe out all the gains. A good countertrend player knows when to throw in the towel on the trade and look to reverse her position and ride with the trend. With this in mind, the exception to the rule will cause minimal damage while she reaps the 80 percent of the countertrend moves that are in her favor.

There will be exceptions in which the 13-minute noodles mini inverse pup attempt gets smothered out and coils back up, suckering in many shorts, only to get squeezed up. This can be a very nasty short squeeze, and it usually occurs when there is a make-or-break situation with a 13-minute moving averages pup or mini inverse pup. The 60-minute noodles stochastics should still be rising, and the moving averages trend should still be up. In cases like these, you need to be very careful. The indices will usually already be up in a rally mode from oversold positions on the daily chart, which makes it even tougher.

EXCEPTIONAL GAPS

You will come upon some days when the daily stochastics is extremely oversold under the 20 band or extremely overbought above the 80 band and a reversal will trigger, keeping the 60-minute noodles stochastics at an extreme band for the majority of the day. These days are treacherous. While an investor may feel great because the Dow is up 300 points, a trader will see this as a very rough neighborhood to be shorting. Usually that 60-minute stochastics on the noodles will be in overbought territory with an uptrend all day. These days usually occur on extreme daily stochastics that are looking to make a reversal.

Be very careful playing against the intraday trends. While these days are few and far between (less than 1 percent), when they do occur, they can be vicious. If you don't want to get mugged, you should simply stay out of the rough neighborhoods, and that means forgetting the countertrend plays and sticking with riding out the trend or staying in cash. A good trader knows when the environment is too risky for his style and will be assertive enough to exercise discipline and patience. You must come to the understanding that there will be days when certain strategies just do not work, such as countertrending a market that is bouncing from an extremely oversold daily condition, as indicated by the 60-minute noodles holding above the 80 band for hours and hours. If you understand and accept the fact that this kind of trading environment does exist and do not play against the intraday trend, you will be much better off.

REVERSAL CANDLESTICK PATTERNS

Candlesticks are an excellent tool for gauging early signs of a reversal. We want to go over some of the key reversal patterns and the rationale behind them. Candlestick charting was not something that immediately grabbed my attention because it seemed as if there was a lot of noise and ambiguity in it. However, when you understand the underlying reactions that create the formations, they become invaluable. *Japanese Candlestick Charting Techniques*, by Steve Nison, should be a part of your trading library.

The rule of thumb is that *a reversal candlestick formation is strongest after a series of green candles (uptrend) or a series of red candles (downtrend).* This series should have at least three continuing candles. It is also very important to note that one candle alone is not enough confirmation most times. For a stronger reversal, there should be at least two reversal candles. Most important, do not be premature in interpreting the candle. Always wait for the candle and the period to close before making judgments. Do not get caught up in trying to read what every candle means because, just as with everything else, there is a lot of noise.

It's most important to filter out noise and just focus on reversal candles at the end of a series of trending candles. The 3-minute and 13-minute candles tend to work best for intraday trading. The 1-minute candles are choppy and have too many wiggles. They can be used for very tight range scalping, but they are not recommended for most traders. Keep in mind that the candlesticks are a good way to interpret the action and help to tip the scales on your trades. These patterns should be used in conjunction with the stochastics and moving averages to create an optimal set of tools.

Shooting Star Topping Candlestick

A very useful candlestick pattern for spotting the top or peak of an up move is the shooting star. This formation usually occurs when buyers are coming in and squeezing a stock to short-term highs (upper shadow) near a pivot, 2.50, or a 200-period resistance. The resistance will initially overshoot and peak, then retrace to where it started and close lower. For example, MSFT's 3-minute candle shows an opening at 47.75, grinds through the 47.85 pivot resistance to peak at 47.89, and slips back to 47.70, where it closes. This would create a candle with a long stem to 47.89 and a body that closes at 47.70, or a shooting star. These patterns tend to occur after a squeeze move up and indicate the last pump on the squeeze before peaking and slipping back down.

We often like to short the next candle after a shooting star is triggered. Remember that the candle simply tells us to be ready. The actual shorting is going to be based on the 1-minute and 3-minute triggers. The candle gives us an early reading that the top may be in, as shooting stars tend to signal the top according to the time frame that you are playing.

Doji Candlestick Reversal Pattern

A doji at the peak of an uptrend is a sign that buyers came in and popped the stock to a high (the upper shadow), then profit takers sold it off to the lower shadow and buyers could take the candle *only* back to where it started from. The doji is a reversal pattern mostly because it is a sign of indecision. Indecision is usually a negative when a trend is concerned. A doji at the end of a long run is a sign that the rally is running out of steam. The best place to short a doji is when there is a doji after a shooting star peak is triggered by the prior candle. Once again, do not be premature; make sure you wait for the candle to close first, and then watch the sec-

Reversal Candle Formations

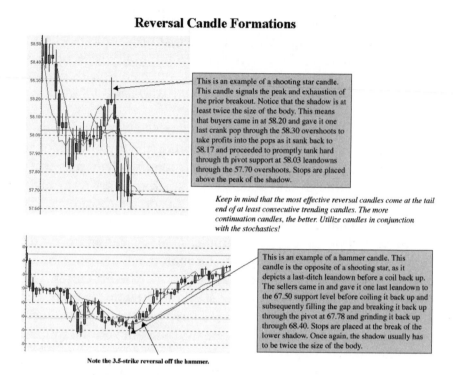

This is an example of a shooting star candle. This candle signals the peak and exhaustion of the prior breakout. Notice that the shadow is at least twice the size of the body. This means that buyers came in at 58.20 and gave it one last crank pop through the 58.30 overshoots to take profits into the pops as it sank back to 58.17 and proceeded to promptly tank hard through th pivot support at 58.03 leandowns through the 57.70 overshoots. Stops are placed above the peak of the shadow.

Keep in mind that the most effective reversal candles come at the tail end of at least consecutive trending candles. The more continuation candles, the better. Utilize candles in conjunction with the stochastics!

This is an example of a hammer candle. This candle is the opposite of a shooting star, as it depicts a last-ditch leandown before a coil back up. The sellers came in and gave it one last leandown to the 67.50 support level before coiling it back up and subsequently filling the gap and breaking it back up through the pivot at 67.78 and grinding it back up through 68.40. Stops are placed at the break of the lower shadow. Once again, the shadow usually has to be twice the size of the body.

Note the 3.5-strike reversal off the hammer.

Figure 9–1 Reversal candles.

ond candle. It is also important to make sure that you catch the doji only after a series of at least three trending candles. The more trending candles you have prior to the doji, the better the reaction.

Hammer

A hammer indicates the bottom of a downtrend. It is basically an upside-down version of a shooting star. It is composed of a long shadow and a small body. Initially sellers came in and made new lows on the candle period, then buyers gap-filled the open and closed the candle at the top of the range. Hammers are most effective after a series of at least three red candles.

PAINTING THE CHARTS—WATCH OUT!

It never ceases to amaze us. The pros will always find some way to manipulate the markets. With more and more traders using candlestick patterns and technical analysis, some market makers take advantage of the newbies by painting the charts. Newbie candlestick readers and chart readers can get suckered by these tricks. Usually these trades will appear as "misticks" on time of sales; however, these out-of-market trades will alter the candle patterns and often the stochastics and moving averages.

For example, let's say MSFT is selling off in a steady downtrend, with the 5-period moving average at 48.70, the 15-period moving average at 48.90, and MSFT trading at 48.68. The 3-minute stochastics is slipping through the 30 band. A crooked market maker may sell himself 200 shares of MSFT at 48.50, which is a pivot support. When he prints this on time of sales, what do you think happens to the charts? The moving averages charts will show a wicked hammer, normally signaling a bottom, and the stochastics will signal a hard reversal coil off the 30 band to the 50 band immediately. A newbie who doesn't realize that this is an out-of-market misprint will dive in head first on a hammer reversal formation and stochastics low-band coil, only to realize that the stock is not moving up for some reason. That's right, that market maker is unloading shares into the sheep. This is why it is so important to *learn the mechanics* of the indicators and methods. Just trying to find patterns and formations with a cookie-cutter mentality is a sure-fire way to get manhandled out there. If you know why and how a reversal candle truly forms, you will not fall for these lame tricks.

CHAPTER 10

The Mental Game

In this chapter, we go over the mental aspects of trading and management. Once again, we give a fresh, realistic approach to how to successfully manage the downtimes as a trader.

STYLES MAKE FIGHTS

One of the reasons that traders get into drawdown slumps is that they are in a period in which the market is conflicting with their style. Your abilities as a trader are a weapon. However, that weapon can be effective only in the right environment. A gun is not effective under water. Use the weapon in the wrong environment, and it can be useless.

In professional boxing, they say that styles make fights. A slugger, like a Mike Tyson, is known for quick, dynamic bursts of power punches in an effort to get the knockout in dynamic fashion. A puncher, like an Evander Holyfield, is known for his jab, weave, and clinch style in an effort to win on the scorecards, and in essence to win the fight, after 12 long rounds. Therefore, when two sluggers meet in the ring, the result is an exciting, hard-fought, dynamic fight with lots of action and volatility that usually concludes rapidly with an early knockout. However, when a slugger gets in the ring with a puncher, the puncher will avoid the power punches, sneak in jabs to score points, and clinch when he is overpowered for the duration of a long, frustrating 12-round match. In the end, a slugger will usually get worn out and lose the fight to the puncher on points.

The markets are very much like a boxing match. Every trader is either a slugger, a puncher, or a combination. From this analogy, you can probably guess that the slugger is the scalper, the puncher is the range/swing trader, and the combination trader is just what the name implies.

The market itself is the opponent. There are times when the market is fast and voluminous, giving fluid follow-through with liquidity. This is the scalper's market and the best environment for him. There are times when the market is in tight ranges and leaning with tiny spurts of volume. This is a range/swing trader's market and the best environment for him. A scalper playing in a range/swing market will constantly get wiggled out. What may appear to be a breakout usually ends up being just a one-candle formation in a range, and the scalper enters and gets wiggled right out. This market version of the jab, weave, and clinch leads scalpers to get shaken constantly until that one time that the scalper decides to stay out turns into the breakout that she should have played. This is a miserable market for scalpers, and therefore they need to stay out of that fight. Tight channel and light volume consolidations are the worst conditions for any trade to play. Consolidations are notorious for headfakes and one-candle pops and drops.

This description is applicable not only to markets intraday but also to markets on daily and weekly time frames. Remember that markets move in phases. They will break out, peak and exhaust, retrace, and consolidate for another breakout or breakdown. It is smart to watch the daily and weekly charts in order to recognize what type of phase the market is in at the moment so that you don't overtrade during consolidation periods on the dailies. Everything you do on a 3-minute moving averages and stochastics chart will apply on the daily and weekly charts. It will just apply on a wider time frame with wider channels. You don't overtrade consolidations on a 3-minute chart. This means that you also don't overtrade during daily consolidation periods, where volume overall will remain light with tight channels. This can be another reason why a trader may be going into a slump.

GAME OF PROBABILITY

This is a game of odds. There's no two ways about it. When you step back and look at the game as a whole, no single trade should ever overshadow all the other trades. We play probability and odds. This means that if you are sticking to the right context and the same setups, then the odds will eventually work in your favor. There will be times when the setups break down on you, as in any theory there will always be exceptions to the rules. However, you can be confident that as long as you manage to stick to the rules, the odds will once again lean to your side. For example, the best setup out there is a perfect storm setup, where you get at least two pups on two time frames and sometimes three. This is a setup that will be effective for profits 90 percent of the time. Given these odds, you must realize that for every 20 perfect storm setups you play, at least 2 of them will reverse and cause you to take a loss. When you step back and see this, it's no big deal.

The problem is that once you are in the trade and it turns on you, it can be easy to write off the strategy altogether and get very emotional about the loss. This is unfortunate. The key word is *emotions*. Probability looks great from a distance, but emotions get involved when someone is in the eye of the storm. It is very important that traders step back and review their trades to determine the success ratio of the setups. Anytime you get into a slump, tighten the filter for more higher-probability trades. It's just like tightening the spigot. It is easy to fall into multiple setups and get lost. It's very effective to step back, tighten the spigot, and refocus on the stronger setups.

TWO COMMON CAUSES OF FAILURE

Most traders who fail at the endeavor usually fall into one of two categories: They are either ignorant (unaware) or lazy (nonassertive). To be ignorant is to be unaware of the potential that looms in the form support or resistance and foreshadowing patterns on a wider time frame. To be lazy is to be nonassertive, either not taking the time to learn the methods patiently and properly or knowing what needs to be done in a trade (e.g., a stop loss) but not taking action. These are the realities of failed traders. If you are aware and assertive, then you may have temporary setbacks and drawdowns, but you will eventually succeed in this game.

The good news is that these two common causes of failure can be dealt with. If you are in an extended slump, it is a good idea to honestly and rationally analyze which category you fall into before it is too late. If you find yourself being unaware, then study the pivots and moving averages as well as the linear formations on the 13-minute and 60-minute charts. Remember that extra emphasis needs to be placed on overlapping levels. If you find yourself being lazy, make the effort to learn the methods and also make the effort to take action when premises do not work out for you. Be premeditated on every trade you make. Assert yourself on paper and slowly build up consistency with smaller numbers of shares until you build up the instincts to react automatically when premises warrant.

CONSISTENCY

Consistency is the key to longevity in this game. What makes consistency so elusive is that traders tend not to be able to judge when the context of the setups is identical. Because they are not able to gauge this, most traders will play the same number of shares on every trade. They may end up winning on eight trades, but then they give back all their profits on the last two trades.

Does this sound familiar? If this has happened to you (and I'm sure it has), go back and review the trades in the *full* context of the 3-, 13-, and 60-minute stochastics and moving averages. That's where you will find the divergence in the context of the setups. For example, the prior eight trades may have been long-side scalps with the 1-minute stochastics where you unknowingly had a rising 13-minute stochastics in the context of a larger time frame uptrend. You may have done the same thing on the last two trades on the low bands without realizing that the 13-minute stochastics had triggered a mini inverse pup down this time and you were actually trying to scalp in the context of a larger downtrend.

See how the difference in context makes the difference in the result of the trades? Your first eight trades may very well have been three-lane highway plays that you didn't recognize. The last two, however, were fractured setups that may have taken a small bounce, only to sell off hard when the 13-minute mini inverse pup foreshadowed the 3-minute moving average inverse pup for a panic breakdown.

As in any play, there is a game plan, and then there is the execution of that game plan. The methods allow you to devise the game plan and see every play in the full context. This context is what allows you to judge the setups to make sure that you are playing apples to apples and oranges to oranges. Most traders can't tell whether they are playing the same setups and therefore are unaware that they are playing a 3-minute time frame versus a 1-minute time frame or a 13-minute time frame. This is a recipe for disaster. As long as you are aware of the context of your trades and the setups, then you should be able to allocate properly.

Once you can allocate properly and pinpoint the type of setups that you play, then the consistency factor can stabilize.

MAKING YOUR OWN LUCK

There are two types of luck in the markets. The first type is random luck, which is very dangerous. This type of luck occurs when someone enters a trade and fails to take a stop when the premises for the trade reverse. Being afraid to take a loss, he holds the position overnight, and luckily the stock reverses and gaps up the next day, at which time he exits the position completely without premises. This is equivalent to being stuck in a minefield and walking out of the minefield in a straight line with your eyes covered. If you make it out alive once, this sets a very dangerous precedent. Eventually, this trader will blow up. This is luck based on hope and nothing more. It is the worst kind of luck there is because it sets dangerous precedents subconsciously, and as much as a trader may say that he will never take that chance again, he usually will, and if he does, his fate is sealed.

The second type of luck is what occurs when a trader enters a trade with the premises intact and a trigger, and instead of her getting a 0.20 scalp, the stock squeezes higher and she ends up taking a 0.40 scalp. In this instance, the trader got a little extra luck on the upside and took advantage of it. If the extra momentum had not come in, the setups were strong enough to allow her to take her 0.10 to 0.20 scalp and exit. She doesn't need luck, but the setup was so strong that she got more than she expected. This is the best type of luck because it happens when one is prepared and takes the opportunity on the trade. Preparation meets opportunity, resulting in a greater profit than anticipated. Traders who structure strong premises into their triggers and setups will often make their own luck by the sheer strength of the move. Make an effort to always make your own luck. If you do get lucky, take advantage of it and cash in the profits or partial profits along the way.

ANALYZING AND RECOVERING FROM SLUMPS AND DRAWDOWNS

Every trader will have drawdown days and weeks. This is to be expected. A slump can be defined as two or more back-to-back drawdown weeks. When you fall into this situation, it is very important that you be patient and methodical in your analysis and recovery process. It is also important that, in addition to reviewing your trades, you take a look at the bigger picture of the daily stochastics and moving averages formations.

Many times, the reason for the slump is a change in the rhythm of the market. For example, there may be extreme market conditions in which the daily stochastics ride 90+ bands or −10 bands for a long period of time. In this case, it is not necessarily the trader who has the problem; it is the market conditions that are causing the trader to trade ineffectively. The market has changed on him, and he hasn't adjusted to it. Most drawdowns in these periods will result from *overtrading consolidations, taking late entries on extreme bands* (shorts under 20-band stochastics and longs over 80-band stochastics), and *playing the dead zone.* Go back and review your trades and check off how many of the losing trades fall into those three categories.

The recovery process starts with an analysis of the market conditions and your trades in those conditions. Knowing that the majority of bad trades fall into the three categories just named, you need to adopt a new game plan in which you make no trades that fall into those categories. To do this, you will need to step back and go back to basics. Remember those prime setups? It's time to tighten the filter, rule out the noise, and focus specifically on three-lane highway setups.

Going back to basics means that you do not make exceptions to the rules–type trades or trade fractured setups. This means that you do not short under the 20-band stochastics and do not go long above the 80-band stochastics in any time frame, especially the 1-minute and 3-minute time frames. Do not play dead-zone periods, where light volume, consolidations, and fractured setups are typical. You may initially kick yourself for not making some of those trades, as they may result in some large moves. However, don't kick yourself too long. Extreme-band moves are exceptions to the rules, and the majority of the time, they peak and fail just as soon as you enter the trade. Would you rather be right 80 percent of the time or 20 percent of the time? The answer should be obvious (déjà vu?). It is sheep mentality to concern yourself with trades you don't make. The woulda-coulda-shoulda syndrome is simply an excuse. You don't concern yourself with the exceptions. By not taking extreme-band positions, you should be able to cut your losing trades column by over 50 percent.

When the markets get into consolidations or extreme high- or low-band daily stochastics, you can get a lot more noise in the markets. It's very important to note when the markets are in extreme periods, like riding under 10 bands or over 90 bands on the daily stochastics. This can cause long periods of indecisiveness and light volume in the markets. Traders need to accept the fact that some market conditions are simply not tradable by them with their style. It is when a trader does not realize that he is in an untradable environment and continues to trade that he gets himself into trouble.

Finally, understand that the most beautiful words in a trader's vocabulary are *closure* and *apathy*. Closure allows you to approach each trading day with a clean slate. Apathy allows you to stay objective with the trade in mind, never crossing the line between conviction, where premises are keeping you in a trade, and stubbornness, where the premises are dead and hope is the only thing keeping you in the trade.

THE ULTIMATE GOAL

The ultimate goal of every trader is twofold. The first goal is to have the ability to be a combination player, which allows the trader to participate effectively in the two types of trading environments: scalping and ranging. The second goal is to increase the comfort zone through the mental threshold to make the transition to larger numbers of shares when the environment (liquidity) is applicable. The obstacles to both of these goals are psychological. As with a trend, the only way to break through the overlapping resistances is slowly, tightly, and with time.

The ability to break the barriers to becoming a combination player will stem from first becoming comfortable with the scalping methods. As you become consistent with the scalping methods, you will find yourself exiting "early," which is normal. From that point on, you will learn to pare out partial profits when the 3- and

13-minute charts are still rising. You will fully anticipate and measure the extent of the wiggle without overlooking the trend.

After you have built up enough success with paring, you will find yourself in many environments in which pure scalping is simply ineffective in that the channels are too tight and do not justify taking scalps that barely cover commissions. In these cases, you will learn to "cast a net" over the range levels, riding smaller numbers of shares for the range breaks backed by the longer time frame premises intraday. As you become more and more comfortable with this method, you will slowly be making the transition to a range-type player who takes profits on momentum moves. When you have done this, you will have accomplished the goal of becoming a combination player.

Range trading is similar to what a professional fisherman does when he casts a large net into the water. You are doing the same thing in a premeditated format, casting a net through the range, hooking a range break with a slow-moving trend. It is very easy not to see the forest for the trees in a tight 3-minute channel environment topped off with wiggles all over the place on Level 2.

The ability to break the larger-share-size threshold is one of the hardest to acquire because the appropriate number of shares is determined by the market environment. Naturally, if the volume is light, you do not want to be going extremely heavy unless you have a very strong underlying wider time frame signal to be heavy. Remember, increasing your share size should be done slowly and incrementally on a weekly to monthly basis. Once you hit 1000 shares, the transition gets a little easier until you reach the 5000 share mark. The larger your share size rises, the less liquidity you will find in a scalper's market, and thus you must already have broken the combo player threshold and be able to pare effectively.

The other point here is that some stocks will by their nature force you to take smaller numbers of shares because of their extra volatility and faster spread moves. All this needs to be taken into account in your trading. If you keep these stocks as your basket stocks, then you will be able to distinguish when you can adjust the number of shares.

As mentioned earlier, your share sizes are based on the setups and the market environment. Just because you have committed to taking larger share sizes doesn't mean that you will take 2000 shares on every single trade. This is apples and oranges again, and it will get you into trouble. A better example would be to take your current trading size allocation and increase each level slightly. For example, if you trade 1000 shares on three-lane highway setups with a good 1-minute trigger in the 30- to 50-band stochastics and you trade 500 shares on 13-minute setups with a 3-minute trigger, then you will look to adjust up to 1400 shares on the 1-minute three-lane highway setup and 700 shares on the 13-minute-based setup. See how we work it up incrementally? In essence, you are trading the same way but increasing the number of shares incrementally. This way you keep apples to apples and oranges to oranges.

PREMEDITATE THE TIME FRAMES

The methods discussed here are linear throughout all time frames, from the 1-minute up to the monthly. However, this doesn't mean that the human emotion factor won't play a big part. When you are playing purely on a 13-minute chart with the backing of the 60-minute trend, it's often wise to block out the 1- and 3-minute time frames and Nasdaq Level 2. It's human nature to watch the shorter time frames too closely when you are trying to play a wider time frame and to get wiggled out in the process. It is wise to have a lay-out page, which you may call the range page, for range trades, using just the 13-minute, 60-minute, and daily charts. By visually having access to only those time frame charts, you insulate yourself from any shorter time frame wiggles. The reality is that a 3-minute stochastics peak will have an influence on the 13-minute chart in most cases, but if the trend is strong, the retracement will be just a wiggle.

FIND A HOBBY

We know it gets boring during the trading day, especially during the light volume throughout the dead zone. Realistically, most traders should be staying away from dead-zone periods. Sitting in front of your computers for 8 hours a day can be strenuous and boring, and this can cause traders to overtrade out of sheer boredom. Our advice is to find yourself a hobby that can take you away during slow periods of the day. This can be a side business, going to the gym, taking a lunch break, or some other activity. This is a game where working harder does not necessarily equate to getting paid much more. In fact, the more you sit and analyze too deeply in periods where there is noise, the more you can get thrown for a loop by losses. This game is about working smarter, not harder. Remember, you don't get paid on an hourly basis as a trader. You get paid for trades that you make in an effective environment. When the environment turns sour during the day (no volume, no trend, no channels), take a walk. This is your job.

Putting It All Together: A Sample Week of Trades

Just as we did in the first book, we document a hypothetical week of trading, giving a play-by-play of 5 days of trading in the equities market with these methods.

DAY 1

Basket Stock: MSFT

Premarket Reading

Reloaded the page at 9:31 a.m. to get the correct pivots. MSFT pivot resistance and 3-minute 200-period resistance sat at 54.60, which was the sticky 5s coil resistance. MSFT's 60-minute moving averages resistance was also at 54.60, overlapping resistances. This will be a spot to short on the first attempts to break.

The 60-minute noodles were crossing up, coiling the 20 band in a tight consolidation; noodles support sat at 997 × 998 for the 5- and 15-period moving averages. The 13-minute noodles were in a consolidation, and the stochastics was sideways at the 40 band. Noodles pivot resistance sat at 1001. The 3-minute 200-period moving average resistance was at 998, the 13-minute noodles 200-period moving average support was at 994, and the 60-minute 200-period moving average resistance was at 1022.

Trades

The market opens up with a small pop as the noodles overshoot the 1001 pivot resistance. Since that 1001 level is a pivot resistance and these usually don't break the first time, I step in and *short 1000 shares of MSFT at 54.32* on the 1-minute stochastics mini pup failure and 3-minute noodles slip at 9:44 a.m. MSFT makes a nice panic overshoot through 54.15, and I *cover the short into the sellers for 1000 shares and +0.17 profit* as the noodles peak and slip back down from 1003 to 993; covered MSFT into the sellers of the noodles 993 coil support.

MSFT bottoms on the 1-minute stochastics and bounces back up for an oscillation move to the overlapping resistance level. The 3-minute noodles are once again testing the 1001 pivot. MSFT takes a full stochastics oscillation and squeezes through the 54.60 level. I *short 1000 shares of MSFT into the overshoots and fill at 54.67 at 9:59 a.m.* in the overlapping resistances as the noodles peak again at 1003 and trigger a bearish engulfing pattern to slip to 990 on overshoots. Knowing that 988 is a coil support, I *cover MSFT on the 1-minute stochastics full oscillation down at 54.25 to scalp out +0.42 at 10:06 a.m.* Phew. Nice action. At this point, the 60-minute noodles are still rising and the 13-minute noodles are rising, so I will not be taking any new shorts or messing with that sticky 5s range on MSFT.

MSFT's 13-minute chart makes a 20-band cross up at 10:11 a.m. I *take MSFT long 500 shares at 54.70* to range this trade, since the triple overlapping resistances finally break. Our stops are placed at the 54.40 coil support, as the 13-minute noodles are rising, the 60-minute noodles are rising, and the 3-minute noodles are rising—a three-lane highway. By 10:37 a.m., the 13-minute noodles are triggering a consolidation breakout as the noodles rise through the 1007 coil resistances. MSFT 13-minute makes an oscillation to the 80 band and triggers a mini pup that squeezes

MSFT through 55 overshoots, where I *pare out 300 shares at 55.05, out +0.30 on 300 shares.* The noodles peak at 1007, retrace to the 5-period moving average, then coil back up to overshoot 1010, where I *pare out the rest of the MSFT longs at 55.20, out +0.50 on 200 shares.*

Nice morning. As the dead zone starts to creep in at 11:15 a.m., I take a break until the afternoon session.

Wow. The 13-minute noodles make a full oscillation to near the 100 band and the 60-minute noodles are up over the 80 band. The 13-minute noodles are showing me a make-or-break situation up here. Noodles are trading here between 1018 and 1022 at 12:45 p.m. If 1023 breaks, then we can have a run to 1027 pivot resistance. If 1018 breaks, then that will give me a 13-minute stochastics 80-band slip on the noodles for a move to possibly 1012, which is the 60-minute 5-period moving average.

The noodles initially attempt to break 1023, and I *take MSFT long 1000 shares at 55.75 at 12.48 p.m.* MSFT makes a small uptick to 55.85, but I am too slow on the trigger. It's a dumb 90-band 1-minute stochastics entry. The noodles take a pop to 1024.50, where they peak and quickly fall before I can lock profits. MSFT quickly downticks to 55.70, where it backfills to let me *take a stop at 55.70, out −0.05.*

MSFT's 3-minute chart triggers a shooting star peak. I don't want to stick around, as the 3-minute stochastics is peaking out on me. The noodles take a 3-minute peak and slip the 80 band, and the MSFT 3-minute stochastics starts to cross back over down. I *step in and short 700 shares of MSFT at 55.52 at 12:58 p.m.,* this time for a 3-minute stochastics oscillation slip. The pivot sits at the 55.37 level; more important, the 13-minute stochastics peaks and slips on MSFT also. As the noodles eventually make a full oscillation slip, MSFT leans and panics to overshoot the 55.32 level, where *I pare out 400 shares of MSFT, out +0.20* as the noodles take a small coil off the 1015 level.

I am still ranging 200 shares of MSFT with a trailing stop up at 55.65 as the 13-minute noodles and MSFT continue lower. MSFT coils off that pivot support to the 15-period moving average resistance on the 3-minute chart, but I am not worried. If the 0.65 triggers, then I will take a small stop; otherwise, I am looking for a 3-minute 200-period moving average support overshoot test near 55 × 55.05. The 13-minute noodles stochastics is still slipping lower, as is MSFT. At 1:25 p.m., I notice that the 3-minute moving averages on the noodles and the 3-minute moving averages on the MSFT chart are setting up an inverse pup breakdown. I check the 13-minute stochastics, and it is still slipping. I *step in short on MSFT again at 55.28 at 1:25 p.m. for 700 shares* with a trailing stop at the 15-period moving average overshoot at the 55.45 level. MSFT and the noodles simultaneously peak and trigger a 3-minute moving averages inverse pup, panicking MSFT down through the 55.05 overshoots and the noodles down through the 1013 coil supports to 1011. *I pare out all my MSFT shorts at 55 into the 3-minute 200-period moving average overshoot panics. Wheeee. Scored +0.52 on the 200 shares and +0.28 on the 700 shares.*

Noodles go into a deep consolidation into the last hour and then have divergence on light volume, so I call it a day, holding the green. Nice scalping opportunities in the morning. The dead zone was active enough to make some nice green on panics and widening channels. The afternoon thinned out into a consolidation range without much of a trend, and thus I kept it light for the rest of the day.

Stats

Shorted 1000 MSFT at 54.32, Covered at 54.15, out +0.17 × 1000 = +170

Shorted 1000 MSFT at 54.67, Covered at 54.25, out +0.42 × 1000 = +420

Bought 500 MSFT at 54.70, Sold 300 at 55, out +0.30 × 300 = +90

Sold 200 at 55.20, out +0.50 × 200 = +100

Bought 1000 MSFT at 54.75, Stopped at 54.70, out −0.05 × 1000 = −50

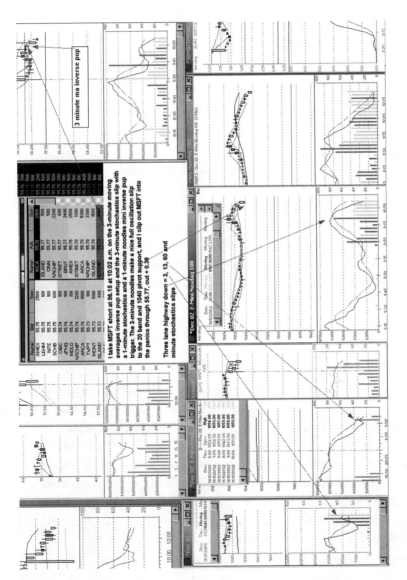

The text within the figure reads:

3 minute ma inverse pup

I take MSFT short at 56.15 at 10:02 a.m. on the 3-minute moving averages inverse pup setup and the 3-minute stochastics slip with a 1-minute stochastics and a 1-minute noodles mini inverse pup trigger. The 3-minute noodles make a nice full oscillation slip to the 20 band and 1040 pivot support, and I clip out MSFT into the panics through 55.77, out +0.38

Three lane highway down = 3, 13, 60 and minute stochastics slips

Figure 11-1 Day 2 trade on MSFT.

155

Shorted 700 MSFT at 55.52, Covered at 55.32, out +0.20 ×
400 = +80

Covered at 55, out +0.52 ×
300 = +156

Shorted 700 MSFT at 55.28, Covered at 55, out +0.28 × 700
= +196

Total Gross Profit/Loss = +1462

DAY 2

Basket Stock: MSFT

Premarket Reading

MSFT hovering just under 56 premarket, nothing much, as it is
gapping up on the open from 55.45 close. MSFT has a pivot
resistance at 56.15 × 56.20 level.

The 13-minute noodles have choppy stochastics but uptrending and the 60-minute noodles have rising stochastics and
uptrending moving averages. Noodles opening strong with a pivot
support at 931.

Trades

The market opens with a large gap; the noodles have a resistance
at 935. MSFT choppy on the open, hovering between 55.90 coil
support and 56.10 coil resistance. At 9:32 a.m. I *short 1000 shares
of MSFT at 56.15* on the pivot resistance overshoot attempt as the
1-minute stochastics peaks and the 3-minute noodles mini pup
gets smothered out at 935. The 3-minute noodles take a nice oscillation to overshoot to 928 as the 1-minute stochastics on the noodles gives me a stair-step mini inverse pup and MSFT makes an
80-band stochastics slip to overshoot back to 56, where I *cover the
shorts at 55.95 overshoots, out +0.20 on 1000 shares.* I don't want to
hold the short too long with a rising 60-minute stochastics and
uptrend and a 13-minute uptrend.

At 9:53 a.m., the 1-minute noodles take a bounce, and I notice the 60-minute chart starting to show an 85-band mini pup. I *buy 1000 shares of MSFT long at 56.05* as the 3-minute stochastics crosses back up, setting up a 3-minute moving averages pup breakout and a three-lane highway on MSFT. The 13-minute noodles stochastics indicates a moving averages pup breakout on a 935 break. The 1-minute noodles take a mini pup full oscillation, taking the 3-minute stochastics to full oscillation up to overshoot 1038 on the noodles as I *sell all 1000 shares of MSFT into the 56.50 overshoots, out +0.45,* wheeee!

At 10:15 a.m., MSFT tries to break the 56.50 resistance. The 13-minute noodles are in an uptrend, though the stochastics is at a high band. The 60-minute noodles are at a high band as well, and MSFT 13-minute stochastics is near the 100 band. I get a three-lane highway, so I *buy 1000 shares of MSFT at 56.52* at 10:20 a.m., only to see it panic back down from the 1-minute stochastics 80-band slip. I keep a tight *stop at 56.42, out −0.08.* MSFT seems to be in a range here, so I switch over to range mode and reenter, *buying 400 shares of MSFT at 56.52.* Seeing how tight the 5-period and 15-period moving averages are on the MSFT 3-minute and 13-minute charts now, I am just going to ride the 13-minute moving averages trend with a trailing stop if the 5-period slips; this is at 55.20, which is also the pivot support, thereby making it an overlapping support. By giving myself 0.30 wiggle room, I am taking fewer shares so that if I do stop out, I won't be hurt too badly.

By 11:30 a.m. MSFT still has not been able to break that 56.50 level, and it has shaken on the 3-minute stochastics full oscillation slip to 56.25. I am tempted to throw in the towel, but I decide to hold on, since the 13-minute stochastics is still rising and the pivot has not been violated. The noodles are holding at an extreme band, trying to break through 1042 coil resistance. Since the 60-minute stochastics and the MSFT chart are still up, although at very high bands, I will continue to range this one higher. By 11:40 a.m., the 3-minute stochastics on MSFT reverses off the 30 band and oscillates up. We are finally getting some steam here as MSFT breaks through the 56.60 coil. MSFT is moving literally in 0.10 increments, but the 60-minute and 13-minute charts are still up. By 1:04 p.m., MSFT finally breaks higher to the 56.85 level, which is just shy of the 56.95 pivot resistance. The noodles are still grinding as it overshoots to the 1045 level, which is enough for me. I *sell into the 56.85 overshoots to exit MSFT 400 shares, out +0.35.* A long wait, but the pivot resistance is there and the noodles are near a real tough resistance level again. MSFT 3-minute chart is tight, sitting with a 0.05 to 0.10 spread between the 5- and 15-period moving averages.

The rest of the day is plain choppy as MSFT holds a 0.20 range under 57 and the noodles are stuck in a range from 1043 to 1048. Nothing compelling shows up on MSFT. However, I notice how strong BRCM is buy fading. The 13-minute noodles make their peak at 1:45 p.m. for a 5-period 13-minute moving average overshoot through 1046, which leads to a slip to the 15-period 1043 support level and the overlapping 60-minute 5-period moving average support. MSFT slips down to the 56.60 level. BRCM's high of the day was 14.22, and it is trading at 14.18 with a pivot support at 14.10. I *buy 1000 shares of BRCM at 14.20 at 1:48 p.m.* in conjunction with the 3-minute noodles 20-band cross and the 1-minute noodles 40-band mini pup back through the 1045 level. BRCM makes a beautiful 1-minute stochastics full oscillation move to the 14.33 level, where I *pare out 700 shares,* as the 3-minute moving averages are still in an uptrend with a 15-period support at 14.15. The 3-minute noodles eventually make a full oscillation and the 13-minute noodles cross back up through the 80 band, triggering a moving averages pup. BRCM breaks through the 14.40 sticky 5s low-range coil resistance as it overshoots 14.50. I *sell the remaining 300 shares into the 14.50 overshoots,* since 14.60 is a coil resistance and the noodles once again are at a 1050 × 1052 coil resistance level.

The morning once again provided some decent scalping opportunities; the afternoon was a choppy range player's market but gave some decent channels to play some scalps.

Stats

Shorted 1000 MSFT at 56.15, Covered at 55.95, out +0.20 × 1000 = +200

Bought 1000 MSFT at 56.05, Sold at 56.50, out +0.45 × 1000 = +450

Bought 1000 MSFT at 56.50, Stopped at 56.42, out –0.08 × 1000 = –80

Bought 400 MSFT at 56.50, Sold at 56.85, out +0.35 × 400 = +140

Bought 1000 BRCM at 14.20, Sold at 14.33, out +0.13 × 700 = +91

Sold at 14.50, out +0.30 × 300

= +90

Total Gross Profit/Loss = +890

DAY 3

Basket Stock: MSFT

Premarket Reading

MSFT closed the day yesterday near its highs of 57 level. Daily support: 5-period moving average sits at 55.60 level and looks like a potential daily moving averages pup trying to form. MSFT pivot sits at 56.30, and the 3-minute 200-period moving average support sits at 56.15.

Premarket the noodles are showing a 3-minute resistance at the 1053 level and a pivot support at 1040 on the nose. The noodles start the morning open near the 945 level.

Morning Trades

The noodles start the morning with a quick dip to 941 and coil back up. MSFT, on the other hand, is showing a sell fade as the 3-minute noodles stochastics opens the day on a high band and is slipping. I let MSFT play out in the opening minutes as it tries to bounce with the noodles off the 56.15 pivot support. Michigan Sentiment report comes out at 10 a.m. and spikes the noodles hard on the knee jerk to the 1059 level, just under the 1060 resistance. MSFT takes a spike to its 15-period moving average on the 13-minute chart near 56.50 and sell fades back down again.

As the 3-minute noodles peak and retrace on the knee jerk, I notice that the 60-minute noodles are trying to form a mini inverse pup. I spot the MSFT stochastics slipping back down, nearing the 56.30 pivot and the 56.15 3-minute 200-period moving average support. As the noodles overshoot the 15-period moving average support at 1047, I spot the 3-minute moving averages on MSFT triggering an inverse pup breakdown with a 3-minute stochastics slip and the 1-minute stochastics triggering a mini inverse pup breakdown. The slipping 60-minute and 13-minute stochastics complete a nice three-lane highway setup. I *short MSFT 2000 shares at 56.15 at 10:02 a.m.* (see Figure 11-2). The 1-minute mini inverse pup alone should give me a nice break through the 200-period moving average. The noodles take a plunge on heavy volume through 1045 and then 1043, and then 1041 overshoots to 1040. MSFT 1-minute stochastics makes a full-oscillation slip as the 3-minute moving averages inverse pup triggers. I *quickly cover 2000 shares on the 55.77 overshoots, out +0.38,* as the 1-minute stochastics gives me a full oscillation and an extreme low-band 1-minute stochastics mini inverse pup climax. Nice fast action on the knee-jerk reaction to the economic report. The noodles 1040 is a pivot support that I respect.

The noodles overshoot to 1039 and then coil back up as they base near that 1043 × 1045 level into the dead zone. By noontime, the 60-minute noodles are attempting to coil off the 20 band. The 13-minute noodles trigger a mini pup at 1 p.m., finally breaking the noodles higher into a 13-minute uptrend. The 60-minute noodles are still showing me the 15-period resistance at the 1052 level. A break there can coil the 60-minute low bands and extend the 13-minute noodles stochastics and uptrend. If 1053 can break, then 1058 × 1060 is the next resistance level, which is the 13-minute 200-period moving average resistance on the noodles. At 1:45 p.m.,

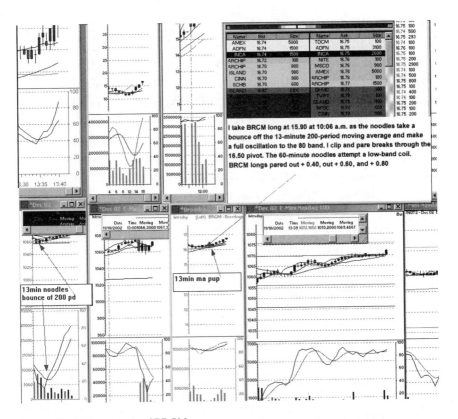

Figure 11–2 Day 4 trade of BRCM.

I step in and *buy 500 shares of MSFT at 56.20* with a stop at 55.90 for a range move with the 13-minute noodles mini pup, and the 60-minute noodles stochastics makes a 30-band cross and a consolidation breakout attempt through the 15-period resistance. MSFT is back over its 3-minute 200-period moving average support and pivot support. MSFT makes an initial pop to 56.37, which is now the 3-minute 200-period moving average. It's very choppy and tight-ranged, providing the rationale for going with fewer shares for a wider-ranged move.

This is a long wait. By 2:22 p.m., MSFT is still only trading at the 56.35 level but is now trying to break that 3-minute 200-period moving average resistance. The 3-minute moving averages are in a slow uptrend on the noodles and MSFT. By 3:30 p.m., the

13-minute noodles are near the 95 band with a potential mini pup, and the 60-minute noodles are up near the 70 band. MSFT grinds through the 56.60 pivot to overshoot to the 56.75 level, where I go ahead and dump my ranged shares, as the noodles also peak out near the 1062 coil resistance. I *sell 500 MSFT at 56.75 at 3:44 p.m., out +0.55 on ranged shares.* That was a long wait. The channels were tight out there, so there was no point trying to scalp anything. The premises with the wider time frames paid off, as MSFT eventually cranked up to a near 57 close as the cranks came in during the last 4 minutes of the day to crank the noodles up to the 1065 level. The day gave a nice scalp opportunity in the morning. The dead zone was truly dead, as the channels were simply too tight on the 3-minute and 13-minute noodles moving averages. The afternoon was dreadfully slow but uptrending, setting up a range trader's environment.

Stats

Shorted 2000 MSFT at 56.15, Covered at 55.77, out +0.38 × 2000 = +760

Bought 500 MSFT at 56.20, Sold at 56.75, out +0.55 × 500 = + 275

Total Gross Profit/Loss = +1035

DAY 4

Basket Stock: MSFT

Premarket Reading

MSFT closed at 56.69 and gapped up this morning to the 57 × 57.10 resistance level. I am also keeping an eye on BRCM premarket, as it is gapping strong and the weekly stochastics is giving me a 40-band mini pup. BRCM closed at 15.45 and is gapping up through 16.30. I *buy 500 shares of BRCM premarket at 16.30* to range. The noodles are gapping up this morning through the prior 973 double top. The 13-minute stochastics triggers a mini pup and consolidation breakout premarket, and the 60-minute noodles are sitting at the 90 band in an uptrend, with support at 1068 × 1063 for the 5- and 15-period moving averages. The 3-minute 200-period moving average support is at 1070, and the 13-minute 200-period moving average support is at 1058. Pivot resistance is at 1076, and support is at 1058. The 1058 level is overlapping supports. Will go long when these first test.

Trades

The noodles open the morning with an initial pop through the 1076 pivot resistance to peak at 1079 and then retrace as the 13-minute noodles peak and oscillate back down. I *buy 1000 shares of MSFT at 56.95 at 9:34 a.m.*, looking for a pivot break. MSFT holds between 56.95 and 57 until the 13-minute noodles start to slip. I *take a stop on MSFT at 56.90, out –0.05*, as the 3-minute stochastics starts to come back down.

BRCM is fading decently so far, as it is holding above 16. MSFT's 3-minute moving averages chart gets very tight as it leans down with the 13-minute noodles. The 13-minute noodles make a full-oscillation slip through 1060 at 10:03 a.m. Spotting the overlapping support, I *buy 1000 shares of MSFT at 56.75 at 10.04 a.m.* and also *buy 500 shares of BRCM long at 15.90 at 10:06 a.m.* to pare the long entry as the 13-minute moving averages trigger a pup breakout on the stochastics cross up (see Figure 11-3). The 13-minute noodles make a nice 20-band cross and oscillation up. My average price on BRCM is 16.10 now. The noodles are taking a very nice pop from 1059.50 to the 15-period moving average resistance on the 13-minute chart at 1067. The noodles overshoot, and I *pare out 700 shares of MSFT at 55.90, out +0.15*, and *pare out 700 shares of BRCM at 16.30, out +0.20*.

MSFT is showing some sell fading as the 13-minute noodles continue to grind. MSFT continues to sell into the buying. Since I am long only 300 shares apiece, I am ranging these with the 13-minute charts. MSFT is showing me a support at 56.57 on the 13-minute chart; that's where I'll keep my stop. The BRCM 13-minute chart is in a nice moving averages pup breakout. The noodles retrace to 1060 and then trigger a 3-minute moving averages breakout at 12:15 p.m. The 13-minute stochastics is still

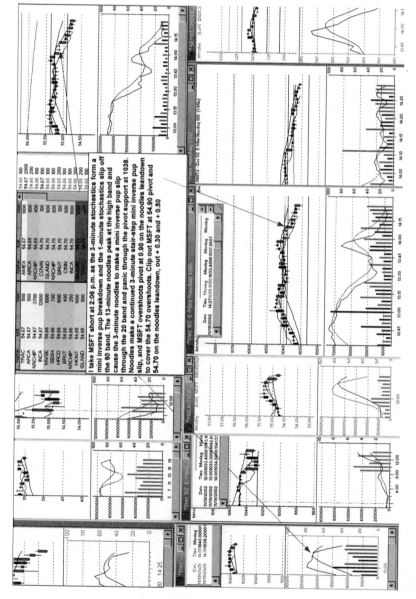

Figure 11–3 Day 5 trade of MSFT.

rising, and I am watching the 60-minute stochastics to see if we get a 30-band crossover back up, which would trigger on a 1073 break and base. The 3-minute noodles make a mini pup at 12:47 p.m. and then trigger a moving averages pup at 1070 that overshoots to 1072. BRCM overshoots the pivot at 16.50 and makes a pop through 16.70, where I *dump the rest of the longs, selling 300 shares at 16.70, out +0.60* on the pared longs.

MSFT is still having trouble getting any higher than 56.80. Looking for the 3-minute moving averages pup to continue to give off some steam, but that 60-minute chart is making me nervous with the potential mini inverse pup. At this point, at 1:40 p.m., if the 13-minute stochastics peaks out, then a 60-minute mini inverse pup is possible. The 60-minute stochastics needs to cross firmly while the 13-minute noodles are up, or else we could break down. At 2:15 p.m., the 13-minute noodles cross back down and slip through the 15-period support. MSFT 3-minute chart gives me a mini inverse pup setup, and the 13-minute stochastics is slipping off the 70 band; it's time to take a stop. I *stop out of MSFT at 56.65, out −0.10 on 300 shares.*

The 13-minute noodles are now making a full-oscillation down move through 1060, and the 60-minute noodles are making a mini inverse pup slip through the 20 band. I spot the sell fading going into the last hour on MSFT and jump in *short 1000 shares at 56.36* at 3:21 p.m. as the 3-minute moving averages form an inverse pup breakdown. The noodles break down through the 1056 pivot to panic to 1053 and then 1051. MSFT makes a nice panic to *56.15, where I scalp out completely, out +0.21* on the nice 1-minute stochastics oscillation slip.

Rangy, choppy action today. We were so close to a 60-minute moving averages pup, but the bears smothered out that 1073 and peaked out the 13-minute noodles for a full oscillation down into the close.

Stats

> Bought 500 BRCM at 16.30, Bought 500 BRCM at 15.90, avg 16.10 × 1000

Sold 700 BRCM at 16.30, out +0.20 × 700 = +140

Sold 300 BRCM at 16.70, out +0.60 × 300 = +180

Bought 1000 MSFT at 56.95, Stopped at 56.90, out –0.10 × 100 = –100

Bought 1000 MSFT at 56.75, Sold at 56.90, out +0.15 × 700 = +105

Stopped at 56.65, out –0.10 × 300 = –30

Shorted 1000 MSFT at 56.36, Covered at 56.15, out +0.21 × 1000 = +210

Total Gross Profit/Loss = +505

DAY 5

Basket Stock: MSFT

Premarket Reading

Noodles gap down this morning; CPI numbers give a small knee-jerk slip. MSFT near sticky 5s level. The 3-minute 200-period and 60-minute resistance overlaps 1048; the pivot sits at 1038. The 13-minute 200-period moving average resistance sits at 1057, and the 60-minute 200-period moving average support sits at 1027. MSFT 55s level very congested, with a daily support at 55.88 × 55.05 and a weekly 5-period at 54.66.

Morning Trades

Hard leandowns on the open as the noodles slip and continue lower; the 3-minute noodles form a moving averages inverse pup as the 13-minute noodles trigger stair-step mini inverse pups breaking through the 1038 pivot to panic to the 1027 overlapping supports for the 60-minute 200-period moving average and pivot. The MSFT pivot is at 55.40 and the sticky 5s low range, but MSFT is sell fading the 1-minute noodles coils, the 13-minute noodles are showing me a mini inverse pup, and the 3-minute moving averages inverse pup on the noodles is too tempting. I *short 1000 shares of MSFT at 55.39 at 9:36 a.m.* for a nice panic on the 3-minute moving averages inverse pup to *55.19*, where I *pare 500 shares, out +0.20*, with a tight stop at 55.45, just above the pivot. MSFT coils and continues to slip lower with the 3-minute moving averages inverse pup. MSFT panics to overshoot 55 as I *cover the last 500 shares at 55.98, out +0.41*. MSFT's next pivot support is at 54.90.

The noodles take a pop near the mood shift to the 1038 pivot, where I *short 1000 shares of MSFT at 55.10 at 10:31 a.m.* on the perfect shooting star peak and noodles suicide doji, for a nice leandown and 1-minute stochastics full oscillation. I *cover MSFT at 54.90 at the pivot support overshoots, out +0.20*. I take MSFT short on the 3-minute mini inverse pup slip at 11:04 a.m. as the 3-minute noodles make a mini inverse pup. The noodles give a nice dual 1- and 3-minute mini inverse pup to the pivot overshoots to clip out MSFT shorts. I *buy 3000 shares of AMAT long at 15.15 at 11:25 a.m.* on the consolidation break attempt on the 3-minute mini pup stochastics at 11:25 a.m. The noodles take a nice pop to the 13-minute 15-period moving average at 1034 and retrace. AMAT overshoots the 1-minute 200-period moving average resistance at 15.30. I *sell 1500 shares at 15.25 and sell the rest at 15.28, out +0.10 and +0.13*.

The noodles make a nice pop to the 3-minute 200-period moving average resistance and the 60-minute 15-period resistance. I *buy 1000 shares of MSFT at 55.40 at 1:02 p.m.* for the pivot breakout. The noodles peak at 1048 and retrace, but MSFT is still fading above 55.30. The noodles attempt a coil off 1043 and stall. I take a *small stop on MSFT at 55.30, out −0.10*.

The 3-minute mini inverse pup triggers for a slip to MSFT's 15-period moving average, which was 55.15. MSFT attempts many times to break the pivot but eventually peaks. I *take 1000 shares of MSFT short at 55.20 at 2:06 p.m.* on the 3-minute noodles mini inverse pup slips (see Figure 11-4). The 13-minute noodles make a nice shooting star peak, MSFT makes a nice leandown through the 15-period moving averages, and the noodles overshoot to the pivot support. I take the clips and go long on MSFT with the noodles spike. The 13-minute noodles give a nice heads up on the slip, and the 3-minute noodles mini inverse pup slip on the 1-minute stochastics slip to pivot on MSFT at 2:12 p.m. Possible 60-minute noodles moving averages inverse pup if we break 1032.50 for a bigger dump. The noodles make a nice 1032 overshoot, and I use the MSFT low-band leandowns to *pare out 700 shares at 54.90 and lock the rest at the 54.70 overshoots, out +0.30 and +0.50*, wheee. The noodles eventually get a slow bleed down to the 1025 overshoots as MSFT leans down to the sticky 5s low-range coil supports. MSFT is too low to short and too weak to go long, so I call it a day. The noodles eventually bounce off the 1020 level and crank into the close up to 1030. Wow.

Stats

Shorted 1000 MSFT at 55.39, Covered at 55.19, out +0.20 × 500 = +100

Covered at 54.98, out +0.41 × 500 = +205

Shorted 1000 at MSFT 55.10, Covered at 54.90, out +0.20 × 1000 = +200

Bought 3000 AMAT at 15.15, Sold 1500 at 15.25, out +0.10 × 1500 = +150

Sold 1500 at 15.28, out +0.13 × 1500 = +195

Bought 1000 MSFT at 55.40, Stopped at 55.30, out –0.10 × 1000 = –100

Shorted 1000 at MSFT 55.20, Covered 700 at 54.90, out +0.30 × 700 = +210

Covered 300 at 54.70, out +0.50 × 300 = +150

Total Gross Profit/Loss = +1110

PART TWO

SYSTEMATIC METHODS

CHAPTER 12

The Need for Method

Traditional market nostrums compounded by market industry self-interest lead the typical investor to disregard time, to discount the importance of investor psychology, and to ignore the fundamental nature and genuine profit potential of the financial markets. Markets are complex psychological phenomena that imperil traders and investors who approach markets without a deep understanding of their own psychology and its pitfalls as well as an understanding of the psychological nature of the financial markets themselves. The only true protection in the markets is "method" rooted in the actual behavior of the markets, not in opinion, expectation, or prediction. Following an overview of the fundamental principles of investment and trading, basic and advanced methods will be explored, that together with hints and helps on practical application will enable traders and investors to take on the necessary personal responsibility for their own investment behavior and its consequences, as well as providing a basis for deeper understanding of the behavior of financial markets.

THE RISK OF RUIN

In August 1999, The National Association of Securities Administrators Association (NASAA) released the results of a carefully documented study of the practice of *daytrading*. In analyzing a representative sample of 27 accounts and 4093 trades in those accounts, the study showed that "seventy percent of the accounts lost money and were traded in a matter that realized a 100% Risk of Ruin (loss of all funds)." The authors concluded: "It is absolutely clear that the average public investor should refrain from short-term trading."[1]

The conclusion raises interesting questions: Are there "non-average" public investors who should *not* refrain from short-term trading? If so, what might the characteristics of such public investors be? Should the average public investor engage in *long-term* trading? If so, what might the characteristics of such trading be?

Before considering these questions, let's look at this report in its historical context.

The report followed by a few days the tragic killing of nine and injuring of thirteen people at two daytrading firms by daytrader Mark Barton. On the day of Barton's rampage (July 29, 1999), prompted by his stupendous losses in daytrading, the Nasdaq100 futures closed at 2658. Eight months earlier (November 24, 1998), the parabolic phase of the "New Economy" bull market had begun in earnest (from 2037) with AOL's purchase of Netscape for 4.2 billion dollars.[2] Eight months later (March 24, 2000), this classic mania reached its peak, more than doubling to 5125. By October 2002, the Naz100 had collapsed, reaching a low of 949, a staggering loss of nearly 83 percent, by far the largest loss of market capitaliza-

---

[1]Report of the Day Trading Project Group: Findings and Recommendations. NASAA, August 9, 1999.

[2]Some might set the "symbolic" start date for the parabolic rise with the FDA's approval of Viagra a few months earlier in March, 1998. This is not as facetious as it may first appear. As will be discussed further on, large-scale collective phenomena (e.g., birth control pill for women, impotence treatment for men) form the psychological background that is among the primary sources of behavior that will find expression in the financial markets.

tion in history, and in percentage terms, exceeded only by the historic bear market in the Dow-Jones Industrial Average from 1929–1932. Not only did the entire "bubble" dissolve, the Nasdaq100 worked its way to price levels not seen since 1995.

By the end of 2002, anecdotal reports indicated that a large percentage of day traders had "faded away." No longer heard were the constant media references to day traders *causing* market volatility. Many trading rooms on the Internet had disappeared. Most of those remaining found their population of traders a stalwart stock, but drastically reduced in number from the bubble days.

What became of the "long-term" investor in the technology rich Nasdaq100 stocks, the home of the "New Economy" companies that were to lead the way beyond the restraints of the "old economy" with its old-fashioned ideas of business cycles, recessions, and growth limits? What happened to the idea that the Naz100 was going to lead the Dow to 36,000, and carry an exploding population of market investors into the land of unending "wealth"?

How did the "average public investor" referred to in the NASAA report—the so-called "buy-and-hold" investor—do?

Well, certainly, if someone had bought Nasdaq100 stocks in March 2000, they too likely would have experienced the "risk of ruin" the NAASP report says is the likely outcome for most day traders. And if one had bought just before the huge acceleration began, not only had 100 percent of the gains evaporated, but nearly two-thirds of the original capital value had disappeared as well. Buy-and-hold investors at the very least lost 7 years and suffered a degree of emotional, if not financial loss, not seen since the depression years of the 1930s. Who is to say the disastrous bear market of the new millennium will not continue for another 7 years, and drag even the most stalwart believer in "the long-term buy-and-hold" approach ever nearer to that "risk of ruin."

What is clear is that the buy-and-hold philosophy purveyed by Wall Street is *not* a safe harbor and if anything is an idea not only undermining investor awareness of risk, but more importantly, an idea that fails utterly to engender the awareness of the absolute necessity for the investor to be responsible for his or her own investment decisions.

"Investing for the long term" teaches the investor simply to ignore losses of value—even losses of value approaching the risk of ruin. Should not a loss in value of more than 80 percent be a risk to be avoided? The investor has been led to *believe* that investing for the long term is the only sure and certain road to growth in the financial markets. Like any other belief, one wonders whether there are *any* circumstances that would lead Wall Street to abandon this proffered faith.[3] But belief and faith are never *willingly* tested for their veracity. Only when reality overwhelms the capacity to ignore disparity is belief broken and the former believer able to look at reality with fresh eyes. If the great bear market of 2000 teaches any lessons, perhaps chief among them is that the individual investor (and trader) must become responsible for their own money at risk. The *good* side of not being able to believe corporate leaders, of seeing the hypocrisy of market analysts, of the revelations of collusion of esteemed brokerages, admired companies, and respected investment banks in grand schemes to defraud investors—the *good* side of this would be not how heavy-handed government can make the markets "safe" for investors, but for *every* investor to realize that trying to make money grow will always and forever be a perilous and risky activity and that the primary responsibility for the fate of any investment must always be in the hands of the investor. This is an unpopular view, perhaps even a dreamy idealism. Investors have no time, no knowledge, no *way* to be responsible. And so responsibility is handed over almost without thought to others. Probably in no other area of life would the "average public investor" be so thoughtless, trusting, gullible, unknowing, and irresponsible.

The reasons why most investors lose money are the same reasons why most day traders lose money: investing *and* trading too often is based on *emotional* factors of fear and greed or stubborn refusal to see what is before their eyes; investors *and* traders refuse to educate themselves in the history and the realities of the

---

[3]The answer to this question is no. There exist no circumstances that will alter Wall Street's recommendation in this regard. We shall see why in the next section.

markets; investors *and* traders do not have a clear and focused plan; investors *and* traders are quick to place blame on others for adversity (market makers, corporate evil doers, brokers, short sellers, the government, etc.).

Investors *and* traders alike refuse to heed three fundamental rules[4] relating to money at risk: (1) specifying the basis of and price and time for *entry* into an investment or trade; (2) specifying the basis for and *target* price and time for the anticipated gain on the investment or trade; and, perhaps most importantly, (3) specifying the basis for and the price and time of an exit point (that is, a "stop") at which the trade or investment is terminated to *avoid* substantial loss. No trade or investment, whether one is a rank amateur or a seasoned professional, should be undertaken without attending to each of these three crucial conditions. Even if the investor hands over total responsibility to someone else (the broker, the financial consultant, the fund manager, etc.), one should endeavor to find out each of these things. There can be no excuse for not doing so. What you will generally find is that aside from making it *easy* to put money in the market, it is difficult to find genuine answers to the above essential conditions. There simply is no investor, from the proverbial grandmother in tennis shoes to the harried physician who has no time at all, who cannot take time to find out at least this much about what is being done with one's money. If those who manage the money cannot answer these three questions, *beware!*

While the NASAA report seems to make bold distinctions between the "average public investor" and the "daytrader," such distinctions are misleading. The *only* difference between investing and daytrading is the relation of one's activities to *time*. The *nature* of what one is doing is exactly the same: *exposing money to the potential multiplying effects of capital markets*. Under all conditions,

---

[4]This is the fist of many examples we shall see of what I call the Rule of Three. Many market methods, strategies, and decisions will be enhanced if formulated in three parts. For example, there are three relationships one can have with any financial market: to be long, to be short, to be out. Specifying the conditions for each aspect will render any investment decision more fruitful.

such exposure entails *risk*.[5] There is *nothing*—absolutely nothing—that guarantees a so-called "long term" investment entailing *less* risk than a "short term" or "day trade" investment. In fact, the degree of risk may actually increase with time and exposure.

More than 30 years ago, J. M. Hurst published the results of his research on this issue in a book called, *The Profit Magic of Stock Transaction Timing*. He showed that, "Assuming accuracy of transaction timing, you will always make more money by short term trades than by long ones." Of course that is one huge assumption! Much of the material in the chapters that follow will be oriented toward making that assumption a reality. As Hurst noted, because of the degree of gains that are potentially possible, "improvement in transaction timing is worth all the effort we can put into it."

Some years ago, Ned Davis, Alan Newman, Yale Hirsch and others, reported studies showing the bi-cyclic nature of equity market performance. They showed in different ways, that there were essentially two periods in the general equity markets: a "best of times" and a "worst of times." Generally, it was found that market performance between November 1 and April 30 (the "best of times") far exceeded the performance of the market between May 1 and October 31 (the "worst of times"). Using this simple strategy, and most especially *compounding* the gains over time, produced far higher returns than *any* version of a buy-and-hold strategy.[6] Some years later, Sy Harding took this a step further showing that being 100 percent long during the "best of times" period and

---

[5]Risk, of course, is the degree of exposure to reverse capital-multiplying effects that diminish the degree of investment value to various degrees of loss and potentially the "risk of ruin" of 100 percent capital loss. An added loss, most often overlooked by "buy and hold" advocates, is the loss of opportunity in markets that are multiplying in a positive direction while the buy-and-hold investment is stagnant, or in a loss, or loss-of-gain position. "Gains not taken" must also be counted as "losses" should such gains be subject to reverse capital multiplying effects.

[6]For example, between 1950 and 1997, $100,000 invested in this manner would have grown to $2,761,113, while the same amount under the buy-and-hold strategy would have grown only to $114,840!

100 percent short during the "worst of times" produced comparative gains that were truly astonishing.

What these studies show is that markets go up *and* down and that even the simplest possible procedure for taking advantage of this oscillatory nature of markets—the *simplest* case of improving transaction timing—increases the capital multiplying effects in contrast to any buy-and-hold strategy. This idea is important to both the investor and the trader. Important to the investor because it suggests a definite method for decreasing the risk of exposure to reverse capital multiplying effects of seasonally destructive markets. Important to the trader because if taking advantage of such oscillations on an *annual* basis produces such spectacular results, how much better might the results be if taken advantage of on a *daily* basis.

Clearly, the root question for either the investor or trader comes down to this: are there methods and strategies that allow one to take advantage of the fundamental fact of markets: prices go up and prices go down. To face this fundamental fact with the idea that "markets will only go up over time" becomes absurd and one must begin to wonder what the motivation behind such an idea really is. The results cited above clearly give the lie to such an idea and only show that this idea has cost the average investor enormous amounts of money, enormous lost opportunity, enormous amounts of wasted time, and enormous pain.

Along with the general admonition to "invest for the long term," is the companion idea that "you cannot time the markets." The results above belie this twin mantra of Wall Street and raise the general issue of whether market timing is not only *possible,* but *essential* to the financial well-being of the investor and trader alike. This of course raises the question of *method* as noted above. Are there methods that enable the investor and trader to take advantage of the oscillatory nature of the markets? Are there strategies that enable the investor and trader to know when to apply the methods and when not to? Are there *combinations* of methods that can increase the returns of money at risk? The simple example above implies that the answer to these questions is *yes.* And if the answer is yes, then Hurst is correct: finding such methods "is worth all the effort we can put into it."

The chapters that follow will introduce the trader to a representative set of methods and strategies that are built on an absolute and fundamental trading rule: On every trade an *entry, a target, a stop.* This principle is applicable to *any* market, to *any* time frame, and for anyone who puts money at risk in the markets. These methods are equally applicable to the short-term *scalping trader,* who enters and exits a trade within minutes; a short-term *trend trader,* who enters and exists a trade during a single trading session; a *swing trader,* who enters and exists a trade over a series of sessions; and, to the *long-term trader,* who holds a position for days, weeks, or months, or longer. All these traders are in fact *investors* doing exactly the same thing: placing capital at risk—only the time frame distinguishes them. It follows that *all investors, for their financial well-being, must be traders.*

The methods and strategies illustrated here will build on and enhance those described in the author's *A Different Style of Trading.*[7] At undergroundtrader.com, we are committed to the idea that constant and consistent education is the key to success and what is offered here reflects that spirit and reveals the "secrets" used every day in confronting the real-time *reality* of the financial markets. The trading or investing neophyte, as well as the seasoned pro, hopefully will find these methods and strategies a useful guide in the difficult task of making money grow.

DESIRE TO MAKE MONEY GROW

Why do we invest or trade? The answer to this question seems simple enough: *to make money.*

All of us realize at some point that, no matter what the size of our labor-generated income, it is difficult if not impossible for labor alone to produce enough money to allow us to fulfill all our

---

[7]In Jay Yu's *The Undergroundtrader.com Guide to Electronic Trading.* New York: McGraw-Hill, 2000.

desires, dreams, and aspirations. At some point, we all have the desire to *use* money to *make* money. Regardless of the amount that we may have available, while we are working at our job or profession, we want our money working too so that it will grow. At some point, most of us will retire, and we will want to have a "nest egg" to help provide for our needs. We want our money to grow so that our kids can go to college, or so that we can buy a home, or so that we will be able to provide a source of support for our families or a legacy for our offspring, or simply so that we can feel more at ease in the world. There are many reasons for wanting our money to go to work for us, to grow for us, to become *much* more than what we have now.

MULTIPLICATION AND THE POWER OF COMPOUNDING

To *grow* our money, we need to *multiply* it. The reason that our labor-generated income is not adequate to this task is that we quickly run into *limits* on the multiplying power of our labor. We cannot work much more than 8 or 10 hours a day, and we often do not have any control over the wage or salary that we receive. Those who have the seeming luxury of charging for their labor, whether they are grass-cutters or lawyers, soon reach limits on the amount they can charge or the amount of work they can do. In a family, the number of incomes is generally limited to one or two. Some people find ways to begin a business, and this always has the promise of multiplying money, but unless the multiplying process increases, money-growth limits impose themselves quickly.

Our earliest experience with attempts to multiply money usually involves putting money into some form of *savings* account. What we are doing is *lending* a bank our cash money. In return, we are accepting a defined arrangement under which the amount of our loan will multiply at some rate, for example, 5 percent per year. If we loan the bank $1000, then at the end of the year our $1000 will have grown to $1050. As everyone is aware, when the multiplying factor is *small* (such as 0.05) and the time period is *large* (such as a year), the amount by which our money grows is painfully small. In the case of savings accounts, this is offset in part by the *relative* security of our money and the *relative* assurance that the incremental growth will in fact be paid to our account and that the account in its entirety will be available for withdrawal in cash form.

Now take a look at what the bank does with the money that we lend it. We all have the impression that somehow banks are "wealthy." And most people assume that this wealth is generated primarily by the *higher* rates of interest that the bank charges its loan customers relative to those that it pays to the customers it borrows from. If the bank takes your $1000 loan and lends this $1000 to a customer at 10 percent interest, then the bank is making 5 percent interest on the difference between what it pays you and what it receives from its loan. That would mean that you and the bank are earning the same amount. True, the bank can multiply its earnings by the number of loans it makes, and as the bank grows, it can add branches and customers, and in this way keep multiplying its money. Is that why the bank appears wealthier?

It's only part of the reason. Since the creation of the Federal Reserve Bank in 1913, banks have been able to use a device called *fractional reserve banking.* Here is how it works. The bank takes your loan of $1000 and *multiplies* it by a factor of 10. This creates a "credit account" of $10,000. From this credit account, $1000 is transferred to a "reserve account" to meet so-called reserve requirements, equal in effect to the original loan deposit. The balance of $9000 is then available for new loans to customers. What this means is that while you have earned 5 percent on one $1000 loan to the bank, the bank will earn 10 percent on the $9000 sum "created" by your $1000. That amount will be roughly 18 times what you earn on your $1000. That is a wealth-generating multiplication of interest.

If you leave your money in the bank to compound annually, it will take about 15 years for your $1000 to double (it will actually grow to $2078.93). During the same period, the bank's balance on your loan will grow to $263,341.94! This illustrates two absolutely crucial factors relating to the growth of money: the power of *multiplying* and the power of *compounding*. The more that money can be multiplied *and* compounded, the more quickly and powerfully it will grow. Clearly, the bank is growing your money *for itself* much faster and to a larger degree than it is growing your money *for you*.

However, even the bank's rate of growth is limited. For example, customers pay back only a fraction of the value of their loans each month. The compounding effect on a bank's growth is thus limited by the amount of inflowing money and the period between inflows (usually monthly).

Obviously, the bank's multiplying of the money we lend it provides miraculous growth indeed. However, consider the growth of a single penny if it is doubled every day for a month. How much growth would occur in that time? Astonishingly, a penny multiplied in this way would become $10,737,418.24 in just 31 days. Now that looks like serious money! Two factors combine to produce such an astronomical sum: the multiplying factor (in this case, 2) and the rate of compounding (in this case, compounding the gain on a daily basis). Of course, while this is simple in idea, there is probably no mechanism available that can double one's money every day for a month. Or is there?

Clearly, the comparison is instructive. If our money is to grow *quickly*, we must *increase* the multiplier, *decrease* the period in which the growth compounds, or *both*.

The next most common way in which people experience the growth of money is generally in relation to the purchase of a home. In this case, we put up some cash in the form of a down payment, for example, $20,000. The bank then lends us $180,000, so we can buy a house that costs $200,000. Now let's consider what happens if the house appreciates, let's say 1 percent per month. In the first month, the value of the house would be $200,000 plus the appreciation of $2000. Notice that it is the *total value* of the house that is appreciating, and since it is appreciating each month, the *compounding period* is once a month.

An appreciation of $2000 does not seem like a great deal in relation to $200,000. Remember, however, that we invested only

$20,000 cash in this arrangement. From the point of view of our cash investment, our $20,000 has increased in value by $2000, or 10 percent. This is another form of "multiplication" that is generally called *leverage*. A small percentage (1 percent) multiplier is being applied to a large amount and compounded monthly, or 12 times a year. By the end of 12 months, the compounded appreciation would be $25,365.00, already more than our entire investment! By the end of the second year, the $20,000 has appreciated to a value of $53,947, more than doubling the investment in 2 years. Now this begins to look like wealth creation, and it is. Compounding a large amount that is leveraged with a small amount has the capacity to multiply the original investment many times in a relatively short period of time.

So here it looks as if we are one up on the bank. After all, it had to put out $180,000—9 times the down payment. Isn't that a bad deal for the bank? Well, look a little more closely. How much of a deposit does the bank need on the *savings* side to "create" this $180,000? Well, approximately $180,000 divided by 9. Therefore, while you make money on the leveraged growth of the value of the house, the bank is going to be making, say, 7 percent interest on the mortgage you owe it—7 percent of 180,000. So in the first month, the interest you pay to the bank is $1050. However, the bank's *true* investment in this arrangement is only $20,000, so in the first month, the bank has earned 5.25 percent on its $20,000! The bank also has leverage in this arrangement. But the bank's gains are *not* dependent on the value of the house increasing, whereas your gains are *solely* dependent on the value of the house increasing. And it must be obvious that unless the house appreciates at a *greater* rate than the interest rate on the mortgage, it will be difficult for the homeowner to have *any* substantial gain on the investment, whereas the bank's gains multiply and compound each month regardless of the value of the house.

Suppose the house does not appreciate, the rate of appreciation is very small, or the house even falls in value. Note that under *all* these conditions, the bank continues to make its leveraged gain, whereas your gain may be very small or even become a loss.

Compared to the risk you assume, the bank has entered into a relatively riskless investment. This is another way in which institutions tend to multiply their investments. When you buy a stock from a stockbroker, you will always have to pay a commission when you open and when you close the trade. You may have a gain or you may have a loss, but the brokerage has *only* gains from your activity and only gains multiplied by all your trades and all the trades of all the clients. The institution earns a commission regardless of the risk level of the investment you are trading. This is the principle of "constant positive multiplication" that is always available to institutions but is never available to the average investor or trader. Constant positive multiplication is a wealth-generating device. In this regard, the investor or trader is always in a position of "constant negative multiplication," a wealth-diminishing device.

Somewhere between an anemic multiplier of 1 percent per annum and doubling daily for a month, there are innumerable opportunities to make money grow. A better way to say this is that there are innumerable ways to expose one's financial resources to the *possibility* of growth as well as the *risk of ruin*.

Chief among these is to *invest* or *trade* in the capital markets, that is, to put money at risk in stocks, bonds, mutual funds, currencies, commodities, options—somewhere in the extraordinary universe of vehicles designed to expose one's money to the hoped-for capital-multiplying effects of the financial markets. There is undoubtedly no more efficient mechanism for the growth of money than the capital markets. The problem is that this efficiency works both ways: in growing and in destroying. Except for gambling and other such activities, there is no more efficient mechanism for the destruction of money than the capital markets. From boom to bust, from bubble to burst, from inflation to deflation, the powerful multiplying effect of the capital mechanism works both to grow *and* to destroy.

The "public" investor is encouraged to invest for "the long term." The rationale for this near-mythic enterprise is that over time, the market always moves higher. In addition, studies show that the long-term investor in the stock markets can anticipate an "average" *compounded* growth rate of 7 to 10 percent per year—sometimes more, sometimes less. We have seen the power of compounding and its multiplying effects in creating wealth. Since the markets always go higher eventually, the rationale includes not only investing at some point for the long term, but continuing to invest for the long term on a regular basis. This is undoubtedly what the majority of public investors do. The IRA, Keogh, 401(k), and all other retirement and tax-advantaged programs are designed for just this purpose, to keep money flowing into the market "for the long term." A simple example would be for someone to invest $10,000 in the market and then continue to invest $2000 or so every year. If we assume an average growth rate of 10 percent per year, after 14 years, the nominal account balance should be approximately $92,925 on a total amount invested of $48,000, or almost double one's investment.

This slow, steady growth is what is meant by "the long term." However, every investor or trader who exposes money to the risk of the financial markets soon realizes that 6 to 10 percent per year is not very much. One sees that particular stocks often increase in value 5, 10, 20 percent or more in a day's time, and that certain stocks increase 1000, 5000, even 10,000 percent or more in a generation's time. It is natural to desire such gains. They are *possible*. This possibility has produced a huge market for financial newsletters, services, seminars, and books encouraging the public investor and trader to join in and receive the "fantastic" profits that are possible in the markets. Everyone has been exposed to the lure of these offerings. However, like the 80 percent or more of managed funds that *fail* to better the market averages, 80 percent or more of the newsletters and such tend to *fail* to deliver the promised gains when tracked objectively.

With such a remarkable degree of failure—a degree of failure that approximates the degree of failure among day traders—how can such a situation persist? To understand this, simply recall the rule of constant positive multiplication. Mutual funds, for example, whether load or no-load, charge handsome fees on an annual basis. These fees are a percentage multiple of the funds' assets and are subtracted from the funds' returns. This is why the average fund underperforms the market by 2 percent or more even when the fund's investments match the market's performance—in itself an uncommon occurrence. That 2 percent represents an *accumulative compounding loss* to the fund's investors and an accumulative compounding positive-only return to the fund's managers. The larger the amount of money that flows into the fund, the larger these gains on the manager's side will be, *regardless* of the fund's actual performance. Again, the institution seems to have found ways to have the public fund riskless constant positive multiplying mechanisms, while the investor assumes the entire risk of capital exposed to the financial markets.

To get a clear picture of this, consider the following. At a 10 percent return over 50 years, an investment in the stock market may be expected to grow from $10,000 to $1,170,000. However, if the public investor puts money in an average mutual fund, the 2 percent fee reduces the return to only $470,000. Therefore, it is costing the average investor $700,000 to be in a "managed" mutual fund as compared to what he could receive with average unmanaged market performance. Add to this insult the fact that most funds, as noted previously, *underperform* the market and the cost is substantially greater.

It is clear that it is the financial industry itself that profits the most from encouraging investors to invest and to continually add to their investments for "the long term." And the industry makes these gains through the vehicle of compounding of constant positive multiplication without regard to market performance. And, most chillingly, since the public investor provides *all* the capital, the industry can profit in this way totally *without* risk. The guaranteed profits from the public's investing for the long term belong to the institutions. The public is guaranteed nothing of the kind.

This may not be the "risk of ruin" that the NASAA report had in mind when it encouraged public investors to stay away from short-term trading, but it perhaps serves as a warning to the public investor of what the challenge of trying to make money grow truly is. The mechanisms for certain money growth are not available to the public investor; they are available only to the institutions. And these very institutions are the ones that encourage the public investor to buy and to keep buying, not to worry about the "ups and downs" of the market, not to attempt any timing of the markets, but only to "keep your money working." For the most part, under these conditions, it is clear that your money is not working for you so much as it is working for the institutions.

THE CHIMERA OF LONG-TERM INVESTING

Moreover, the oft-quoted 10 percent historical average gain to be expected from the equity markets is a chimera. While this may be true for the market average on a statistical basis, it is clearly and manifestly *not* the case for any real-world investor—or fund manager, for that matter. The average returns are extraordinarily affected by the initial starting point of the investment, whether dividends or gains are reinvested, and when the investments are liquidated. Studies show that about 80 percent of the historical gains in equity performance are the result of a constant positive multiplier (such as a quarterly stock dividend), rather than the presumed and inevitable "the market will always move higher over time."

So is the trader any better off? Suppose an active trader makes 30 trades a day and pays a discount commission of $15 for each complete trade. This is a guaranteed income to the brokerage of $450 per day and more than $100,000 a year *regardless* of the success or failure of the trader—unless the trader runs out of money. Whether the individual is a trader or an investor, the factor of constant positive multiplication, and its compounding, will work *only* for the benefit of the institutions. Too often, this is the reality that the individual public investor or trader is unaware of when he or she puts money at risk in the capital markets—that is, that he or she is funding huge profits for the financial industry. Of course, the financial industry will do everything possible to continue this charade.[8]

---

[8]It will pay the public investor to carefully study the advertising of financial institutions encouraging public participation in the markets. Nowhere is the art of manipulation of belief as successful as in these advertisements, which harness the power of suggestion to the lack of awareness on the part of the investing public.

There is a fatal flaw in almost all the studies of market returns upon which the recommendations to "invest for the long term" are based. To understand this flaw, one must first see the overall results of investing for "the long term" and what the components of long-term "growth" actually are. From 1802 to the present time, an investment of $100 would have grown to $700 million, assuming that all dividends were reinvested. What's not to like about this? However, if you subtract the effects of monetary inflation, the gain drops to $37 million. Still, this isn't a bad deal. If you subtract dividends, however, that original $100 invested 200 years ago is now worth only $2099. This is what reflects total "growth." That's not such a good deal. Moreover, in 1982, the value of this investment was only $400. That is, more than 80 percent of the current value came in the last 20 years, during the longest bull market in history. Clearly, the compounded return on equity investment comes largely not from capital appreciation, but from the compounding of dividends and from the increases due to inflation.

This fatal flaw results from the overwhelming tendency to *ignore* the profit potential of the declining phases of stock market cycles. Downward cycles and long-term bear markets are seen as "interrupting" the sought-for bull trends. Clearly, the ravages of periodic bear markets are destructive to investment value. But why insist on holding investments during these destructive phases? Even more to the point, why ignore the *profit* potential of these declines in value? Is the "bullish bias" simply so content with a long-term average return of 6 to 7 percent (most of which is due to inflation and dividends) that it refuses to deal with the fact that bear trends are as strong and as recognizable as bull trends—if not more so? What is going on here to make an inevitable *natural* part of price fluctuation be simply *ignored,* as if it were not something to learn from, to make use of, to act on, and to gain from? If the aim is to make money grow, why not include *both* aspects of the market's *natural* behavior in that effort?

The simple fact is that if anything other than the "permabull" perspective were to gain any wide acceptance, it would be a financial disaster for the financial industry and the whole elaborate structure that has been carefully built to inveigle the public's money into the system. Money under management would decrease drastically, as would the fees collected. But if the Great Bear of 2000 is not sufficient to teach the investing public that some other way must be possible, then no amount of broker, or banker, or company, or analyst scandal is going to do so either. The ingrained belief in the "rightness" of bull markets and the "wrongness" of bear markets simply has no empirical basis for falsification. Merrill Lynch wants you to be "bullish on America." And that means to buy.

Anything else is, by implication "bearish on America," and who wants to be in that camp? Never mind that even if one is a permabull on America, stock prices will still decline, and often decline viciously, as has been the case since March 2000. Being bullish on America does *not* repeal the natural law of growth and decay of financial markets. But the belief has generations of believers, and new recruits are added daily. Wall Street will never let go of this mantra, this gold mine, this huge income stream that is so totally unrelated to performance and accountability.

Is something else possible?

I want to look at the task in general terms before we turn to illustrating the methods and strategies that will be the focus of these chapters. Consider Figure 12-1. Here we have a plot of value as a function of time. The value of what? And, over what time periods? At this point, it could be almost anything: my weight over the last 18 months, the number of solar storms in the last 18 years, the number of violent crimes in the nation's capital in the last 18 days, the price of Microsoft in the last 18 minutes, the children born in the world in the last 18 seconds. Unless it's labeled, there is, of course, no basis for knowing from the chart itself what is plotted here.

BASIC PRINCIPLES OF MARKET BEHAVIOR

Yet, without knowing anything at all about *what* is plotted, we can gather a great deal of information about the behavior of whatever it is. Let's run through some observations based on this nameless

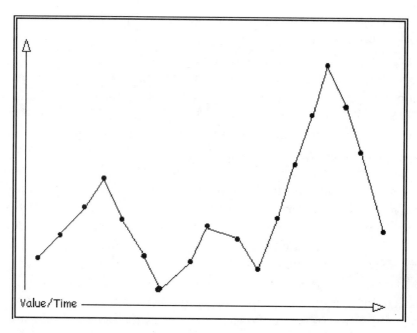

Figure 12-1 A plot of changing value over periods of time.

chart and develop a set of provisional *principles* to use as a framework for the task.

The first thing to observe is that values *change* over time—
whatever the time frame might be. I'll call this the *principle of
change*. Prices are in continuous flux from one moment to the next,
from one day to the next, from any one period to the next. The
second thing to observe is that values both *increase* and *decrease*. I'll
call this the *principle of alternation*. In the unlabeled chart, there is
absolutely no way to place a value judgment on what is seen. If this
is a chart of my weight, I may be extremely pleased at data point 7
and greatly displeased at data point 15. But if this is a chart of
MSFT, and I am *long* MSFT, I'll be pretty happy at data point 15
and not so happy at data point 18.

What is clear is that this rising and falling, this increase and
decrease, this alternation is a *natural* characteristic of continually
changing values. Alternation *belongs*. Certainly, to fully understand
the change in values, knowledge of what factors are involved in

decreasing values is as important as knowledge of the factors involved in increasing values. *There is no basis for preferring one over the other or for excluding one and embracing the other.* If this is a chart of my weight, clearly I ought to learn something about what I am doing between data points 4 and 7 and between data points 15 and 18 that is *different* from what I am doing between data points 11 and 15. I can learn from both and profit from both. For the same reasons, I ought to learn something about both why MSFT increases in value and why it decreases in value. By what perverse logic should I pay attention only to the increases in value and disregard the decreases in value? To restrict one's attention (and, by implication, one's *actions*) to only one aspect of changing value would seem to be a sure way to cripple one's understanding and right action altogether.

Of course, as soon as any kind of label is put on what is charted, the question of value judgments comes into play. If we are long MSFT, the price increases are "good" and the price decreases are "bad." "It was a good day on Wall Street," the nightly news tells us, but *only* when the market goes up. "It was a bad day on Wall Street," it tells us, but *only* when the market is down. Such value judgments invariably become core aspects of belief systems, and belief systems *invariably* lead one away from genuine understanding of what is happening in the chart. Objectively, there is absolutely no difference between money growing as a function of rising prices and money growing as a function of falling prices. Both are merely ways of taking advantage—*if one can*—of the changes in price behavior.

A third feature of this unlabeled chart is that the changes in value seem to be orderly. The values do not appear to be random. This orderliness is created by the consistency and persistence of values *moving in the same direction.* At each data point, the probability on a random basis of the next data point's being in the same direction (e.g., an increase) is *always 50 percent,* so that at each successive data point it is a "coin flip" as to whether the value will increase or decrease. Yet clearly, as the number of data points moving in a consistent direction increases, the probability of such persistence occurring *by chance* diminishes rapidly. The first four data points exhibit this consistency and persistence. Does this in any way guarantee that the fifth data point will exhibit the same character? Not at all. But we do know what to look for. I'll refer to this condition as the *principle of order.*

When values change in the same direction and persist for two or more data points, it becomes possible to speak of this orderly relation as a *trend.* The first four data points in Figure 12-1 define such a trend and clearly give us a basis for projecting that trend into the future. We *know* that a prediction of the next data point still has a 50 percent probability of being wrong.[9] Would we bet the farm on that next data point's being up? Of course not. Not only do *we* not know whether the next data point will be up or down, but *no one else does either.* This also means that we can never know what the *duration* of a trend might be, that is, how long a trend will last. After all, if anyone could predict this with any regularity, the problem of investment or trading would be solved immediately—not to mention the fact that whoever had such an ability would soon control all the markets. The crux of the matter is this: *Consistent prediction of trend duration or trend alternation is impossible.* I shall call this fact the *principle of chaos.* This image is not meant to imply "disorder," for as we can see even in this simplest of charts, there exist specifiable patterns of order (*trend* being just one such pattern) even within structures in which consistent prediction of trend duration and trend alternation is impossible.

In this simple chart, it is relatively easy to see what defines the "end" of a trend. Consider the relationship between data points 3, 4, and 5. Point 3 is a "high" point, point 4 is a "higher" point, and point 5 is a "lower" point. This specific relationship between *three* successive periods defines the end of the initial trend. I will call this the *principle of structure.* An uptrend will continue and persist until it "structures." Looking at data points 6, 7, and 8, the relation is low, lower, higher low. This relationship would characterize the "structuring" end of a downtrend. Note that these "end-of-trend"

[9]Further on I will elaborate on the important distinction between *projection* and *prediction.*

structures are an example of the Rule of Three, that is, the structuring point is defined by a *specific* relationship between *three* successive periods.

Another significant feature of this simple chart is that the alternation of trends forms "higher-order" structures. This is another example of the Rule of Three: Such a higher order structure has a *beginning*, an *extreme*, and an *end*, with each of these points being defined by simple structures. This cycle produced by alternation of structures can be referred to as a *wave*. We can think of a complete "cycle" of an up and down alternating trend as forming a wave. Figure 12-2 illustrates the three waves of Figure 12-1 defined in this manner. The arrows indicate the direction of the trend as defined by the structuring points. Note that the relationship between wave 2 and wave 3 produces a "rising trend." This will occur whenever the end structure of each succeeding wave is higher than the preceding end structure. From this observation we denote the *principle of wave dynamics*. As we shall see, this principle will lead into questions concerning the relationships between waves. In addition, it is clear that within larger trends (such as the rising trend encompassing wave 2 and wave 3), there will be trends in the *same* direction and trends in the *opposite* or *alternate* direction. We can refer to the latter trends as *countertrends*. This alternation between trends will be referred to as the *principle of oscillation*.

Certainly a question that arises when we look at even the nameless chart is, "What causes trends to end and reverse direction?" While the fact of trend reversal is clear, the cause or causes are decidedly not clear—an example of the principle of chaos at work. In relation to the financial markets, the search for causes is unending and produces a huge amount of literature every year, as well as a seemingly compulsive need to "explain" why the market did what it did today. The news reports, the commentators, the newspapers will never simply report that the Dow went up 168.97 points today. There is always a need to "explain": "The Dow was sharply higher today as investors were encouraged by the Federal Reserve's decision to lower interest rates by one-quarter percent."

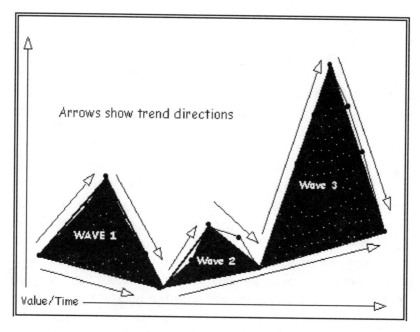

Figure 12-2 Complete trend structures produce waves.

And how do we know that investors were encouraged? Well, because the market went up. And if the market had gone down? "The Dow was sharply lower today as investor worries over the impending war overwhelmed the market in spite of the Federal Reserve's decision to lower rates by one-quarter percent." And how do we know that investors were worried? Because the market went down.

These kinds of "explanations" are not explanations at all and add *nothing* to an understanding of the behavior of the market. But the problem of explanation remains a genuine concern. We shall see that how one approaches this problem has a great deal to do with the use of certain methods and strategies. While the facile explanations always seem certain and assured, the fact is that the degree of *uncertainty* about the cause(s) of market behavior is extremely high. For this reason, I will group all of the efforts to "explain" market behavior under the label of the *principle of uncertainty*.

Figure 12-3 illustrates the observation that the three peaks in value are spaced more or less equal distances apart. Such an observation would lead to the question of whether there might be a "time" effect on the values, such as seasonal factors or some other time-related factor (such as a presidential cycle). Such uncertainties about the causes of market behavior lead to another principle. We have seen earlier that Wall Street's twin mantras of "invest for the long term" and "you can't time the market" essentially lead to *ignoring the market altogether*—except for the "always timely" behavior of putting more money into the market. I hope to show that another perspective is likely to be more productive and profitable, and that this perspective flows from a *principle of curiosity*. Most investors and traders are focused on *price*. Being curious about the ups and downs of the market, about the beginnings and ends of trends, and about the relationship between waves brings the trader and investor face to face with the question of *time*, the least understood and perhaps the most important factor relating to the behavior of the financial markets.

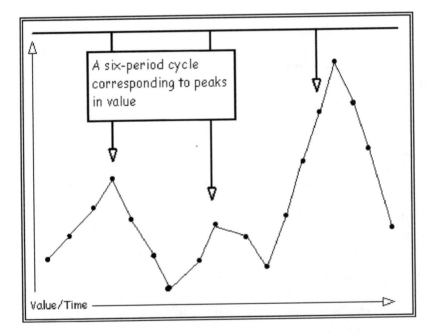

Figure 12-3   Possible time effects relating to peaks of value.

There is much more that can be gleaned from this nameless chart, but the principles gathered thus far are sufficient to frame the task of how to make money grow. Before moving into the background material necessary for the effective use of the methods and strategies to be presented in the following chapters, it will be useful to consider the results of an idealized trading scenario. Recall Hurst's admonition: "Improvement in transaction timing is worth all the effort we can put into it." In order to tell how well one is doing, one needs to know what "perfect trading" would produce if it were possible.

Consider Figure 12-4. Here is a chart of prices over 30 periods. This could be a chart of 30 days, or 30 weeks, or 30 months, or 30 years. Whatever the time frame, the "long-term" investor is one who buys at point 1 and is still holding at point 8. This investor's net gain over the 30 periods is nothing. At various times, the investor would have seen substantial percentage gains; for example, at point 6 the investment would be up more than 28 percent. But since the long term remains indefinite, there is no clear indication as to when such gains should be taken. The investor has not lost anything, but there has seen no "profit" whatever from the price movement over the 30 periods, and that 28 percent gain has now evaporated.

Now let's consider the opposite situation. Let's imagine that we have a method that enables us to buy at points 1, 3, 5, and 7 and to sell our position at points 2, 4, 6, and 8. This clearly is an idealized example of Hurst's "improved transaction timing" that requires *shortening* the interval between trades in order to increase gain potential. The results of Hurst's studies refute the usual admonition against "trading" and the recommendation that investors hold for "the long term" (see Figure 12-5). As applied to the present example, our method enables us to buy at the low and sell at the high of the different price waves. Under these conditions, the value of our account at point 8 would be a gain of more than 54 percent. Moreover, if instead of just buying a constant amount at the buy points, we *compounded* the gains—that is, the gains taken enabled us to buy a larger position (and in this way *multiply* the position)— by point 8 the gain on the position would be more than 60 percent in only four trades.

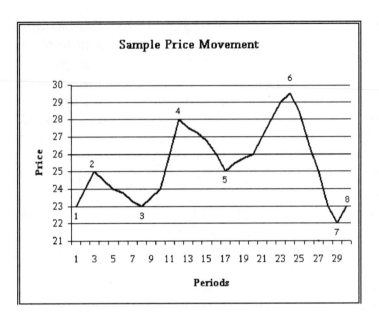

Figure 12-4 Price peaks and valleys as a function of time periods.

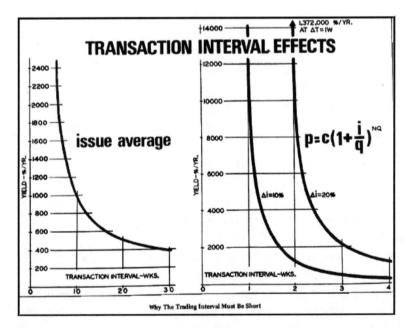

Figure 12-5 The graphic results of Hurst's studies on the effect of transaction interval and potential gains and the result of such gains compounded at different rates.

Consider further that the method not only lets us know when to buy and when to sell, but further enables us to sell *short* at points 2, 4, and 6 and to cover these short positions at points 3, 5, and 7. In this example, we are trying to profit from both the up *and* the down trends. By point 8, the gain under these conditions would be 109 percent, more than doubling the original investment. And if these gains were compounded, the gain would grow to 145 percent.

If this were a single trading day, the gains available through trading both the up and down trends and compounding these gains would begin to approach a doubling of the amount at risk on a daily basis—similar to the penny example noted earlier. The idealized case illustrates that taking gains more often can produce a larger percentage return than "holding" over periods of price oscillation. And if one trades both the upward and downward trends and compounds these gains, the wealth-generating potential becomes truly astonishing. This is why Hurst said that "improved transaction timing is worth all the effort we can put into it." I'll consider all issues relating to taking advantage of price oscillation and alternation to be under the *principle of transaction timing.*

Of course, in this idealized example, we have traded perfectly, and everyone knows that this is impossible. There is no suggestion here that it is possible. The question is, what percentage of the idealized results can be achieved in practice? This idealized example also makes other things clear. For example, it should be evident why "the long term" is always indefinite and why the best time to buy is always "now." You can see that the long-term trend of rising prices (about 10 percent per year if all dividends were reinvested over the last 200 years) will inevitably affect the value of the investment positively, but how long this takes is dependent entirely on *when* in the cycle of oscillating values the investment is made. For example, if one begins investing at point 6, it will take significantly longer to have a positive return than if one invests at point 7. If this is a yearly chart, the person who invests at point 6 will have 5 rough years, losing 22 percent of the invested value. The person who has invested at point 1 has not yet lost anything, but has, after 30 years, also gained nothing at all. Thus, even for someone who is contemplating buying and holding, it is clear that attending to Hurst's principle of improved transaction timing will serve to increase returns. The chart shows the three types of risk clearly: the risk of loss (from point 6 to point 7); the risk of gains not taken, that is, the risk of vanishing returns; and the risk of lost opportunity, that is, perhaps failing to discover a market in which the trend over the period was an ever-rising one even with oscillations.

The main point of this highly arbitrary example is to call attention to the value of what Hurst pointed to, that is, the *effort* to improve transaction timing. The comparative rewards are so compelling that trying to improve transaction timing and compounding the results of such improved timing can bring the wealth-generating factors of multiplication and compounding to bear on money at risk. This necessarily requires the investor or trader to be more active with regard to money put at risk. Letting "the market" do all the work of multiplying and compounding and making no effort whatever to improve transaction timing subjects the money at risk to undefined procedures for gain taking, undefined methods of entry, and undefined ways to avoid losses. Wall Street makes this extremely easy to do. What is the best time to invest in stocks? *Now.* When should one sell? Sell? Why sell? Stay the course. You are in for the long term. You can't time the market, so just *buy, now!* And keep buying!

Of course, a portion of each dollar you put in is subject to constant positive multiplication and compounding—not for *your* benefit, but for that of the institution. As long as the money rolls in and stays in, this factor alone will enrich the institution without regard to what happens to your money at risk. This has been pointed out sufficiently now to turn our attention more directly to the task: how to improve transaction timing.

CHAPTER 13

Requirements of Method

Market behavior is chaotic in nature. Nonetheless, there are patterns of order in the complexity of price and time relationships. Method is the means of synchronizing and harmonizing the trader's and investor's behavior with the behavior of the markets. This chapter will discuss the foundational assumptions relating to the psychological, philosophical, and historical antecedents of method so that the necessity of method for trader and investor alike is clear.

FOUNDATIONAL ASSUMPTIONS

From the cursory analysis of the nameless chart in the previous chapter, especially the results available from perfect trading, it is clear that *oscillations of trend* are the capital-multiplying mechanisms of any market and therefore are at the root of any effort to make money grow. It follows that it is in the trader's or investor's interest to seek out the very best methods and techniques of *early* trend detection, along with methods and techniques that warn of trend exhaustion and reversal. While the disciplined use of almost any method is likely to be better than no method at all, methods vary widely in their capacity for and sensitivity to this task.

One reason that the traditional investor tends not to consider method is that as soon as one gives technical analysis even a cursory glance, one finds literally thousands of methods competing for one's attention. The choice of methods is literally more difficult than the choice of investments. And the typical investor has even less background available for making any kind of rational decision concerning methods. Even if he gives methods any consideration at all, the typical investor, after looking at this pandemonium called technical analysis, is likely to turn away and to embrace the simpler, easier, and more understandable buy-and-hold method: Buy at any time; keep buying at any time; don't worry about selling; one is in it for the long haul. That's a pretty simple method, and it's obviously the method of choice for most investors.

Of course, the reason that there are so many methods is that from the very beginning of the first financial market, the history of investing and trading has been replete with extraordinary efforts on the part of thousands of individuals and groups to discover the key to the *principle of transaction timing.*[1] All these methods are trying to do what Hurst implored investors to do: improve transaction timing. Has *the* key been found? No. Will the seeking continue? Absolutely. Are some methods better than others? Without question.

RULES FOR ASSESSING METHODS

After studying the endless variety of methods for many years, I have developed my own set of eight rules that I use for assessing the value of any method or combination of methods. Before focusing on the specific trading methods, it will be helpful to review this set of rules.

---

[1] Perhaps the best general introduction is John J. Murphy, *Technical Analysis of the Financial Markets: A Comprehensive Guide to Trading Methods and Applications* (New York: New York Institute of Finance, 1999).

Rule of Applicability. The method(s) must apply to all markets and all time periods. This has the value of allowing you to learn *one* method or set of methods that will have a wide range of applicability in seeking opportunities across markets and across time periods.

Rule of Objectivity. The method(s) must be entirely objective and not subject to variable interpretations depending on how the market behaves. Many methods fail this rule because they change as the outcome changes. This undermines the projective value of the method and ends up being similar to the constant stream of explanations emanating from the financial channels as to why the market did this or that. Such methods soon become quicksand for the trader or investor. The rule of objectivity ensures that the method generates unambiguous conjectures that are subject to refutation, not an "explanation" that cannot be refuted. "For the long term," for example, because it is always indefinite, cannot be refuted and therefore fails the test of objectivity. Similarly, a statement like "investors sold heavily today on war fears" not only is untested, but does not explain the actions of those who bought all those same shares. Such commentary fails the test of objectivity and therefore cannot be successfully used as part of a trader's or investor's method.[2]

Rule of Discrete Signals. The method(s) must use actual market prices as well as time points involving averages, statistical variables, or other derivative values. Because the latter are always lagging the present behavior of the market, action signals often become fuzzy and uncertain. In contrast, a specific price signal indicating clearly what to do and when to do it has clarity and helps the trader and investor to be decisive. Where possible,

---

[2] Of course, such commentary in the public press, by market gurus, or from other sources becomes part of the "market environment" (and thus part of the chaotic structure that we call markets), even if it cannot be used as method. It certainly becomes part of the psychology of the market and the psychology of the trader and must be appreciated as such.

methods that provide either concurrent or leading indicators are favored.

Rule of Trade Parameters. The method(s) must be capable of providing not only action signals for *entry* into a trade or investment, but also discrete signals for *gain taking* and *loss avoidance* (stops). To the extent possible, these three essential conditions should be specifiable in *advance* of entering into any trade or investment. Typically, failure to follow this rule is the beginning of the loss of discipline that undermines many traders and investors and ultimately leads to the "risk of ruin."

Rule of Market Condition. The method(s) must *objectively* and *unambiguously* identify trends, trend exhaustion points, and trend reversals and must do so for any market and any time period. The trader or investor should always know the condition of the market before entering the trade, and certainly during the exposure of financial resources to market risk.

Rule of Projection. The method(s) must not rely on predictions from *any* source. Instead, *projections* of future market behavior must be made from market behavior only. Because the future is unknown, and because the market is chaotic (unpredictable) by nature, investors and traders are always subject to *anxiety* about future market behavior. This anxiety is the seedbed for whole industries of market prediction, from media analysts to the get-rich-quick schemes flooding the mailbox. The most productive basis for projecting future market behavior is the market itself.

Rule of Action. The method(s) must at all times provide the trader with specific and unambiguous action signals so that the trader or investor knows what the "trade state" is, whether she is in the market or not. Generally, this rule will lead to knowing whether the current market state is "long," "short," or "out."

Rule of Incorporation. The method(s) must be sensitive to and incorporate the basic principles outlined in the previous chapter.

This will assure the trader or investor that the methods are consistent and coherent.

These rules ask a great deal of any method. No method by itself will satisfy all of them. It is even quite possible that no combination of methods will do so. But as with perfect trading, the impossibility of satisfying all of these rules should not discourage one's efforts to improve methodological coherence and consistency as a basis for improving transaction timing. The set of principles outlined and the set of rules described here form an idealized framework within which one may develop a meaningful, consistent, and coherent approach to the markets that can be applied to a wide range of trader and investor circumstances and conditions in the effort to improve transaction timing and to make money grow.

CHAOS, COMPLEXITY, AND CURIOSITY

There is probably no area where the application of mathematical, statistical, and modeling techniques has been more fruitless than that of the financial markets. The goal, of course, has been the ever-seductive lure of increased money growth available for compounding. I say fruitless because the results of this historical compulsion have proven to be of such little constant and consistent value. The vast majority of these attempts have involved the application of mathematical approaches (from the very simple, such as a moving average, to the very complex, such as advanced transformative functions) that aim to treat the market as a mechanical system. The idea behind this is that if such a mechanical system could be found, then mechanical trading actions would become trivial. Under such conditions, one could simply set up the computer to recognize the signals and have the computer call the trades into the order desk. The operator would have no responsibility other than deciding how to spend all the money that would flow into his account.

This dream has led to a whole industry of system development, back testing, and attempts to *automate* trading in order to take the trader's emotion and lack of discipline out of the trading equation. I believe this seeking after mechanical solutions is self-defeating. The market is not a mechanical system at all. The market is *alive*. Just as most cause-and-effect approaches to living organisms flounder as a result of the complexity of living systems, these approaches to understanding the behavior of the market are likely to flounder as well. Living systems are complex largely because their behavior is constantly affected by experience, and thus the system *changes* over time, often in unpredictable ways. This feature of unpredictability is the hallmark of any system that is called *chaotic*. The chaotic character *increases* as the degree of complexity of the system increases.

Any approach that seeks a mechanical solution to this problem is likely to be doomed to failure in the long run because the system to which the mechanical solution is applied will change, if not through the application of the system itself, then through other factors. In this respect, the market is not a closed system at all, but an open system that embodies a fundamental principle of *change*—not just change in prices, but also unpredictable changes in the underlying structures that determine prices. I will call such structures "deep structures," partly because they remain invisible and most likely unknown. They are similar in many respects to the concept of the "unconscious" in the language of psychology. While we may be able to look at someone's dream and link its imagery to various *known* aspects of the dreamer's life and world, it is an entirely different task to predict on the basis of what we know what the next dream will be. Predicting the market is like that.

A person's dreams may in this sense be considered a chaotic system. Yet, in any dream, there are patterns of order, instances of structures, qualities of theme, and senses of meaning. The market is like that as well. It is like that because it is the result of the collective behavior of human beings who buy and sell for all kinds of reasons, who get emotional and get greedy and panic and do things under the influence of the crowd that they wouldn't do on their own. This *human* thing that we call the market is alive with all this complexity, and there simply is no way to reduce it so that it is amenable to simple mechanical understanding.[3]

What is important for *every* investor or trader in the face of this uncertainty is *not* to look for certainty at all in relation to the financial markets. When the commentator on the nightly news explains a falling market by saying, "There just is no certainty right now, and understandably investors are cautious about buying until there is more certainty," this is just another version of *bullish bias* masquerading as explanation. Investors can be "certain" when the market is going up—because they understand that. Uncertainty occurs when the market goes down—because they do not understand that.

Of course, there is no more certainty in relation to a market that is going up than there is in relation to a market that is going down. The future of the market is *always* uncertain. This is a part of its inherent complexity. An investor's or trader's certainty is misplaced when it is applied to the market. The only area where certainty has a place is not the market itself, but *how the investor or trader relates to the market*. That is useful certainty. This would always take the form of a conditional: *If the market does this, then I'll do that.* There is no certainty whatever that the market will do this. But *if* it does, then the trader and investor is well served if there is certainty that the action called for will be carried out.

Strangely enough, I have found that a most useful attitude toward the market was articulated by the English poet John Keats. This was not his purpose, of course, but we can make use of it nonetheless. In a letter to his brother, dated October 27, 1818, he wrote,

---

[3] Once this basic idea in relation to the market is grasped, it is not necessary for our purposes here to go more deeply into chaos or complexity. The interested reader will find Bill Williams, *Trading Chaos* (New York: John Wiley & Sons, 1995), to be a useful introduction, and Edgar E. Peters, *Chaos and Order in the Capital Markets* (New York: John Wiley & Sons, 1991), a good second step. More literature is being published that brings the value of chaos theory, complexity theory, and other nonlinear approaches to bear on the financial markets. What the outcome of this will be is, of course, unpredictable.

At once it struck me what quality went to form a Man of Achievement, especially in Literature, and which Shakespeare possessed so enormously—I mean Negative Capability, that is, *when a man is capable of being in uncertainties, mysteries, doubts, without any irritable reaching after fact and reason.*[4]

It is precisely this "reaching after fact and reason" that leads to such a plethora of mindless commentary on the markets that can be so misleading and does such an enormous disservice to the investing and trading public. These explanations are not genuine explanations; rather, they are defensive "explainings away" of the very phenomena one might wish most genuinely to understand.[5] Note how *certain* these explanations are. There is no *doubt* and no *mystery*—only that "reaching after fact and reason."

So how does one hold the doubt and the mystery and the unknowing in the manner suggested by Keats, the manner of *negative capability?* One quality that I have found enormously valuable for both the trader and the investor is *curiosity.*

What do I mean by curiosity? First of all, it is a *desire* to know or learn something one does not yet know. Second, the word itself is derived from the same root as the word *cure*, which means "restore to health." Most investors and traders are overwhelmed with information coming at them from TV, newspapers, the financial press, magazines, gurus, commentators, analysts, books, seminars—the whole panoply of the industry. This tidal wave of stuff makes it very nearly impossible for a trader or investor to experience anything like what might come from that state of negative capability.

I like to suggest a little experiment. Almost anyone now has access to the market. Turn off everything, whether live or delayed—

---

[4] Keats, John. *The Letters of John Keats: A Selection.* (Ed.) R. Gittings. Oxford: Oxford University Press, 1970 (p. 43).

[5] I don't mean to undervalue genuine attempts to understand market behavior. There are many analysts and financial observers who are doing outstanding work and for whom I have enormous respect. Nonetheless, even the most astute and in-depth commentary and analysis typically fails to produce signals that meet the aforementioned requirements and rules of method.

the news, CNBC, everything—so that it is just you and the chart. Watch the chart in some small time interval, such as 5 minutes or 13 minutes. Pick something to watch that you have no investment in, no stake in. What do you see? What happens? Without the ready explanations that are steadily applied by others, what comes into your mind as you watch the oscillations, the ups and downs of the price? What catches your attention? Do you see patterns as you watch the chart form? Do you wonder what will happen next? Go ahead and predict what will happen next. Did it? If so, why do you think it did that? If not, why did it not? Would you be just as happy trading or investing in this chart based on what you see, or do you need something else? Do you really need to hear what others are saying about this? Be curious about your own needs in relation to what you are seeing. Would you trust the chart itself to tell you *everything* you need to know? Could you learn from the chart so that you would know what to do *next* if you had actual money put at risk?

If you put money at risk in what you are seeing, what do you see happening in the chart *then*? How is it different from what you saw when you were only watching? What is happening in your experience as you watch the chart unfold? What happens to you is as important as what is happening in the chart. Being curious about your own reactions and your own behavior is just as important as being curious about the chart.

What you will find as you do this, really do this, is that your own experience and behavior are *also* a complex chaotic system. This is an enormously important observation because it then poses the question of *harmonizing* chaotic systems—that is one way of characterizing the task of trading and investing. Most traders fail and most investors lose money because of this failure to *harmonize* their own chaos with the chaos in the markets.

How to do that is the subject of the remainder of this book.

The inevitable interface between the chaotic market and the chaotic trader or investor is filled with uncertainty, mystery, and doubt—just those elements that Keats pointed to. Without belaboring the issue here, the *cure* for these "problems" is not the "irritable reaching after facts and reason"— most particularly not those facts and reasons that are trumpeted by the market's self-interested cheerleaders—but rather opening yourself to *curiosity*. Hopefully, curiosity will drive you to seek out those methods that *you* as an individual chaotic system can use as you confront the chaos of the financial markets.

There is no one method or set of methods that will fit all individual traders or investors. Everyone, however, will find him- or herself face to face with the *necessity* for method. The methods to be presented here are the result of a curiosity-led exploration of the financial markets as "teacher." Take the results as an example of such a *process*, not as something to be adopted or followed mechanically. The market is a great teacher. It has endless lessons. Always be curious!

THE FUNDAMENTAL RULE

There is a simple *fundamental rule* in trading or investing that if followed rigorously will improve trading results regardless of the type of trading, the markets traded, or the time period. I referred to this rule in the previous chapter, but it will be useful to focus on it more directly.

In its simplest form, it is this: On every *entry*, there should be a *target* and a *stop—no exceptions!* For shorthand reference, I will refer to this rule as ETS.

For each of the three elements of ETS, both investor and trader need to articulate the *basis* for the trade or investment and a specific *price*. It is absolutely essential that you *write these down in a trading or investment journal.*[6] Do this for every trade or investment without fail. Many investors and most traders will lose money because they do not do this. Beginning traders ignore this burdensome task, to their detriment. Professional traders who hit

---

[6] The importance of the trading journal will be considered in more detail in later chapters.

a bad patch always find returning to this fundamental act helpful in the recovery of good trading habits.

Consider using the ETS format to describe the anatomy of a trade that an average investor might have done in March of 2000. A broker advises the investor to buy CSCO because it is "the backbone of the Internet," because "it has always beat earnings," and because "the Internet just isn't going to work without CSCO in the driver's seat." The broker says, "No need to worry about the price—let's just buy it." On the basis of this "entry signal," the investor buys 1000 shares at 80. When asked about the target price for selling, the broker says, "Put this one away and forget about it. This is your ticket to *real* wealth. Remember Microsoft? Don't ever sell this baby."

Thus, the *target* becomes indefinite. But what if CSCO goes down? "Buy as much as you can on any dips. Don't worry about the price. You'll be averaging a gold mine here." Instead of a stop loss, the investor is encouraged to dollar-cost average, and in this way always to buy. This is the standard practice of "buy and hold" and "buy some more." Under these conditions, there is no target, and there is no stop. Without a target and without a stop, there is no way to assess the potential reward of this investment against its potential risk. Without an assessment of risk, the "risk of ruin" increases.

The investor never buys more of CSCO because he is *feeling* upset about the loss in value and can't bring himself to put more money into it. Here the investor's psychology is taking over control of the investor's actions. But he can't sell it, either, because "maybe it *will* come back." Here, once again, the investor's psychology and belief are taking control of his actions. He can't seem to just "forget about it." The failure of this investment has become an emotional burr. Worry, fear, hope, and prayer have become "methods."

When CSCO hits 40, he gets up the nerve to call the broker and tell him to sell it, but the broker says, "The bottom is in; this market's ready to fly, and CSCO will fly higher than any. What you really need to do here is buy more!" So he does not sell, but he does not buy more because he does not have more cash to buy anything. In October of 2002, he needs cash desperately to pay an overdue tuition bill for one of his kids. He uses the brokerage's Internet site to sell CSCO at 8.25 because he can't face talking to the broker. He just has to do it. It's a staggering loss of more than $70,000, about 90 percent of his capital. The devastating loss causes problems for him both financially and personally as his secret shame about this investment begins to destroy his marriage and depression begins to eat away at his vitality. Table 13-1 summarizes the ETS for this trade.

Table 13-1 ETS for CSCO Trade

	Basis	Price	Action
Entry	Broker said, "This is the backbone of the Internet"	"Just buy it"	Bought 1000 shares at 80
Target	"Put it away and forget about it"	Don't ever sell this "baby"	None
Stop	"Buy more if it goes down"	"At whatever price" "Averaging a gold mine"	Sold at 8.25—needed cash for kid's tuition

Every trade has an ETS that can be specified in the trading journal. It is always revealing and is the key to understanding one's trading behavior.

This all too common scenario and many like it that create the "risk of ruin" are avoidable. The essential problem is that the investor is acting on belief and faith and on entirely speculative predictions about the future. Whether these come from the broker, the broker's research department, the market guru, the latest magazine article, the endless promotions one receives in the mail, or even one's own wild greed or fantasies, they are nothing but beliefs about the future. Belief is seductive; it has the capacity to pull one into itself. Once one is inside a belief, one looks only for conviction, certainty, and security. However, this is not the "uncertainties, mysteries, [and] doubts" that Keats wrote of—quite the contrary. Once one is in a belief state, one seeks to banish uncertainties, mysteries, and doubts. The financial industry is fully obliging in providing conviction, certainty, and security—in a word, something to *believe* in.

The investor or trader falls prey to this seduction at great risk. This risk is never pictured as such. In many ways, the seductive power of the financial industry is the greatest risk of all. Falling into these belief systems tends to short-circuit and disable investors' and traders' capacity to see for *themselves* the reality of the markets. It paralyzes curiosity. The one thing the financial industry *cannot* obscure is the actual behavior of the financial markets—the *reality* in the chart of prices.

Wall Street apologists tend to discourage looking at the price chart or paying any particular attention to analyzing the price chart, preferring instead to focus investors' attention on lists of currently favored equities with simple-to-understand "ratings" like "accumulate," "market outperform," or "strong buy." One notices the strong emphasis on *buying* and the almost total absence of recommendations to *sell*. These recommendations reflect so-called fundamental analysis of markets, the economy, and the prospects for the future.

All fundamental analysis is speculative. Predictions about earnings, predictions about the growth in equity prices, predictions about return on investment, predictions about the economy, predictions about interest rates—all of these, in spite of their trappings of rigor and research, are simply speculative and rest on foundations of belief. All belief systems proselytize for additional believers. This is the lifeblood of Wall Street. *Vampiric* is not too strong a word for it.

For this reason, in relation to the ETS table, we add a simple rule: *All information in the ETS table must originate entirely from methods derived from or applied to the chart of prices.*

Before one enters into a trade or investment, there must be something *in the price chart* that supports going long or going short. One does not buy CSCO because the broker says, "It's the backbone of the Internet." That simply is not in the price chart. CSCO may indeed be a good buy, but before you buy it, there must be something in the price chart that is not only providing a buy signal, but also telling you the precise price at which to *enter*. When the buy signal occurs, then it is necessary to be explicit about the *target*. "Put it away and forget about it" simply is not in the price chart. If the target must also originate in the price chart, then the trader needs to have methods available that provide a meaningful target. The target must be a specific price. In addition, as soon as the entry price is known, it is necessary to explicitly set an initial *stop*. Again, the trader must have some method using the price chart to do this. "Buy more if it goes down . . . at whatever price" is not an effective stop.

Table 13-2 illustrates the ETS values for a trade using methods that meet these requirements. The methods will be described further on. The point here is simply to compare and contrast the explicit instructions that the trader and investor will ideally follow with the trade illustrated in Table 13-1. The basis for the entry, the target, and the stop and the specific prices for each element of the trade are the result of applying specific methods to the price chart. Once the trade is completed, the investor or trader then has the task of determining what to do *next*. As we shall see, how to answer this question is one of the most important things that the trader or investor must learn.

Table 13-2   Ideal Form of Trade Journal Entry

	Basis	Price	Action
Entry	Upside structure complete; on trigger	Trigger = 13.25	Bought 1000 shares at 13.25
Target	Wave 3 high	Calculated target = 16.50	Sold at 16.50
Stop	Wave 2 market structure low	Wave 2 low = 12.38	Not stopped

IMPLEMENTING THE FUNDAMENTAL RULE

The fundamental rule is: On every *entry*, there is a *target* and a *stop—no exceptions!* Added to this is the requirement that each element of this rule—entry, target, and stop—must originate entirely from methods applied to the chart of prices. Before we detail the methods, it will be useful to formulate what the trader or investor ideally might seek from the use of methods, that is, what does the trader/investor need methods *for?* In the context of implementing the fundamental rule, there are eight areas for which the trader/investor *needs* methods. These needs have guided the development of the methods and strategies that I employ at undergroundtrader.com.

Trend. Ideally, the trader/investor must *always* know what the trend is, how mature the trend may be, and at what price and point in time the trend will change, and must know these things instantly for any market in any time frame.

Trigger. Ideally, the trader/investor needs a method (or set of methods) that will provide a *specific* price that, *if* seen in the market, signals an entry into a trade. In addition, based on this trigger price, the method ideally provides for setting a specific *market-based initial stop loss trigger price,* in any market and in any time period.

Target. Ideally, the trader/investor needs a method (or set of methods) that will provide a *specific* price, price zone, time, and time zone that, *if* seen in the market, signal the *taking of gains* or the implementation of *gain-preservation* strategies, in any market and in any time period.

Context. Ideally, the trader/investor needs methods for determining the most relevant factors that are likely to influence the dynamic behavior of the market in terms of both price and time. This is essentially the "story line" of the market: the "setting," the "plot," the "cast of characters," the "dramatic tension," the "crisis," and the "lysis" as the market's story unfolds. The market is a human drama, and for this reason dramatic theory has an applicability to method that has not been fully appreciated.[7] The "twists and turns" of a story are

---

[7] The market is at times like a group of Pirandello actors rebelling at the confines of Wall Street's script. Sometimes the play itself seems to have "a mind of it's own" and to want to go somewhere other than where the author intends it to go, and the actors beg for direction and there is none. All the issues in the history of drama play themselves out as well in the history of the financial markets.

very similar to the chaotic and unpredictable nature of the market.[8]

Convergence. Ideally, the trader/investor needs methods to enable her or him to be aware of the *nodal* and *cluster points* in price and time where trends, triggers, and targets *converge* within crucial contexts. These nodal and cluster points in price and time are the moments when market dynamics undergo significant changes through exhaustion, reversal, or expansion. Convergence in price and time above current market prices will tend to attract prices upward, while convergence in price and time below current prices will tend to attract prices downward. Without the price and time convergence information, these often-sudden moves seem inexplicable.

Commitment. Ideally, the trader/investor needs methods to enable understanding of the *psychology* of the market, his or her own psychology, and the interface between these two major psychological systems. In general, a greater understanding of the psychology of the market, one's own psychology, and how these factors interface will make it possible for the trader/investor to be more committed to the trades signaled, the gain-taking signals generated, and the stops that are signaled. When commitment falters, trading becomes ever more perilous to the trader/investor.

Curiosity. Ideally, traders and investors need methods that work against the dulling effects of habit on the mind. One might initially think that being *habitual* in how one approaches trading or investing would be beneficial. However, habitual activity tends to act as a depressant on the mind, and the mind itself will respond by increasing "novelty." Such habituation-induced novelty, when it enters into the trading arena, is often detrimental to the trader. For this reason, methods for

---

[8] This may also be the reason why art is typically a leading indicator for developments in other areas of a culture, from politics to science. The understanding of the deep structure of financial markets as following developments in art has not been sufficiently appreciated.

engendering curiosity and keeping the trader and investor as aware as possible of those things that Keats referred to (uncertainties, mysteries, and doubts) will keep the mind alive and awake and involved in ever-greater understanding of the psychological realities of the market and the trader.

Consistency. Ideally, the greater the degree of coherence among the methods the trader/investor employs, the more consistent the trading results will be. The market may be chaotic and unpredictable. However, if the trader/investor's methods are chaotic and unpredictable, the outcome is certain: *failure.*

DYNAMIC ADAPTATION TO CHANGE: SYNCHRONY AND HARMONY

Another way to formulate the idea of the market as *chaotic* is to say that "the market is always right." A great deal of market commentary expresses the opposite idea: The market is overvalued, or oversold, or overextended, or due for a rally; the market is discounting the fall in the interest rates, or fearing the negative possibilities for the economy too much. What most such commentary and analysis amounts to is, "The market is not doing what I think it should be doing." If the market does not "behave," then of course the market is being perverse, unreasonable, irrational, emotional, absurd, and so on.

Well, of course! The market is *alive.* The market is behaving as an emotional animal. To picture the market's behavior as *rational* is so much wishful thinking. It may appear rational at times, but a few minutes or a few days later it may appear not so rational. Market participants may like to picture *themselves* as acting rationally and to develop all sorts of models for acting rationally. This has little to do with the market's actual behavior. Rather, all attempts to treat the market rationally will be plagued by the market's "misbehavior." Plato's attack on the irrationality of poetry and *poiesis* in general lives on in the modern belief in the rationality of financial markets and the resulting faith that "things are under control."

There is much more to be gained from a deeper perspective on the *poetics* of financial markets and the irrationality underlying this major human enterprise.

Part of the difficulty comes from *insisting* on the correctness of the methods or theories or models that are applied to the market. One can develop a model, for example, then "back-test" the model and even reach 100 percent accuracy with regard to past performance. Going forward, however, the accuracy always deteriorates, because any model becomes a static model, and when this occurs, the performance of the model will deteriorate. There is a very good reason for the disclaimer that one sees everywhere: *Past results do not guarantee future results*. If they did, the market would in fact be predictable, and if the market were ever to become totally predictable, it would cease to *be* a true market.

In the absence of total predictability, the trader must become aware of the principle of *dynamic adaptation*. This might be an attitude, or it might even be a method. In a sense, what this means is that every method (and most certainly every trader/investor) has something to learn *from* the market's behavior—perpetually. There are two crucial elements that characterize dynamic adaptation: synchrony and harmony.

Synchrony means that two things are occurring simultaneously in period or in phase. For the market, the two things are the market and the trader. When the market decides to go long, then the trader/investor will be *in synchrony* if her methods have provided signals to go long and she *follows* the methods. This mantra, *"follow the methods,"* will be the trader/investor's best friend. Naturally, the success of this synchrony depends on the sensitivity of the trader/investor's methods to the market's behavior and the capacity of those methods to track the chaotic behavior of the market, that is, to dynamically adapt to the "irrationality" of the market's behavior.

Harmony comes from a root word that carries the image "to fit together." There is a style of trading, and even of investing, that considers trading to be a kind of battle, a war in which there is conflict for gains. Sometimes the market is pictured as the adversary;

sometimes other traders are the enemy. This approach is described beautifully in the first part of the present volume. The principle of dynamic adaptation, however, strives for a different relationship to the market, one that aims toward "fitting together" with the market, so that the trader/investor's behavior and that of the market become a pleasing combination of elements of a larger whole.

This sense of "fitting together," this articulation, is also the root of the word *art*. In addition to the methods and strategies for dealing with the chaotic nature of the markets, there is some quality of art lying at the root of the principle of harmony. This is the *art of trading.* This art is always expressing a creative synergy arising from the tension between the chaos of the markets and the chaos of the trader.

PERSONALITY, METHOD, AND THE SHADOW OF FAILURE

What shadows almost every trader/investor at every turn is *failure*—failure of systems, strategies, and methods; failure of will in carrying out systems, strategies, and methods; failure of advice, recommendations, and following "the experts"; failure to be responsible for one's own investment/trading behavior; failure to act when it is necessary to act; failure to withhold action when that is necessary; failure to overcome the patterns of loss, emotional decisions, and reckless disregard for common sense. Failure abounds in the world of investment and trading. About 90 percent of day traders fail. Most investors fail to achieve what they had hoped or dreamed of. Most fund managers and professionals fail to match the performance of unmanaged funds. Failure is the greatest challenge for most traders and investors, no matter what degree of expertise or experience they have.

Success causes few difficulties for investors or traders. Of course, success can lead to failure quite abruptly in the financial markets. For example, during roaring bull markets, one may imagine that one has learned how to trade or invest successfully because one is racking up gains hand over fist. However, when the tide turns, one soon discovers that one has learned nothing at all, except perhaps the cost of greed and frenzy.

The financial industry is well equipped to mask failure, while individual investors and traders are not. The immediate consequence of this is that the trader/investor is immediately thrown into a state of personal crisis. When money is on the line, the full range of an individual's personality and character becomes "invested" right along with the money. The individual does not have the luxury of trading or investing "other people's money." This is not the place to go into these issues at any length, but it is necessary to take note of the degree to which trading and investing engage one's character and personality "difficulties" because this is at the heart of failure.

Many of the problems that lead to failure are related to projecting one's self-worth into one's trading and investing performance. This leads to many self-defeating processes that hound traders and investors and that traders and investors try to blame on others. The root problem is that while most traders and investors understand themselves to be engaged in investing and trading in order to make their money grow, the fact is that most of them are trying to work out personal psychological problems in the context of the financial markets. This factor is the genesis of failure. Traders and investors who wish to be successful will have to face this difficult truth and work as hard on themselves as they do on the market. In the pages ahead, these issues will be noted and methods and strategies for dealing with them will be detailed along with the methods and strategies for the markets.

Building the Fundamental Methods

If methods are to be genuinely useful, they must be simple, coherent, and effective in dealing with the chaotic nature of the financial markets. The methods illustrated here are designed to be useful for both the trader and the investor. The methods described in this chapter are considered "fundamental" primarily in the sense that they follow from and embody the foundational assumptions, principles, and rules articulated in the previous chapter, "Requirements of Method," and also serve as preparation for the more advanced and specialized methods described in the next chapter. No effort is made here to compare or contrast or even consider the wide range of methods vying for the attention of traders and investors. There are plenty of sources available for that purpose.

In any event, the purpose here is to illustrate the methods taught and used daily in the context of the real-time market at undergroundtrader.com.

THE IMPORTANCE OF CANDLESTICK CHARTING

As specified in the previous chapter, all information in the ETS table must originate entirely from methods derived from or applied to the chart of prices. Interest in a particular market may originate from any source at all: a broker's recommendation, an advertisement for a phenomenal stock-selecting service that promises 500 to 1000 percent growth or more, a stock touted in a chat room, a tip from the grocer's mom, or whatever. Whether the stock that is of interest is selected at random, is found through high-powered scanning searches using complex criteria, or comes from a supposedly reliable source, adherence to the fundamental rule and its supplemental requirement will save the investor and trader no end of grief, no matter what the market and no matter what the time period.

Of course, this makes the chart extremely important. Perhaps the most important characteristic of the chart is its *truth value*. Companies may distort earnings and balance sheets to bedazzle investors. Brokerages may issue urgent buy bulletins while privately thinking and doing something else. A market guru may trumpet the year-end targets. A popup advertisement may advertise fantastic returns on a stock that is about to fly, so you had better get in early. A trading-room play caller may call for a short sale. Whatever the source of the recommendation, consult the chart. The chart *never* lies. The chart is *always* telling the truth. What you see in a chart is what the market has done. No one can argue that the chart of prices is wrong. To begin on truthful ground, one must begin with the chart.

Now, whether the present chart can tell us about *future* behavior, what features of the chart are the most important to attend to, and how to relate what one sees in a chart to what one actually does in the market are all important considerations that are open to good, solid debate. They are all good *empirical* questions that are subject to testing and evaluation. Opinions, speculations, forecasts, and all manner of predictions about the behavior of the market are very difficult to test. "Yes, I would accumulate IBM here, because if the economy improves and capital spending returns to its more normal levels and people start to feel confident again, this stock will be a winner!" There is no ETS in this statement for one to act on. There are too many conditionals. Indeed, even if capital spending and consumer confidence continue to tank, IBM could still rise because it reported higher earnings—even if those earnings are only the result of IBM's buying back its own stock and not really earnings at all.

A market does *not* need rational conditions to be in place in order to move. It can move on rumor, or it can move when people buy for no other reason than that the market is rising. In a chart, none of this is hidden. It is all there in plain view for anyone to see. All markets are *naked* in this sense, even if the greater portion of the financial industry is devoted to clothing the markets in one illusion or another. Both the investor and the trader must see through to the "truth of the tape" that is displayed so nakedly in the price chart. If all methods must be applied there or be derived from there, one can at least be confident that the ground on which one is operating is true ground.

Because of the importance of the chart, we must consider just what sort of chart to focus on and why. There are many ways to picture prices as they occur in and through time. The most common chart is the *bar* chart (see Figure 14-1). In the bar chart, the overall impression is the sense of *wavelike* behavior as the market oscillates from lows to highs and back again. The details of the individual bars and the relationship between them are visually subsumed in this larger gestalt.

A very different visual impression is gained from looking at the same prices plotted as Japanese *candlesticks*. In the candlestick chart (see Figure 14-2), the individual bars are treated as if they were candles with wicks at both ends. The candle body consists of a vertical rectangular box bounded by the open and the close. Price behavior beyond these body points is shown by thin "wicks" above and below the body points. These wicks are also called *shadows*, emphasizing their insubstantiality or the fleeting quality of

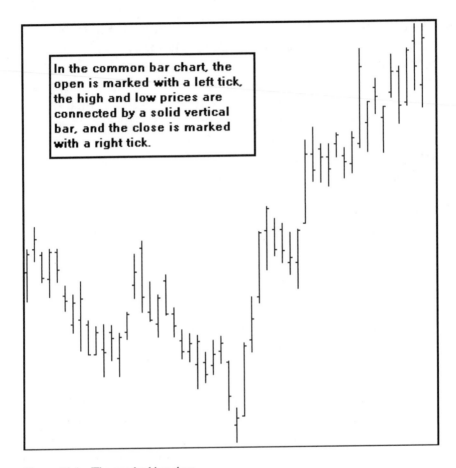

In the common bar chart, the open is marked with a left tick, the high and low prices are connected by a solid vertical bar, and the close is marked with a right tick.

Figure 14-1   The standard bar chart.

prices that could not be maintained. It is well to remember that candles are used for lighting, and for that reason there is an importance to the behavior of the candle wicks that I will return to shortly.

In the candlestick chart, the wave action is still evident, but now the specific candles in the chart, the relationship between them, and the differences in their behavior draw the eye. Because of this capacity of the candlestick chart to produce more visual information than the bar chart without trying, this will be the preferred chart form for the methods described here. Many of the

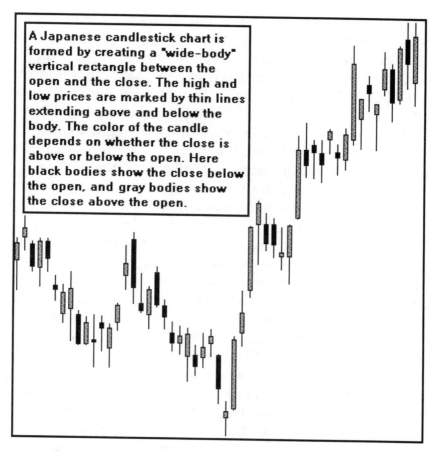

A Japanese candlestick chart is formed by creating a "wide-body" vertical rectangle between the open and the close. The high and low prices are marked by thin lines extending above and below the body. The color of the candle depends on whether the close is above or below the open. Here black bodies show the close below the open, and gray bodies show the close above the open.

Figure 14-2   The Japanese candlestick chart.

patterns that catch the eye will become very important tools in the trader's and investor's toolbox.

READING A CHART

Reading a chart begins with asking questions. The most elementary thing shown by a chart of price behavior is that prices will move up to certain points, then down, then up, and so on endlessly. A reasonable question in relation to this basic phenomenon would be, is there anything *in the chart* that would indicate or *signal* a change from one direction to the other? In effect, we want to know whether the market itself hints at what it will do *next*.

Before addressing this question directly, it will be useful to introduce a few features of any chart, a *language* of charts, if you will. Look again at Figure 14-2. Notice first that there is no indication of *what* is being charted or the *period* of the charting. We could be looking at the monthly chart of General Motors or a 5-minute chart of pork bellies. While that may seem ludicrous on first hearing, it actually reveals a profound feature of the price chart: The principles that will be derived from the price chart or applied to it will be the same no matter what the market and no matter what the period.

What this means is that the important characteristics of price behavior seen in the price chart are "unitary" across markets and across times. These *features* of price behavior remain coherent and self-similar for all markets and all times. In effect, this is the first and primary level of *order* in the behavior of financial markets.[1] Moreover, once one has learned what to attend to in *one* price chart, one has learned the basic approach to *all* price charts. In other words, one can glean almost everything of value from the detailed study of a single price chart. To illustrate this, I will use the price behavior in Figure 14-2 to indicate the salient features of the fundamental methods. This price chart is in no way a special case. Almost any chart will exhibit the same features, some more, some less. In any event, as the chart is read, the reader is encouraged to be curious about *everything* in any price chart and to formulate this curiosity in the form of questions to explore. In this reading, I will give names to the specific elements or relationships that become the object of attention. Some of these names may be different from those used by other people. If so, the purpose is to emphasize certain features or characteristics that will become important later on.

---

[1] This level of order is termed *fractal*. This term refers to both this feature of price charts and other characteristics of the methods illustrated. There is a definite preference for methods that are fractal to all markets and time periods.

THE PRINCIPLE OF EXHAUSTION

When prices are moving up—as, for example, those shown by the first and second candles in Figure 14-2 are—why do they stop doing so? Why is it that the third candle in this chart does not move higher? We may never know the precise reason—if there is one. However, we can formulate a possibility: The *energy* or *force* of buying is *exhausted*. Many factors may contribute to this energy or force of buying. However, the chart indicates that whatever the source of this buying may be, it has, for a time, become exhausted. A price high followed by a *higher* high and then by a *lower* high defines the momentary exhaustion of buying. The first candle sets a high, the next one goes yet higher, but the third candle *fails* to achieve a new high. This failure is the first evidence of exhaustion of the energy of buying.

THE PRINCIPLE OF MARKET STRUCTURE

This leads to the formulation of one of the most important features of price behavior: *market structure*. In this simplest of cases, we can see the market rising until it forms a market structure. A *market structure high* (MSH) is *three*[2] consecutive candles with the form high, higher high, lower high. When the energy for buying is exhausted, this means that no one will pay yet higher prices *at that time*. Someone has clearly offered to *sell* at higher prices—buyers *always* have to buy from sellers. In effect, the buyer is saying no to the price asked by the seller.

If the seller is motivated to sell, then he will lower the price. However, when the buyer sees this, she may reason that if prices have gone lower because she has said no, maybe they will go lower still if she continues to say no. This is a momentary "buyer's strike," sufficient to produce a lower high. It follows that market

---

[2] This is the first chart-reading example using the Rule of Three discussed earlier. As you will note throughout this chapter and the next, the Rule of Three is intimately involved in many of the methods and approaches to be illustrated.

"tops" will always be of this nature and will reflect the failure to recruit buyers who are willing to pay higher prices.

When buying energy is exhausted, it is natural for prices to move lower. The same buyers who failed to buy at higher prices may be quite eager to buy at lower prices. These would be "bargain buyers." However, what about those who bought "at the top," at the peak of the market structure high? They may not be so eager to see falling prices. Instead of feeling that they are getting a bargain, they may now feel that they overpaid. If prices continue to fall, fear of still lower prices may begin to play a part. In order to avoid a greater loss, these buyers may decide to sell, thus adding to the selling pressure. As prices fall further, buyers begin to expect lower prices and reason either, "Why buy now when it may be cheaper later?" or "If prices are going to continue to fall, why buy at all?" More and more buyers go into neutral or turn away entirely.

With buying pressure becoming further exhausted, selling pressure naturally increases. Selling increases to avoid losses, but because buyers are not so eager, prices will fall even further and faster. Moreover, some hardy souls may even begin to sell short, meaning that they will sell in the market even though they do not have anything to sell. They will "borrow" shares for a period and sell those. If prices go down further, the short sellers become motivated to buy in order to pocket the difference. This natural ebb and flow of buyers who become sellers and sellers who become buyers creates the price chart.

Obviously, every transaction is between a buyer and seller. What is different is each party's "eagerness" or "desperation" to make the transaction. When a market is falling continuously or rapidly, sellers become desperate to sell in order to avoid further losses, while buyers may, at any point, become eager to buy. This oscillation between the psychological condition of buyers and sellers happens to a small degree in every single transaction between a buyer and a seller. A buyer may be buying in some state of desperation, while the seller in that transaction may be desperate as well. There is no way to track every single transaction to determine the motivation for it on both sides. However, the *net* effect of all these transactions is seen clearly in the price chart. When that third candle fails to make a new high, we *know* that buying pressure is becoming exhausted, that selling pressure may increase, and that the probability of *lower* prices ahead increases.

The price level at which buying is exhausted is marked by the peak of the market structure formation. It is always an exact price. No one knows where the market will go in the future, but we can know with precision whether prices are above or below this price line (see Figure 14-3). This initial market structure provides the chart reader with the first *context* method.

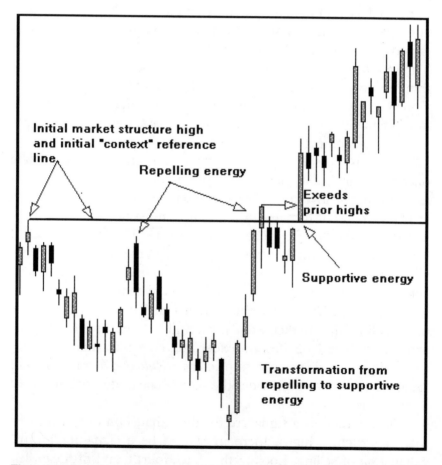

Figure 14-3 The initial market structure high provides the first context price line, illustrating the market's "memory" of that price point on subsequent price moves and the phenomenon of repelling and supportive energy.

Context methods are those methods that reveal the market's *memory*. Note that after the market fell following that first market structure high, it then rose sharply, but as the price approached the context line, the market backed sharply down to even lower prices. Then it once again challenged the price line, peeked above it, fell back a *short* distance, and then broke through resolutely in a strong move much higher: three "failures" and then "success." It is as if the market "remembers" this price line. In its second attempt, it did not quite return to the same level before forming another market structure high *lower* than the first one. Does this fact have anything to do with the market's going still lower? Then, on the third attempt, prices moved above the price line but could not be sustained and fell back below it, forming yet another market structure high, but this one *above the prior attempts*. Does this fact have anything to do with prices' finally moving resolutely beyond the previously "repelling" or "resistive" price line? What is it about that *third* failure that might hint at why the market was able to break through the context line?

It is easy to see the context effects of even a single price line once the chart is complete for the period being examined. In real-time trading or investing, however, the context methods, although available for what has *already* happened, must necessarily be projected into the "blank space" of the future. The question is not whether the trader or investor can *predict* future price behavior, but whether the trader or investor will *know what to do* when the market behaves in certain ways in relation to the context methods. For example, note that *after* the third market structure high neared the context line, the market went powerfully to the upside (see the arrow in Figure 14-3). Might exceeding *three* prior market structure points in testing a context price be a *Rule-of-Three* buy signal? If so, the market itself provides the signal. The trader/investor must then decide to *act on the signal*.

Just as there is a signature for the exhaustion of buying (the market structure high), there must also be a signature for the exhaustion of selling. Look at the third, fourth, and fifth candles. In this set of three sequential periods, there is a low and a lower low, followed by a *higher* low. This pattern formally defines a *mar-*

ket structure low (MSL). If you observed that in this instance the market structure high and the market structure low shared a candle in common, you have good eyes. If you are wondering whether that matters—that's a good question! It is detailed observation like this that leads to becoming a good chartist. Later, I will explain why this *commonality* of a candle in opposite structures tends to create structures *weaker* than those built from more widely separated candles. Note that in this instance, the next candle fails to move higher, but instead falls abruptly, opening even *below* the market structure low. This typifies the weakness of a shared candle in alternating structures.

Market Structure Bull and Bear Lines

Just as the market structure price line drawn horizontally from a single market structure high (illustrated in Figure 14-3) established a context for "reading" price behavior, lines drawn between market structure points and extended will also provide powerful context lines. Figure 14-4 illustrates the construction of a line between successive falling market structure points. This produces a "bear" line, meaning that prices will continue to fall until this line is "violated."

Note that given this context of a downward-sloping line, it is strikingly clear when a move above this line occurs (circled candles). Note that the *entire* body of the first candle to "break out" above the bear line is above the line. In this first instance, the market went up considerably. In the second instance, the whole body is *not* clear of the bear line, and the market fell to new lows. In the third instance, note that again the whole body is not above the bear line. However, there is a pronounced difference in the candles. In the prior case, the candle has a small body and a small range, whereas in the latter case, the candle has the largest range and largest body since the chart began. It is clear that there is something about this candle that is different from any prior candle. Note also that after the market went higher (but not as high as the first market structure price line), it also fell to new lows. However, the original bear market structure line was not touched or penetrated. In that sense, even though prices went lower, that downward-sloping line was supportive.

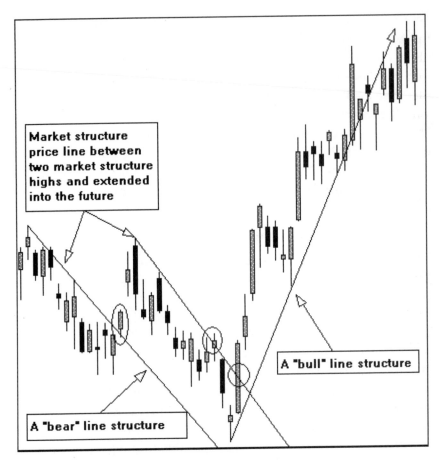

Figure 14-4 Lines drawn between falling market structure highs produce "bear" lines, whereas lines drawn between rising market structure lows give rise to "bull" lines.

Market Structure Events

For ease of reference, downward-sloping market structure lines drawn from higher to lower market structure highs will be termed *bear* lines, signifying a downward tendency of prices. Similarly, lines drawn from market structure lows to higher market structure lows will be termed *bull* lines to signify the upward tendency of prices. Any *close* of a candle *above* a bear line in a declining market (or a close *below* a bull line in a rising market) is a *market structure event*. Such events require immediate action on the part of the trader or investor.

This is equally true for the short-term trader and the long-term investor. The first candle close above the initial bear line occurs at the 14th bar. If this is a 5-minute chart, this is occurring at 70 minutes. If it is a monthly chart, that breakout candle is occurring at the 14th month since the chart began. For a mutual fund buyer, for example, this is the first point where the chart *itself* signals a move into the long side of the market as the market closes above the "ruling" bear line for the first time.

Reading completed charts is *always* misleading. The purpose of doing so is *only* to learn what to pay attention to and to learn from the *history* of the market in question. Under actual trading conditions, the future is always a blank into which one projects the methods. Again, whether one is trading in 5-minute periods, daily periods, or monthly periods, this will always be true.

ANALYSIS OF CANDLE TYPES AND PATTERNS

Even a cursory glance at a candlestick chart reveals a wide range of different candle types and different patterns of relationship between the candlesticks. Ideally, the trader and investor would be able to use candlestick types and patterns to *anticipate* the movement of market prices. Of course, as with *all* methods or tools, such anticipation *must* be in the form of conjecture and refutation.[3] That is, if we *conjecture* that a certain pattern is associated with market declines, we must avoid locking into a stance of certainty that this will be so. Most particularly, we must know precisely what conditions will *refute* its being so.

With this in mind, let us return to a fresh version of the chart and review some important candlestick features, types, and pat-

---

[3] The rule of "testability," formulated by the philosopher Karl Popper in the form of requiring that conjectures be expressible in a form that can be refuted by evidence, is extremely useful to the trader and investor. All the methods illustrated here lead to testable conjectures that can be refuted by the evidence of the market. Generally, beliefs are not expressible in conjectures that can be refuted. This is why belief is so dangerous to the trader and investor.

terns (see Figure 14-5). The purpose here is to specify some of the
ways in which these candle features will be used in conjunction
with other features of the price chart, not to give an in-depth
review of candlestick analysis.[4]

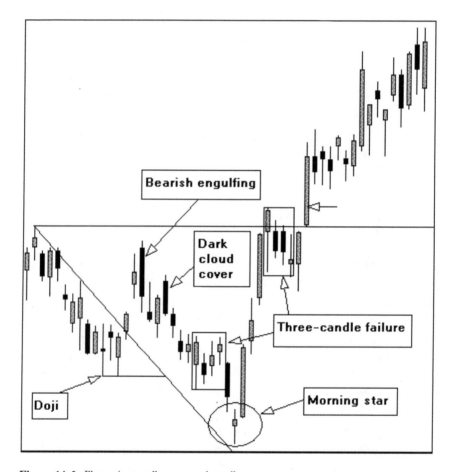

Figure 14-5 Illustrative candle types and candle patterns.

[4] For an in-depth treatment of candles and candlestick methods, see Steve Nison,
*Japanese Candlestick Charting Techniques: A Contemporary Guide to the Ancient
Investment Techniques of the Far East* (New York: New York Institute of Finance,
1991), and *Beyond Candlesticks: New Japanese Charting Techniques Revealed* (New
York: John Wiley & Sons, 1994).

Doji Candle

Many types of candles differ in their *body* characteristics. When the body is very small relative to the range of prices, or, better yet, nonexistent (that is, the close is equal to the open), the candle is called *doji* (literally, "the same") in Japanese terminology. This type of candle is frequently a *reversal* candle because the bullish and bearish factors end the period in a "draw," and a draw represents a waning of the trend in progress. In the chart, a doji candle sets a low for the market structure bear trend that is in progress. The trader can use this doji as an early warning signal of a potential reversal. The doji sets up a *conjecture* that the market will turn higher. At this point, the trader/investor will want to set up two conditions: (1) to specify exactly what price behavior will *confirm* the conjectured move, and (2) to specify precisely what price behavior will *disconfirm* the conjectured move. We know that *any* conjecture about market behavior is a probabilistic one, not a certainty. For this reason, putting money at risk requires the specification of both conditions.

What confirms the reversal potential signified by the doji candle? Answering this question requires attention to another question: How long does the doji warning of reversal last? Here it is best to think of candle types and candle patterns as "warnings" or "signals" that *persist,* as if a warning light comes on and stays on until the matter is resolved. This is the single best way to approach the significance of candles and candle patterns. The market has made a new low. It has gone higher than the previous candle and lower than the previous candle, and it has nearly set a new closing low, but not quite. And the bullish and bearish forces have battled to a draw, forming the doji.

However, as noted, a draw is evidence that the trend in progress and its bearish energy is *weakening*—that's the conjecture. Note that the *opening* of the next candle is higher than the close of the doji. Note also that the *close* of the next candle is higher than the close of the doji. Therefore, in relation to the price points that define the candle's body, both points reflect higher prices. However, note that the high did *not* exceed the high of the doji candle.

Since the market did not make a new high price, we have to con-
clude that the degree of confirmation is not yet strong. Indeed, in
the next period, the market opens substantially lower and moves
lower yet, before closing strongly on the day near the high.

As noted earlier, the trader/investor needs to specify not only
what would confirm a reversal, but also what would *disconfirm* it.
Certainly, the primary disconfirmation of this reversal doji would
be if prices in fact went *lower*. Thus, in that period, after opening
down and then moving lower, the "warning light" nature of the
doji is demanding the trader/investor's close attention to the low
price achieved. If the price goes lower than the low of the doji candle, then the doji reversal is disconfirmed. As can be seen, in this
example, the price came back down to meet the market structure
context line, but did *not fall* further, and prices moved quickly and
sharply away from the context line. It is as if selling pressure suddenly evaporated in spite of a substantially lower opening and
within a tick of making a new low in the bear move down. That a
new low did not occur illustrates the weakening of the bear energy,
as anticipated by the doji candle. With these conditions in place,
the next candle breaks above the bear line with its whole body—a
strong bullish signal. This "breakout" leads to a substantial gap
opening (called a *window* in candlestick language) leading to a new
high, followed in the third candle by yet another window and a new
high.

The principle of alternation works exquisitely in the markets.
It is at work in the minute examination of successive candles in
whatever time period, as well as in the alternation of trends lasting
many years. The trader/investor who tends to favor only one direction (e.g., bullish) will fail to genuinely appreciate and profit from
the fundamental alternating nature of market behavior.

It is useful for the trader/investor to formulate the bullish and
bearish "task" at any point in the analysis of market behavior. For
example, as the market broke above the bear line and began to
move higher, the bullish task became one of surmounting the original context price line set by the first market structure high. In
order for this to happen, buyers must be willing to keep buying at

higher prices. Such buying progressed until it reached a more than 90 percent return to the original market structure high. At that point, buyers *failed* the bullish task.

The Engulfing Candle

The candle that formed when the context line was not breached is called an *engulfing* candle. The body of this candle goes both higher and lower than the body of the prior candle, completely engulfing it. Because the close is below the open in this case, it is called a bearish engulfing candle. In contrast to the doji, which involves a single candle, the bearish engulfing candle is a candlestick pattern that involves two candles, the engulfing candle and the engulfed candle. This is a major reversal candle pattern; it implies that buying energy is exhausted and that the probability of selling energy will increase. Once again, the principle of alternation suggests that the trader/investor must now anticipate lower prices.

Of course, as before, this is a conjecture. In addition, one must go through the whole process again in the reverse direction. Shortly after the bearish engulfing candle, the market attempts to regain the bullish momentum by forming a market structure low— the first evidence of the exhaustion of selling, as we have seen. However, the third candle of that market structure low is another major bearish candle pattern, this one called a *dark cloud cover*. As you can see, this candle pattern is formed when the second of two candles opens higher than the prior close (and often above the prior high), only to fall substantially and close well within the body of the prior candle.

As prices continued to fall, another bearish candle pattern emerged. This is one that I call the *three-candle failure* pattern. Note the candles in the box. Following a new low, there are three successive candles with their entire *bodies* (and most frequently the wicks as well) contained within the *range* of the first candle. If such a pattern produces a new *body* low, prices may be expected to fall further, exactly as seen in this case in the next two candles, which reach the ultimate low for this charting period. Note the three-candle failure in the opposite direction as prices moved above the original context line. Here, after establishing a new high above the context line, there are three lower candles whose bodies are contained within the range of the first candle. Once the market had a body close above the high of the first candle, the bullish task was accomplished.

As the market fell to the low of the chart, the bearish task was relatively easy to specify: a *close* below the first market structure bear line. If this occurred, there would be a very high probability of the market's regaining *angular momentum* to the downside. This would simply mean that prices would continue to fall to new lows below the declining bear line, as the bearish trend would intensify. Without knowing where the market structure bear and bull lines are in a chart, traders and investors are often left in puzzlement as to why prices have started to climb abruptly instead of falling or vice versa. The answer often lies in the market's exhibiting "contrary" behavior at critical junctures (an aspect of the principle of alternation).

Morning Star Candle Pattern

In this example, the bearish energy *failed* to drop prices below the ongoing bear line. Such a failure will embolden those bullish traders/investors who are eager to buy at "bargain" prices and provide a warning to those traders who are profiting from the decline (short sellers). If this *is* a critical juncture, the market will often provide a distinctive candle type (e.g., a doji) or candle pattern (e.g., a bullish engulfing candle). At this particular bottom, the market did form a distinctive pattern—in this case, a "morning star." This refers to the light of Venus as it announces a "new day" and the "rising sun," the language itself indicating the quality of what is expected to happen. In the language of Japanese candlesticks, much is made of "light" and "dark" as imaginal icons for the rising and falling emotional "moods" that turn the markets.

This pattern is a three-candle pattern, formed most essentially by a candle with a small body (the "star") bounded by two larger candles, with a body gap between the two outside bodies and the star. There are many variations on this theme, and some of these variations give strong hints as to what is to come. For example, you can see that the third candle is an engulfing type in relation to the first candle of this pattern. This relationship between candles "at a distance" often indicates the strength of the coming reversal. This strength manifests itself clearly in the ensuing major move to new highs through the end of the chart.

The purpose of this brief excursion into candlestick types and patterns is to illustrate their capacity to *anticipate* market reversals. As the methods develop, candle analysis will become an integral part of the context of the analysis of price behavior and preparation for trader action.

MARKET STRUCTURE TRIGGER

The fundamental rule (on every entry, there should be a target and a stop) requires the specification of a method for *entry* into every trade. In the course of developing the methods, several different procedures for trade entry will be specified. Here I will introduce one of the most important entry methods: the *market structure trigger*. If a market structure high indicates buying exhaustion, and the conjecture is that prices will subsequently fall, there is a natural entry point: *a tick below the low of the third candle in the market structure pattern*.

To illustrate this, consider Figure 14-6. The market structure highs (MSH) and the market structure lows (MSL) in the first periods in this expanded view of the chart are marked. The first market structure high in the chart sets a trigger (to sell or sell short) at a tick below the low of the third candle, shown by the arrow. The conjecture is that the market will go lower upon the completion of the market structure high. The trigger *requires* the market to do just that. If the market does not go lower, the trigger is not hit. In this case, the market did indeed go lower and the trigger was hit, signaling a short position or, if the trader was long, a sale. If one were waiting for a signal to go long, one would continue to wait. The trader or investor looking for a signal to go long would be waiting for a market structure low trigger. In the MSL trigger, the entry triggers when the market moves a tick higher than the high of the third candle of the market structure pattern.

As noted, in the fourth period, the market structure high triggered. The trader or investor enters a short position in order to take advantage of the profit opportunities from a decline in market prices. The market initially moves lower, but by the end of the period, the market has moved higher. Recall the fundamental rule: On every entry, there should be a target and a stop. To this rule we have added the requirement that the decision *must be based on what we see in or can apply to the chart.* Where is the stop? The most obvious place to place the stop is a tick above the market structure high price. While the trader/investor may choose any stop method, in practice the trader/investor will find that stops based on actual

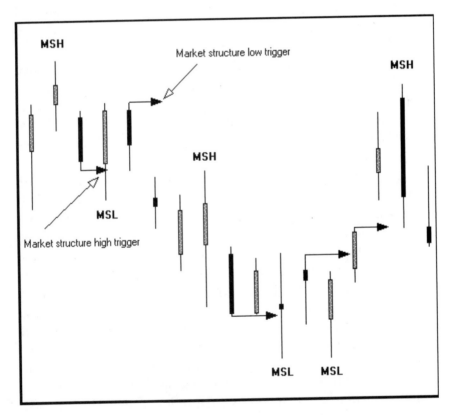

Figure 14-6   Various market structure low and market structure high triggers.

market behavior are likely to be more effective and profitable than stops based on arbitrary point sizes or dollar values. The popular-stop setting methods of point sizes and dollar values are not in the market's chart behavior.

One cannot expect the market to be so accommodating that as soon as one enters a trade, it rewards one with an immediate and large profit. Most important, the trader/investor must always be aware of the principle of alternation. That is, as soon as a market structure high is set, representing the exhaustion of buying, the *market structure event* that is likely to occur next is a market structure low, indicating the exhaustion of selling. No one knows when such a market structure low might occur.

The market's fundamental way of functioning is to oscillate between market structures. The major issue becomes one of the *relationship* between market structures. If the market's behavior is characterized by lower market structure highs and lower market structure lows, then the market is in a downtrend ("bear" trend). If the market's behavior is characterized by higher market structure highs and higher market structure lows, then the market is in an uptrend ("bull" trend). In this example trade, sometime following the opening in the fourth period, a tick below the trigger price was hit, and that point signaled *entry* into the trade.

In this first trade, then, as in all trades, one method of setting a stop is to use a market structure point. This first example of a market structure trade illustrates something that every trader and investor sometimes experiences: As soon as a signal is given, the market moves in the "right" direction, but then suddenly reverses course and moves substantially against the trade.[5] By the end of the period, the trader/investor is in a loss position. From the per-

---

[5] This "contrariness" of the market typically sets off the most troublesome emotional difficulties that traders must learn to discipline through method. Regardless of the validity and accuracy of the method used, the trader must learn to tolerate this contrary behavior of the market. The best methods will give this contrariness room to play out without disconfirming the veracity of the signaled direction. Naturally, if the contrariness becomes extreme, then all methods employed must provide a rational or market-based stop or stop-and-reverse dynamic adaptation to the changed conditions.

spective of *method*, however, the trader/investor has acted correctly by following the method, entering on a signal, and setting a stop. *There has been no signal to do anything else*. From the perspective of method, the trader/investor is in the correct position, even if there is a current negative equity in the position.

Every trader and investor must learn a fundamental lesson: The *discipline* of method lies first and foremost in *following* the method. There is *never* a guarantee that a signaled trade will be profitable, any more than there is a guarantee that it will be unprofitable.

In this trade, it would not escape one's attention that the fourth candle is a *bullish engulfing* candle, portending higher prices. This candle turns on a major *warning* light for the trader or investor in a short position. With this warning, what should one be looking for? The first thing to look for is what sort of follow-through there is on this bullish engulfing candle. Why? There are two reasons: the trade in progress and the potential *reversal* of the trade in progress. As indicated previously, the trader/investor will *always* want to know what the immediate bullish and bearish task is in relation to the structure and trend of the market. One of the major reasons that traders and investors lose is that they become *single-minded* about their position. The point of being aware of both bullish and bearish tasks is that it teaches the trader or investor the profit potential from being *objective* about the market. This is the primary way one becomes a *disciple* of the market. This is the ultimate origin of all *discipline* in relation to the market.

This is a lot to bring to the first few candles of a chart. Yet, as noted earlier, reading a *single* chart closely will yield most of the valuable secrets of chart reading.

After the fourth candle, the bullish engulfing candle, the immediate bullish task is to *confirm* the bullish candle. What is confirmation? For a bullish candle, irrefutably, *strong* confirmation consists of a higher high *and* a higher close in the next period. Anything less than this must be characterized either as *weak* confirmation (e.g., a higher high, but a lower close) or as *disconfirmation* (a lower high and a lower close). The bearish task is clearly to disconfirm this bullish candle and establish a *lower* market structure high, and therefore to put in place the initial condition for a downtrend. The trader/investor *knows* this before the next period begins, so there is clear preparation for what to look for.

Note that in the fifth candle, the period opened about where the prior candle closed. This is the first hint of possible weakness. Solid buying follow-through on such a strong candle signal (the bullish engulfing candle) should produce an open higher than the previous close in the following period (a "gap" or "window"). Following the open, one can see that the market went to the prior period's high and *stopped*. For whatever reason, it did not go higher.[6] Buyers said no to higher prices. Moreover, the close of the period was well into the body of the bullish engulfing candle. Buyers failed the bullish task and disconfirmed the bullish conjecture. However, the low of the period was higher than the prior low, and this established the first market structure low in the chart. This formation establishes a market structure low trigger for the following period (see arrow in Figure 14-6).

After each period, it is important to reassess the bullish and bearish tasks. This is the *work*, the necessary *adaptation* to the dynamic conditions of the market. Given the new structure, the bullish task is clearly the triggering of the market structure low. The immediate bearish task is to drive the market to a lower low and a lower closing low—first in relation to the just concluded candle, and then in relation to the prior low of the trend. It should be clear that the bullish and bearish tasks are always expressible in terms of specific prices, enabling the trader/investor to be entirely objective about the state of these forces in the market.

The short position established at the first market structure high trigger has survived a potential bullish reversal. As a result, the trader or investor would experience some relief. It is often just such relief that leads the trader/investor to lower the guard and become lax. It is extremely important not only to formulate the

---

[6] In Japanese candlestick terms, this consecutive sequence of two highs at the same price is a "tweezers" top. It signals exhaustion of buying.

bullish and bearish tasks, but also to articulate the specific events—most particularly market structure events—that would *disconfirm* the validity of the short position going into the next period. Certainly one element of disconfirmation would be the triggering of the market structure low. Thus, each new period provides the trader/investor with *specific* price behavior to watch for. This objectivity is both an important feature and the basic objective of chart reading.

The sixth period opens substantially below the close of the prior candle and serves as ample evidence of the significance of the bullish failure in the prior candle period. Not only is the market structure low *not* triggered, but the market makes both a new low and a new closing low. In the next period, the open is substantially below the close of the prior candle and the close is again at a new low. This candle, however, has a substantial *bullish* body (closing above the open), and this feature of a candle turns on a *warning* light for the trader/investor with a short position. The large bullish body is evidence of considerable buying *in spite of a new low*. Typically, this is *speculative* or *emotional* buying simply because prices are lower. It is not typically buying from *strong* buyers. Nonetheless, the bullish candle body has the potential to attract new buyers.

In the next period, the market once again opens lower and makes a new low, before buying again pushes the market to a new candle high and a higher candle close. This form of candle (where the open is within the body of the prior candle and the close is above the prior candle body) is one that I call the *sunshine* pattern and is typically bullish. Note also that the range of this candle is the largest in the chart to this point and that the range completely engulfs the range of the prior candle. Range engulfing is a reversal signal *if* it is confirmed.

Confirmation is a higher high and a higher close. As can be seen in Figure 14-6, the next session opened substantially lower and closed near the low of the day with a new low and new closing low. This again is a bullish failure. This forms a new and lower market structure high, with the trigger a tick below this candle's low. This lower market structure high provides the first formal evidence of a downtrend. The stop is quite naturally lowered to the peak of this lower market structure high.

The trader with a short position is now extremely pleased. The market made a new low, closing nearly at the low. The trader may envision a gap down in the next period and imagine that this will induce extreme selling. The vision of large gains now dances in the trader's mind, and this begins to excite the emotional background leading to *greed*. As the emotional prospect of a large profit begins to take hold, the trader/investor may forget to articulate the bullish and bearish tasks. The bearish task is straightforward: Trigger that market structure high! The bullish task is a higher high and a higher close.

The next candle opens about where the prior candle closed, but does *not* go below the prior candle low and therefore does *not* trigger the market structure high. Instead, prices rise to close substantially higher, putting a *tweezers* low in place. The trader and investor's greed is jarred, and this emotional *disparity* is again something that every trader needs to learn to control through method. This candle exhibits both bear and bull failure. It exhibits bear failure because the market structure high failed to trigger—particularly because it required only a few ticks to do so. It also exhibits a partial bull failure, because in spite of a potentially bullish candle[7] and a higher close, the buyers failed to reach a new high.

The next candle is a shock to the bulls because it opens substantially lower than the prior close and moves to a new low for the trend. It is also shocking to the bears because it moves to a new high. It is a shock to all traders because the degree of bull failure

---

[7] This is a *harami* candle. *Harami* literally means "pregnant" and refers to the image of the second candle's entire body being "inside" the prior candle's body—the mother candle. The harami formation means that "something is about to be born." And as with all births, there is a certain mystery as to what this might be. Very often a harami candle leads to greater volatility, as expressed by expansion of range—as was the case in this example.

and bear failure equalizes at the close, forming the doji candle described earlier.[8] It was noted there that the doji is commonly a *reversal* candle—particularly at extremes. This candle thus portends higher prices *if* the signal is confirmed. We know that confirmation will require a higher high and a higher close than the doji candle.

The next period was partially confirming (a higher close), but failed to set a new high. However, a market structure low was formed, and a trigger for a long-side position (or covering a short position) was set in place. The next candle *failed* to hit this trigger, moved lower to the same low as the doji candle, and then closed substantially higher. The lows at the same price *one* candle apart form a *wide-tweezers* bottom. This formation is important for several reasons. First, in spite of the failure to trigger the prior market structure low, the market did *not* achieve a new low. By the principle of alternation, a bullish failure should be followed by a bearish success. This implies that when a new low did *not* occur, it became a bearish failure. One can see that since the doji candle low, the degree of bearish failure has been increasing. The second reason that the wide-tweezers bottom is important is that it contains a "candle at a distance" pattern that is bullish. In this case, the third candle forming the wide-tweezers bottom is a bullish engulfing candle to the first candle of the wide-tweezers bottom (the doji). This should be sufficient *anticipatory* information for the trader/investor to *take gains* or to institute *gain-preservation* strategies. Moreover, the trader/investor should be prepared to go *long* if the prevailing market structure low triggers—which it does in the next period.

---

[8] Certain aspects of bull and bear failure can be measured precisely. For each candle, the degree of bull failure is the distance between the high and the close (High – Close), and the degree of bear failure is the distance between the close and the low (Close – Low). This allows the computation of a value for each candle that represents the degree of bullishness (Bear Failure – Bull Failure). Accumulating this value across candles provides a bullish index. How this will be used in trading will be illustrated further on.

The purpose of this candle-by-candle analysis has been to illustrate the nature of market structure formation and the concept of the market structure trigger as a basis for *entry* and for a *stop* on a signaled trade. It is clear from this analysis that while the next candle is *not* predictable, a *pattern of order* emerges in the flux of rising and falling prices. One expression of this order is in the formation of a *trend*. In any methodological approach to markets, trend definition ("identification"), extent of trend, and trend reversal naturally become the central focus of the trader's attention.

THE CONCEPT OF TARGET

In the analysis of the chart thus far, certain *entry* and *stop* procedures have been illustrated. The third requirement of the fundamental rule (on every entry, there should be a target and a stop), the *target*, has not yet been specified. In many ways, the target is the most difficult concept. Since the target must be based on the market's behavior as shown in the chart, many forms of "target" will not qualify. For example, "my target is a gain of 10 percent above my entry" is not a target that is in the chart. It is in the mind of the trader/investor, to be sure, but it is not in the chart.

Understanding the principle of target will require consideration of several additional methods and concepts. The concept of target will always embody some effort to specify the features of trend *exhaustion*. For this reason, methods that will *unambiguously* keep the trader and investor informed of the nature and extent of the trend in the time period of interest are required. While one may think of a trend as being only *up* or *down*, the reality is that within a trend, the market is rising and falling, falling and rising in *wave-like* fashion. Thus it follows that the trader/investor needs *wave analysis* methods as part of any trend analysis method. Market structure bull and bear lines are natural trend-determining methods. The oscillations in relation to those trend states are wavelike in nature. In approaching this double aspect of trend and wave analysis, I'll first consider the trend analysis methods and then go into the wave analysis methods used at undergroundtrader.com.

A Rule-of-Three Trend-Determining Method

The "three-period" trend-determining method is one of the simplest trend analysis and trading methods available. It is a *Rule-of-Three* method. After the first set of three periods establishes a high and a low limit, either the market will signal long or short in the next period or no signal will occur. With each successive complete period, a new set of range limits forms. This is a "rolling" three-period method of trend tracking and signaling. Figure 14-7 shows the signals this method provides in each trend phase on the chart.

Like all the methods illustrated here, the three-period method is fractal to all time periods. Whether one trades this method or

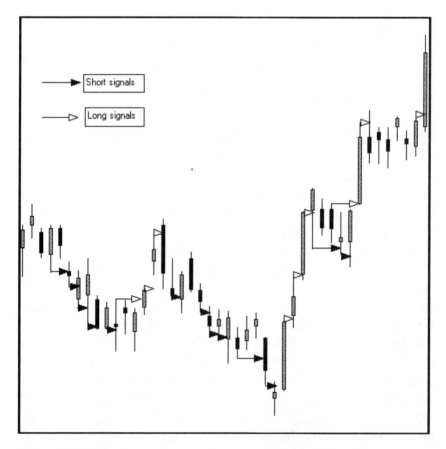

Figure 14-7   Rolling three-period range triggers as a trend-determining tool.

not, it is an excellent *contextual* support for other methods, often providing an early warning of trend change. In tracking the three-period range method, the trader will become aware of the trend "extent" associated with reversals: commonly at 3, 5, 8, or 13 entries. What this means is that after three new lows, five new lows, and so on, the trader or investor should be especially attentive to trend change. In the first trend sequence in the chart, for example, five new lows occurred and then the trend reversed, followed by three new highs before it reversed again. In the second downtrend phase, six new lows occurred. Generally, if more than five new lows occur, the market will *not* rise above the fifth new low price point, but will go to eight lows. If the fifth low price line is violated (as is the case here), the market is very likely to reverse (as it did in this example). Shortly, I'll consider why these particular "ordinals of trend" are important.

The three-period trend is extremely useful because it answers the trend question in any time period. Thus, if you want to know what the yearly trend is and you look at a yearly chart, the method will indicate the current trend state without ambiguity. The same is true for any other time window. This adds to its contextual power. As a trading method, this is an *always-in* method. The trader or investor is always either long or short the market of interest. Or, if this is used as *contextual* information, it may support trading decisions using other methods of trade entry.

Three-Price Break

Another Rule-of-Three method is drawn from a very old Japanese rice-trading method that I call *three-price break.*[9] The three-price break chart begins with two immediate distinguishing features: First, only the *closing* prices are used, and second, time is not a factor in the chart of prices. Every three-price break chart begins with a "start" price. In the example illustrated in Figure 14-8, this will

---

[9] This method has many names, among them being Shimizu's "three line break new price" and Nison's "three-line break." I prefer "three-price break" for its simplicity and its direct focus on price.

be the *close* of the first period. The start price is shown as a short horizontal line. Relative to this first start price, if the next candle has a higher or lower close, then this counts as a three-price break "event," and a new data point is marked. In this case, the close is higher, so a box is constructed on the original base. This box has two prices: the original starting price and the *new* higher close. At this point, the trend is long and has one high.[10] The third candle

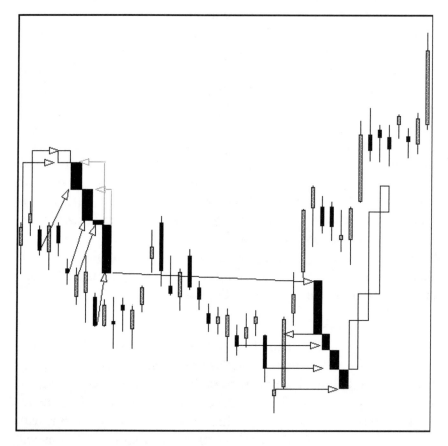

Figure 14-8   Illustration of the three-price break method of trend determination.

[10] A trend is minimally defined by two data points, in this case, the starting price and the direction of the first three-price break event. A Rule-of-Three definition will require three data points to establish trend; this will be evident in the next section, when the concept of wave is defined.

closes *below* the start price. As you can see, this down candle "breaks" both below the last close *and* below the first close. The uptrend is now broken; a downtrend has started and has one low.

The fourth candle does not make a new closing low, nor does it go above the prior closing high. Therefore, the fourth candle is a *nonevent* as far as the three-price break trend chart is concerned. If the trader is short, the trader remains short. The fifth candle closes lower, but it does not close lower than the third candle, so it is another nonevent. This illustrates how time is extracted from the chart.[11]

Two periods have gone by, but neither of them has produced a three-price break event. However, the sixth candle does indeed close lower, and so a new low is marked. At this point, consider the bearish and bullish tasks in terms of the three-price break method. The bearish task is very simple: *a new closing low*. It would not take much to make a new closing low. Even a tick lower would do it. The bullish task at this point is considerably more difficult. First, it must close above the low just set; in addition, it must close above the prior low; and, at this point, it must also close at a new high in the chart. That would be quite a large move in one period. Therefore, the probability favors the short side.

The seventh candle gaps down on the open, goes to a new low, and then rallies. Nonetheless, the *close* is in fact a lower close, and so this counts as a three-price break event. This close produces only a small addition to the three-price break chart. With the three down boxes, it may become easier to see why the method is called "three-price" break. In order to break the downtrend at this point, the market now need not close at a new high, but only above the top of the first box down in this trend, marked by a gray arrow. At this point, there is an evident downtrend with three new lows. For the trend to reverse, the market must close above those three closing price points. The eighth candle makes a new low in the trend but not a new closing low. The ninth candle,

---

[11] It should be apparent that the three-price break method automatically creates a range within which price movement is considered "noise."

however, makes a new closing low and so is a three-price break event. Now there are four new lows, and the new "break price" is moved lower as well. The bullish task here is to close above the highest price point (the top) of the third box from the low. This is again marked with a gray arrow.

Now something very interesting happens. Over the course of the next 14 periods, the market fails to make a new closing low, makes a strong move up but fails to break the three-price break trend, and then begins falling again. There are 14 periods of "no change." These nonevent periods I call "skip" periods. Later on, I will go over the rules for holding a position or exiting it based on certain skip-period characteristics. Long skip periods are ineffi- cient for money at risk and will often be periods of countertrend moves against the trend position, as is the case in this chart.

Fifteen candles later, the market puts in a new closing low, the fifth low. And if you follow the progression of new lows, you will see that the trend comes to an end with seven lows. The large upside candle that completed the morning star candle pattern described earlier is the first candle to close above an upside break price. From this point to the end of the chart, the market makes new closing highs (to the seventh new high at the chart's last can- dle). In terms of the three-price break trend method, there was one sizable downtrend (to seven lows) and one sizable uptrend (with seven highs). The method is very precise and always yields a defi- nite trend determination of long or short in *any* time period of interest to the trader or investor.

MARKET STRUCTURE AND THE CONCEPT OF WAVE

The outstanding feature of any financial market is the rise and fall of prices. Even when prices are moving strongly in one direction (the trend), the market persists in exhibiting an unceasing ten- dency for prices to rise and fall along that trend. A rising market has similarities to a high tide; a falling market, to a low tide. Yet even at the highest or lowest tide, the ebb and flow of waves, in and out, persists. In effect, the tidal rhythm is a larger and more persistent version of the waves one sees on the surface of the water.

The word *wave* derives etymologically from the Indo-European root -*webh*, meaning "weave." The essential nature of weaving involves the "back-and-forth" movement of a shuttle interlacing the warp threads and the woof threads, gradually growing into a pattern. Likewise, the up-and-down movement of prices gives rise to *structures* that grow into *patterns*. The images embedded in this statement are crucial to understanding the nature of price behavior in and through time and the necessity for a method that will reveal structures, growth, and patterns. In this section, each of these elements—structure, growth, and pattern—will be considered.

Earlier, one method of establishing the direction of a trend was the use of bull and bear lines, or projections drawn between market structure points (see Figure 14-4). Trends are *always* defined by *two* points. Extending the use of market structure to *three* points (a Rule-of-Three procedure) identifies *triangular* market structures (see Figure 14-9). An *upside* structure is defined as a market structure low followed by a higher market structure low, with the triangular point being the highest price *between* the two. A *downside* structure is defined as a market structure high followed by a lower market structure high, with the triangular point being the lowest price *between* the two. It should be clear that an upside structure will always project a bull trend line and a downside structure will always project a bear tend line. Once a triangular structure fully forms, its "projection" (properly considered a *vector*) divides the "future" price/time space into two domains: bullish (e.g., above a bear line and above a bull line) and bearish (below a bear line and below a bull line). Figure 14-10 illustrates this division of price/time space.

Note that going forward, the bear zone (that below the bull line) *also* rises. Thus, entering into the bear domain *even at higher prices* alerts the trader or investor to the potential weakening of the upside movement. This weakening becomes manifest when a downside market structure triangle develops.

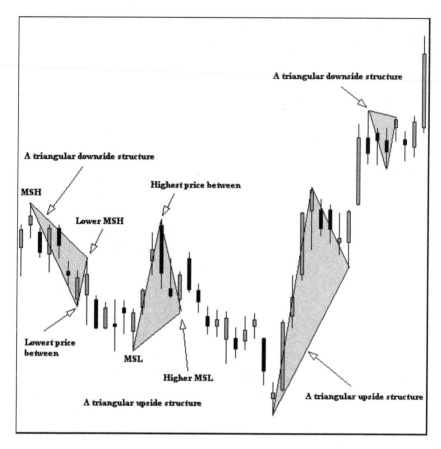

Figure 14-9   Illustration of triangular structures developed from a sequence of market structure points.

It should now be clear that a market structure *triangle* is the formal definition of a *wave*.

The Concept of Wave Growth

When a market reaches a low point, rises, and then falls to a higher low, the conditions for an upside structure exist. The low point, the high point, and the higher low point form a triangular structure that can be considered an upside or bullish wave. A line drawn from the low through the higher low forms a bullish trend line, projecting a bullish vector rising into the future. This rising line supports prices moving higher into the bullish domain pictured in Figure 14-10. An

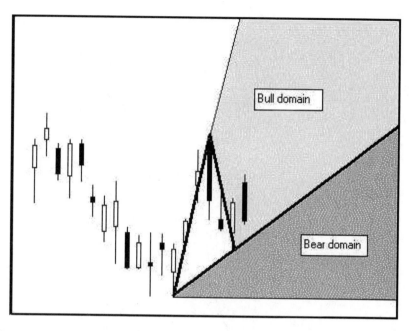

Figure 14-10 The triangular array following the formation of an upside structure, showing the projected bull and bear domains.

upside structure or wave illustrates two objective conditions: Buyers have shown the capacity to move the market higher (that is, to the market structure high peak between the low and the higher low), and *after* this, sellers have *failed* to move the market to a new low. This higher market structure low is a critical market event, as it forms a *higher-order* market structure low. (See Figure 14-11.) This higher-order structure, formed by a low market structure low, followed by a lower market structure low, followed by a higher market structure low, implies even more strongly the typical meaning of a simple market structure low—the exhaustion of selling. It is this setup that sets the stage for buyers to "build on" the initial upside structure. The essential *meaning* of growth is that buyers will be willing to buy at a *higher* price than they did in the initial wave.

Factors in Wave Growth

Buyers who bought at the low of the initial wave may be considered *aggressive* or speculative buyers. After all, this new low

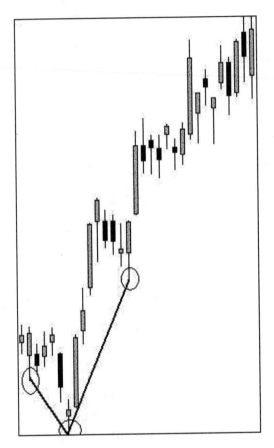

Figure 14-11   Higher-order market structure low composed of three market structure lows.

(referred to as the *reference* low in Figure 14-11) follows a prior low, and there is nothing structurally or in the trend to suggest that the market will turn here. These buyers are *anticipating* a potential alternation move—perhaps because the market has moved so far away from the highs. The next candle, setting up the bullish morning star candle pattern, vindicates and rewards these early buyers. Generally, such traders are short-term traders and so will be increasingly likely to take gains as the market moves higher and runs into context resistance, such as the original context line.

The bulk of the traders in an initial upside wave may be thought of as *anticipatory* traders, who act on their anticipation of market turns. Such traders may easily become short sellers as the market moves higher, once again anticipating a short-term reversal. For this reason, we may characterize the initial wave as the *anticipatory* wave. Once the anticipatory wave completes the upside structure and forms the projected bull line and creates the bull domain in the future, what is it that the anticipatory wave anticipates? When this market structure is completed, the short-term traders are ready to go long again.

Moreover, many more buyers are now likely to come into the market *because* a new low did not occur. These traders are not as speculative as the anticipatory-wave traders. Moreover, they are more likely to be committed to the upside *trend*. It is likely to take more to get these traders to leave a trade than it would take to get the anticipatory traders to leave. Generally, upside structure traders will be larger in number and will buy more eagerly than anticipatory traders. In effect, they are buying more confidently because they believe that the trend has turned, and they are looking for larger gains.

As the market moves higher, more trend buyers are recruited as the trend begins to confirm itself by moving higher. As the new upside trend breaks through important context resistance points, yet more buyers are recruited. This influx of steady buyers will eventually attract buyers who are buying not because they are committed to the trend, but because the market is moving up. These *emotional* buyers cannot resist buying when the market is moving higher. They are the "greed" buyers. The higher the market move goes, the more greed buyers will become a part of the move. These buyers will also exit very quickly if the market begins to oscillate down, as they are not committed to the trend, but only to the emotional state. Greed can quickly turn to fear, so as a market turns, the emotional traders tend to provide fuel for any subsequent down move as they panic and become active sellers.

With all the fresh buying for the various reasons indicated, the next wave is likely to move higher than the anticipatory wave. I call this wave the *impulse wave*, partly because it typically appears to be a simple wave, with each successive period likely to produce a new high and a new high close, and partly because this is the feature in a chart that attracts impulse buyers—buyers who are buying because the market is moving strongly higher. Nothing seems simpler in trading than buying when period after period the market is making new highs and new high closes.

As the impulse wave extends its growth, it will begin to encounter fresh areas of context resistance. This is likely to turn the shorter-term anticipatory traders into sellers as they take gains. Any slowdown or turn in the market, and certainly the formation of a market structure high, may begin to unsettle the impulse buyers because the market now appears to be headed lower. This may also be a cue for short-term anticipatory short sellers to step in and begin selling. The market's moving down may cause the impulse buyers to sell as well. Only those who are more strongly committed to the uptrend will stay committed through an oscillation down; they are particularly likely to stay if prices remain in the bull domain.

At some point the impulse wave will end, more than likely at a price level higher than the peak of the anticipatory wave. What is likely to happen *next?* The Rule of Three suggests that we should expect *three* waves. Certainly most things that we think of as "growing" tend to grow in three basic stages: immature, mature, and old. While each stage may be broken down further (e.g., infant, child, adolescent), in studying the growth of most living things (and many nonliving things as well), the existence of three major stages appears to be ubiquitous.

Applying this rule to the financial markets, we may begin with the assumption that following an initial anticipatory wave and an impulse wave, we may expect to see a third growth wave. Figure 14-12 illustrates an idealized version of three-wave growth. I have termed the third wave the *limit wave* because it is likely to contain the limit to which the initial anticipatory wave will grow.

In any natural growth function, growth tends toward a limiting condition. Typically, growth in a limiting condition tends to be different in various ways from that in earlier growth periods. One way to characterize these differences is to consider the limit wave to be *complex.* In relation to the financial markets, one way in which this complexity exhibits itself is in the fact that the limit wave is itself

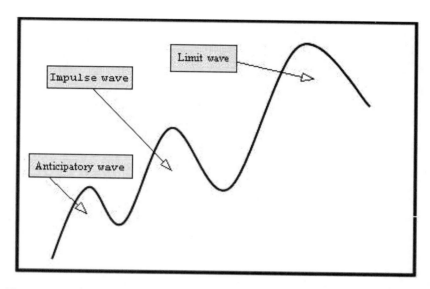

Figure 14-12   Idealized Rule-of-Three growth pattern showing the anticipatory wave, the impulse wave, and the limit wave.

frequently composed of three distinct subwaves. Figure 14-13 shows an idealized form of a complex limit-wave growth pattern.[12]

The Concept of Wave Failure

Once an upside anticipatory wave is complete, the first bullish task is to move prices higher than the peak of the anticipatory wave. I call this market event *registration*. When this occurs, we may say that the impulse wave has registered. Likewise, when the limit wave exceeds the peak of the impulse wave, we may say that the limit wave has registered. If the impulse wave does not register, then we may say that the impulse wave has *failed*. Likewise, if the limit wave does not register by exceeding the limit of the impulse wave, then we say that the limit wave has failed. Generally, limit-wave failure is more common than impulse-wave failure, and impulse-wave failure itself is uncommon.

---

[12] Keep in mind that these characterizations of wave growth are fractal, which means that this same patterning of wave growth is expected to be seen regardless of period, whether one is looking at a 1-minute chart or a monthly chart.

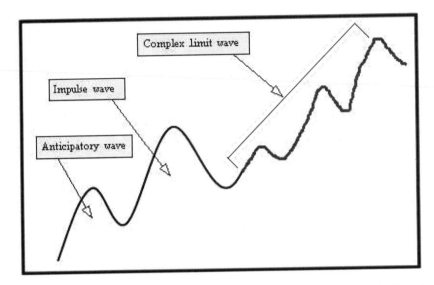

Figure 14-13   An idealized version of the more typically complex pattern shown by the limit wave.

Wave failure is important because it quickly sets the stage for the formation of a *downside* anticipatory wave that may reverse the uptrend in progress. The trader and investor should be particularly watchful for wave 3 failures, as this can lead to dramatic trend reversal. Wave 5 failure seems to bring with it a period of quiet indecision before the downside anticipatory-wave function is completed. This is an additional aspect of the complexity of the limit wave. It follows that the impulse wave, whether formed in upside structures or downside structures, is likely to be the easiest wave to trade, as it tends toward simplicity and infrequent failure.

THE CONCEPT OF TIME LIMIT ON WAVE GROWTH

How does the trader or investor know how long to wait before determining that the impulse wave or the limit wave is going to be a failure? How long should one wait for the formation of an anticipatory wave? How long should one wait for the completion of the limit wave? These questions are equally applicable regardless of the period traded, whether one is looking at a 5-minute chart or a monthly chart. Each of these questions has to do with the issue of time limiting. Is there a way to answer these questions other than by imposing some arbitrary scheme? Is there some *natural* approach to time limits that can be adapted to the financial markets, in the same way that there may be natural limits on growth in prices as discussed in the prior section? These *time* questions are similar to the price questions relating to the growth limits of the waves. That is, is there a way of estimating the peak of the anticipatory wave? Can we use the size of the anticipatory wave to estimate the growth peak of the impulse wave and the limit wave?

Fortunately, an approach is available that will be of major value in answering both the price and time questions and will prove to be of major value to the trader and investor.

The Fibonacci Number Series and the Growth Spiral

Plants and animals do not grow in a haphazard manner. There is an order of some kind, in terms of both the rate of growth and the ultimate size of growth. This order occurs at all divisions or multiplications of scale, from the microscopic to the telescopic. Indeed, many elements of the solar system, galaxies, and other inconceivably large elements of the universe grow in time and in size in very orderly ways. Everything in the universe grows and decays, and it is remarkable that this enormous range of growth and decay is describable in terms of a strikingly small number of mathematical functions.[13] Clearly, the financial markets grow and decay like everything else in the universe. Perhaps one or more of a small number of mathematical functions may serve useful purposes in answering the questions just raised regarding price and time.

---

[13] Sir Martin Rees, Britain's Astronomer Royal, in his book *Just Six Numbers* (New York: Basic Books, 2000), theorized that at the moment of the "big bang," an inconceivably small number of mathematical functions—just six numbers—determined the form of everything to come.

Chief among this small set of growth functions is the Fibonacci[14] number series. Everyone is familiar with number series, even if they do not know it. For example, one's age is a number series. The series has the form 1, $(1 + 1)$, $(2 + 1)$, $(3 + 1)$, ..., $(n + 1)$. As you can see, each number in this series is generated by adding the constant 1 to the number before it. In this way, if one knows that one's age is 56, then at one's next birthday one will be $56 + 1$, or 57. We *know* that financial markets do not "grow" in this way, although hours in the day, days in the week, days of the month, and days in the year *do* grow in this fashion. This integer growth system has many important applications, but it is not particularly useful in the financial markets.

Now consider the Fibonacci number series:

0, 1, 1, 2, 3, 5, 8, 13, 21, 34, 55, 89, 144, ..., (????)

How is this series generated? The rule is quite simple. Starting with the *initial* pair $(0, 1)$, the sum of the pair is determined, and that sum becomes the next value in the series. Thus, $0 + 1 = 1$; $1 + 1 = 2$; $1 + 2 = 3$; $2 + 3 = 5$, and so on. As this series grows, the numbers become quite large. However, what is striking about this series of generated sums is that after a certain number of sums, the *relationship* between the numbers becomes a constant. That is, each number divided by its predecessor (e.g., 144/89) will have the same constant value, 1.618, and each number divided by its successor (e.g., 89/144) will also become a constant, 0.618. If we skip one over (for example, 144 divided by

---

[14] Leonardo Pisano Fibonacci (1170–1250). The famous number series first appeared in his *Liber Abaci* in 1202. For a modern treatment of the power of Fibonacci principles in trading, see Robert Fischer's *Fibonacci Applications and Strategies for Traders* (New York: John Wiley and Sons, Inc., 1993) and *The New Fibonacci Trader: Tools and Strategies for Trader Success* (New York: John Wiley & Sons, Inc., 2001).

55), we get the constant 2.618, and dividing the other way yields the constant 0.382.[15]

The first degree of growth factor in this series is 1.618. That is, we can take any particular value in the series x and determine the next value by multiplying x by 1.618. We can get the following value in the series by multiplying x by 2.618. The sequence works in reverse as well, and so we can get the prior number in the series by dividing x by 1.618. Doing this repeatedly produces a series of numbers that become infinitely small and infinitely large.

Dividing a line x of any length by 1.618 divides the line into two parts with lengths $0.618x$ and $0.382x$. This division of the line is called the *golden section,* and it is the most important division of distance both historically and psychologically. Historically, this golden ratio division is the central mathematical principle in architecture, perspective, and almost all art forms. Psychologically, this ratio produces the most emotionally pleasing division and characterizes the most productive degree of creative tension. Moreover, enormous and diverse categories of plants and animals grow and reproduce in accordance with this growth function: The distribution of plant leaves, the growth of the snail's shell, and the growth of galaxies all grow in size, density, number, pattern, and so on as a function of the Fibonacci spiral.

We will use the Fibonacci growth spiral to make some normative assumptions about the growth of waves in the financial markets. We shall assume that the anticipatory wave will be equal to size x. This is the wave that will "grow." We shall assume that the impulse wave will grow to $1.618 \times x$ in size, multiplying the size of the anticipatory wave by 1.618. We shall assume that the limit

---

[15] These properties are not limited to the Fibonacci number series but are a feature of any summative series beginning with any pair of numbers. After a certain number of summations (typically the eighth pair), these constants will begin to characterize the series. I will focus here on the Fibonacci sequence because its ordinal values (1, 3, 5, 8, 13, 21, 34, etc.) have been found to have special applicability to the financial markets.

wave will be limited to the second-degree growth factor of the Fibonacci series, or $2.618 \times x$.

How do we apply this to *time?* The first question about time has to do with the temporal definition of the anticipatory wave. How many periods apart must the reference low and the structuring low be in order to qualify? Is there a minimum? A maximum? We shall use the Fibonacci number series itself to help answer these questions. It was noted earlier that a structure sharing a candle in common with another structure was weak. The minimum number of periods between structures with no period is 4. If we add a further requirement that no common members can be adjacent, then the minimum number is 5. Since 5 is a Fibonacci number, this will be considered the *minimum* requirement for wave structuring: 5 periods, counting from the reference structure to the structuring period.

In the Fibonacci series, it is at the eighth ordinal point that the ratios between the series values become constant values. The eighth ordinal is the number 13. Since this point is the point in the series at which there is no further change in the growth constant, this would seem to be a reasonable basis for taking 13 periods as the maximum number of periods by which a reference point and a structuring point can be separated in order to constitute a "coherent" wave.[16]

This provides us with a window of 5 to 13 periods from a reference low for the complete formation of an anticipatory wave. If

---

[16] There are other approaches as well that arrive at the number 13 as defining the limit of a coherent structure. The pyramids, for example, are built according to the "growth" of the number 13. Stonehenge is built precisely on the spot where 13 describes the hypotenuse of a triangle (the sides being 5 and 12) with the base at the Blue Stone in Wales and at Lundy Island in the Bristol Channel. The point at the Channel's Calday Island divides the base 5 precisely into 2 and 3. The length of the hypotenuse drawn from this point to Stonehenge is 12.368. This is exactly the number of full moons in a solar year. It is extraordinary that Stone Age peoples would be able to build such a sophisticated "clock" as Stonehenge is and to locate it at precisely 13 units from the Blue Stone origin in Wales. Astonishingly, the continuation of this line crosses precisely at the location of the Great Pyramid at Giza, which had not yet been constructed at the time of the completion of Stonehenge.

we take the maximum period and multiply by 1.618, we arrive at 21 periods. This will become the nominal time point by which time the impulse wave should reach its growth limit. Multiplying 13 by 2.618 yields 34 periods, which will be considered the nominal time point by which the limit wave should reach its growth limit. Figure 14-14 illustrates these relationships.

This 34-period window in any time period (34 five-minute periods, 34 monthly periods, and so on) will be referred to as the *price/time box*.

APPLICATION OF FIBONACCI TARGETS AND WAVE REGISTRATION

The nominally expected limits on the growth of the *impulse wave* and the *limit wave* are price and time *targets*. The lowest low in the chart we have been studying occurred in the context of the for-

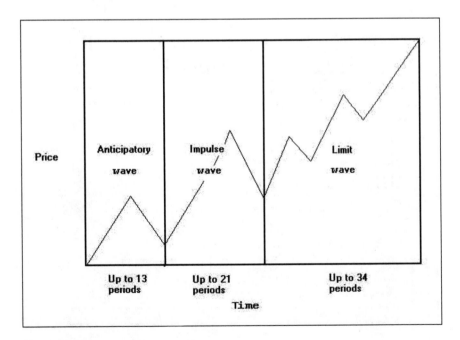

Figure 14-14   The nominal price/time box.

mation of a bullish evening star-candle pattern. Figure 14-15 begins at this point and follows the *daily* price chart of Verizon Communications (VZ) from September 26 through December 13, 2002.

The bullish evening star formation produces the subsequent gapping body windows to the market structure high of the anticipatory wave, from the reference low at 26.75 to 33.65. This 6.90-point wave is what will be projected to grow into the impulse wave and the limit wave. Of course, we cannot tell where the peak of the anticipatory wave will be until a higher market structure low occurs. This occurred in the 9th candle from the reference low and was completed with the 10th candle. Note that the impulse wave registered when it went a tick higher than the anticipatory wave. In

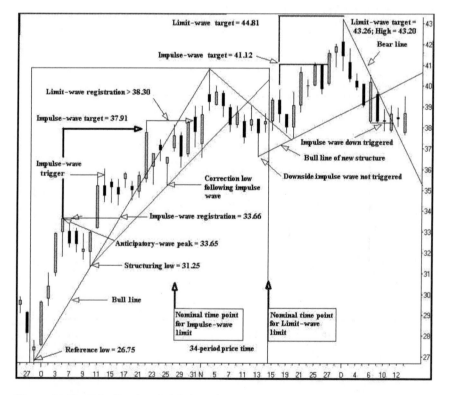

Figure 14-15   Price/time box for VZ from September 26 through December 13, 2002.

this case, the market behavior set up a very high impulse wave trigger, just above the high of the 10th candle.[17]

Once the peak of the anticipatory wave is known, the impulse wave target can be calculated: $6.90 \times 1.618 = 11.16$. This is the projected growth from the reference low. Thus, $26.75 + 11.16 = 37.91$. The chart shows that this target was hit in the 17th candle period on a high at 38.30. Note that there was a slight overshoot on the high, but that the close was at 37.75, below the target. In the next session, the open was substantially below the close. This illustrates a general rule: *When the market hits a wave target, take the gain promptly.*[18]

Notice that following the impulse-wave high at the target, the market begins to fall below the rising bull line and thus falls into the bear domain. This will be true until a *new* higher market structure low is formed, which will be the correction low following the impulse peak. We won't know exactly where the correction low will be until it forms and is triggered long for the limit wave. The limit wave will be registered only if there is a price rise above the high of the impulse wave. Once this occurs, or a market structure low triggers, then the correction low can be determined precisely.

Once this low is known, a *secondary* bull line is drawn from the original structuring low through the correction low of the impulse wave. This creates a secondary bull domain that is the general province of the limit wave. The limit wave was triggered long and registered at the same price point, that is, greater than 38.30. The high that was reached following this point was 40.74, with the limit-wave target being 44.81 ($6.90 \times 2.618 = 18.06 + 26.75 = 44.81$). Recall that the limit wave tends to be complex, and therefore the first wave up in the limit-wave phase must be assessed carefully. For example, following the trigger and registration, the market closed lower. The next session it opened lower and

---

[17] This illustrates that a wave can register before it triggers on a market structure trigger basis. For this reason, both the trigger and the registration are entry points, either separately (i.e., whichever comes first) or compounded (dual entry points).

[18] In a later discussion, I will describe how to use gain-preservation strategies as an alternative to taking gains. However, in most instances, taking gains when the target is hit is the simplest and best strategy.

put in a lower low, before closing higher and forming a bullish engulfing candle. Since the stop was likely to be placed at the correction low or the next higher market structure low, one would still be long and would be long into the high in the following session.

After the high was hit the following day, prices moved to close below the open and formed the pattern called a *shooting star*. Generally, if a shooting star forms in a long-side trade and one remains long, the stop should be raised to a tick below that candle. In the next session, there is a small bullish engulfing candle, but a market structure high formed. This requires raising the stop to the market structure high trigger point, and the trader will need to make a decision as to whether this is a stop only or a stop and reverse.

The typical problem with limit waves, and why they become complex, is that as time goes by, downside structures form. This will not happen in a strong limit wave, and it is quite rare in impulse waves. Another complication with the limit wave is that it will be limited by the 34-period time limit for completion. Figure 14-15 shows the 34-period price/time box with an arrow pointing to the nominal time limit for the limit wave to reach its nominal peak at 44.81. The impulse wave reached its peak prior to its nominal time limit (21 periods). It is rather common for the impulse wave to reach its peak on or before the nominal time point, but for time to run out on limit-wave completion.

This relates to what I term *wave coherence*. After the high occurred, several sessions went by before a downside structure formed near the end of the box. A fully formed downside structure that is *triggered* is the formal definition of the *end of wave*. The formation of downside structures occurs most often in limit waves, and for this reason they begin to lose coherence as upside waves and begin to unfold as full-fledged downside structures.

DYNAMIC WAVE ANALYSIS

Since the publication of Ralph Nelson Elliott's monograph entitled *The Wave Principle* in 1938, and the subsequent development of

Elliott wave analysis by Robert R. Prechter, Jr., and others,[19] the fundamental approach to wave analysis has remained essentially unchanged. That is, a complete major wave cycle is considered to consist of three advancing waves followed by two declining waves— with each peak and trough included, a total of eight major waves, as shown in Figure 14-16. Each major wave in turn consists of subwaves. The analysis of the order and relation of waves has led to enormous complexities in attempting to determine a proper wave count and degree that can be objectively agreed upon. In many

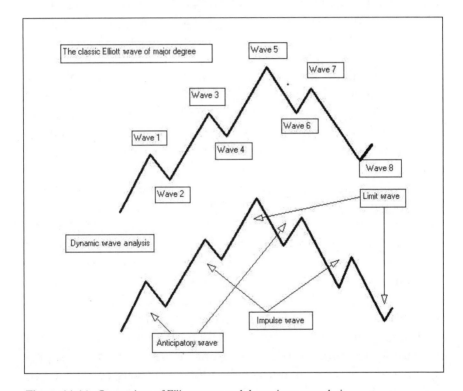

Figure 14-16 Comparison of Elliott waves and dynamic wave analysis.

[19] For further study, see Robert R Prechter, Jr., *The Major Works of R. N. Elliott* (Chappaqua, N.Y.: New Classics Library, 1980); A. J. Frost and Robert R. Prechter, Jr., *Elliott Wave Principle: Key to Market Behavior* (Chappaqua, N.Y.: New Classics Library, 1978); and Robert R. Prechter, Jr., *Conquer the Crash: You Can Survive and Prosper in a Deflationary Depression* (New York: John Wiley & Sons, 2002).

circumstances, the uncertainties and multiplicities of Elliott wave analysis have made it difficult for traders to act on the resulting conclusions. Traders are often frustrated by "reconstructed" wave counts following the market's unanticipated behavior.

In seeking a simpler approach, yet one that is nonetheless based on the underlying Fibonacci principles of wave generation and growth, I have developed the Rule-of-Three approach to dynamic wave analysis. As has been shown in the prior sections, this approach proposes that there are always three basic waves in market behavior: an anticipatory wave, an impulse wave, and a limit wave. This is true for *both* the bull and bear phases of a market cycle. The bull cycle is *symmetrical* to the bear cycle, with each cycle being nominally composed of three waves: anticipatory, impulse, and limit. In addition, dynamic wave analysis, following the requirements of wave coherence, places wave development in the context of time limitations on growth. Moreover, wave failure can cut short the completion of a wave cycle and lead directly to the next three-wave cycle. Dynamic wave analysis is fractal to all time frames, from minutes to any longer period of time.

To illustrate a downside structure, consider the Nasdaq 100 price behavior between March 2000 and December 2002, as shown in Figure 14-17. Here the anticipatory wave completes its structure after 7 periods (peak to lower market structure high) and is triggered short in the 9th candle from the peak. The impulse wave completed its low by forming a monthly market structure low in the 14th period. The complex limit wave was triggered short in the 17th period, was registered in the 19th candle, and achieved the lowest point in the 32nd candle. The price/time box expired at the end of December 2002. This meant that from a price/time perspective, the great bear market of 2000–2002 was coming to an end prior to the completion of the third wave down in the complex limit wave. Time cuts short the completion of the limit wave. A new downside structure may form, in which case it would be a *new* structural bear market.

From the end of December 2002, a new 34-month price/time box begins. Whether this will be a bull cycle or a new bear cycle,

Figure 14-17   Downside market structure for monthly Nasdaq 100.

no one knows. A bull cycle is unlikely to begin, however, until a monthly upside wave structure forms. Notice that there were no triggered monthly upside structures throughout the duration of the bear market of 2000–2002.

This chapter has been focused on an initial set of tools for the trader's toolbox. The critical tools are those that allow the trader to immediately assess the *trend state* of any market in any time frame (three-price break, three-period range, market structure bull and bear lines). In addition, these tools enable the trader to pinpoint the entry price into a signaled trade (market structure and candle pattern triggers), to identify meaningful price points for stops (market structure triggers, candle patterns, three-price trend breaks, three-period range breaks), and to meaningfully identify price targets for gain taking (Fibonacci wave growth targets, three-price break ordinals of trend, candle patterns).

This initial set of tools works well together in practice. In the next chapter, the tool set will be developed further, and examples will illustrate how the methods can be combined to increase the effectiveness of the tool set in trading in any market and in any time frame.

Advanced Methods for the Trader's Toolbox

The basic methods raise questions that lead to the analysis of the deeper structures of market behavior and require the trader and investor to have a more complete awareness of the context variables in order to more fully appreciate the behavior of the financial markets. In addition, there are practical issues related to putting the basic and advanced methods to work, assessing trading behavior, and dealing with the necessity for discipline. Play-by-play illustrations will detail the use of the methods in both intraday and longer-term trading. The ever-changing nature of the financial markets is a challenge to every trader and investor. The key to success lies in discovering those elements in human behavior that are relatively unchanging and that, in the end, determine how the markets behave. The fundamental methods learned here will serve any trader or investor as solid ground on which confidence and trust in one's own behavior can become the basis for a profitable and enjoyable experience in the markets—no matter how perverse the markets may seem.

DEEP STRUCTURE

Before illustrating examples of the use of these methods in different markets under various conditions in more detail, it is important to consider additional context variables that will enable the trader and investor to better understand the behavior of the financial markets. We have seen that there is a constant effort to "explain" the market's behavior and that, in general, these explanations are always "after the fact"; thus, they cannot be used successfully in actual trading, and their explanatory potential is minimal at best. The reason for this is that the *actual* determiners of market behavior are hidden from view in the "deep structure" of the market. Deep structure is similar in many ways to the concept of the unconscious in psychology, the deep structure in humans that determines what is visible in human behavior. The behavior of the financial markets is more likely to be the *result* of causative factors (e.g., cultural mood states, general crowd phenomena, collective emotional expectation and extremity, and so on) than to be a causative factor itself. Of course, the complexity involved is such that market behavior will become an interactive factor as well, with major declines or rises interactively contributing to these other factors.

The important point, however, is that the actual causes of market behavior cannot be precisely known. While social mood may play a large part in determining market behavior, it is often only in retrospect that this can be seen clearly enough to be understood. In many respects the mechanisms of these factors lie hidden in the market's deep structure and are of no practical or immediate use in trading, even if they are actual trends that will eventually materialize in the market's behavior.

What *is* of use in trading is the transformation of these larger causative factors into phenomena that can be *seen in the chart of current prices* and *acted upon*. That is, no matter what the hidden causes of market behavior may be, the trader or investor cannot trade on the results of analyzing these factors—to whatever extent such analysis is possible. The trader or investor must *always* require the appearance *in the chart* of correspondences to any deeper analytic insights. For example, we know that both social and emotional mood and collective trends rise and fall, moving from one extreme to another with interludes of seeming uneventfulness, and that these *extremities* of mood and emotion may be part of the causative nexus of major market movements.[1] But discerning these factors is at least as complex as discerning the movements of the market itself. However, it would prove useful if the trader and investor had a tool that could provide context information indicating when prices have "gone extreme" and that would satisfy all the methodological requirements previously described and be applicable to all markets in all time frames. For this, we make use of a modification of a long-standing technical analysis solution to this question—what I have termed *extreme Fibonacci Bollinger bands.*

EXTREME FIBONACCI BOLLINGER BANDS AND MOVING AVERAGE SHIFTS

The essential reason that the trader or investor is interested in the *extremity* of any market movement is the foreknowledge that such movements to extremes are the essential conditions for major *turns* in the market. Extremity will always be one of the major conditions of market exhaustion and market reversal. Measures of extremity always involve some measure of the "standard," "usual," "expected," or "normal" *range* of trading (the so-called measures of central tendency), as well as some way of assessing when prices have "gone out of bounds" (that is, measures of inordinate degree of variance).

John Bollinger developed one of the earliest and most enduring measures of extremity. The basic method involves calculating a moving average and then plotting a value of 2 standard deviations

---

[1] A major contribution to this area of study is Robert Prechter, *Socionomics: The Science of History and Social Prediction* (Gainsville, GA.: New Classics Library, 2003). This work is highly recommended to all traders and investors.

above and below the moving average, referred to as "bands." This method uses one of the most popular moving averages (20 periods) and a standard statistical value for measuring deviation (1.96 standard deviations, rounded to 2).[2]

My suggested values for this indicator are significantly different, and for this reason I refer to the method as the *extreme Fibonacci Bollinger bands* (EFBB). Several features are different. First, the measure of central tendency is based on a 13-period moving average, which reflects the maximum number of periods for forming coherent wave structures, as described earlier.[3] Second, the degree of deviation used for constructing the upper and lower bands is the second-degree Fibonacci growth constant, 2.618. Thus, both the exponential moving average (ema) and the degree of deviation are based on Fibonacci values. Third, the calculated moving average is shifted *forward* in time by 3 periods, again a Fibonacci-based value. Fourth, a second moving average is added. This is a 3-period exponential moving average that is shifted *backward* in time by 3 periods.

The purpose of the use of *shifted* moving averages is to minimize the "whipsawing" effects of prices in and around measures of central tendency. The use of the 13-period, 3-shift (forward) moving average has this purpose.[4] However, the 3-period, 3-shift (backward) moving average has a different function. It is recognized that markets will not always go to an extreme and reverse at once. Rather, quite often markets will *stay* in an extreme condition for several periods. The purpose of the 3-period, 3-shift (backward) moving average is its *intersection* with the EFBB envelope.

---

[2] This degree of deviation is a standard statistical test for determining the likelihood of an event's being sufficiently different from a "chance" deviation as to be considered "significant."

[3] In computing the moving average component, the exponential method is used to give greater weight to the successively later values in the series. Most charting programs enable exponential moving averages to be computed as easily as simple moving averages.

[4] I am indebted to Terry R. Davis and his *Commodity Method* (private publication, 1989) and his teachings on the value of time-shifted moving averages.

This can be seen and its significance appreciated more readily from an illustration.

Figure 15-1 shows the daily price chart for MSFT from September 10 to December 27, 2002. Note that at the end of September, MSFT reached the low of the downtrend in the bear market to that date, and that this low rested on the lower EFBB. Over the next few sessions, MSFT formed a 5-period upside structure that was triggered long in the 7th candle from the low. The market did not trigger the stop set at a tick below the reference low. In the 9th candle, the market took off strongly to the upside, closing above the 13-period 3-shift (forward) ema. Over the next 3 sessions, the market moved substantially higher. Note that as the market advanced quickly, the 3-period-shifted (backward) ema "crossed" the upper EFBB line.

This cross may be taken as a warning light, and the trader or investor needs to plan gain-taking strategies. Remember, in real time, when that cross occurs, the candle in progress will be 4 periods ahead. It is at about this point that the market begins to move away from the upper EFBB as the extremity move begins to consolidate. Typically, this is a good point to take gains. When the 3-period-shifted (backward) ema crosses back below the upper EFBB, this can be taken as a final signal to take gains. The arrow points to the candle where gains would be taken in real time as the 3-period-shifted (backward) ema crosses back below the upper EFBB. When that cross occurred, MSFT had reached 53.20, and the limit-wave target from the earlier anticipatory wave was at 52.81. This is an excellent example of the convergence of the basic method (wave targets) with a powerful context factor (the 3-shift recross of the EFBB).

MSFT had formed an upside anticipatory structure that was triggered after hitting the lower EFBB. Here the lower EFBB can serve as strong *contextual* information, even instruction. That is, with MSFT having reached a bearish *extremity* (the lower EFBB), the trader or investor begins to look for signals to go long. One major signal would be the triggering of an upside anticipatory wave, as is the case in this illustration. A second signal in this context would be a close above the 13-period 3-shifted (forward) ema,

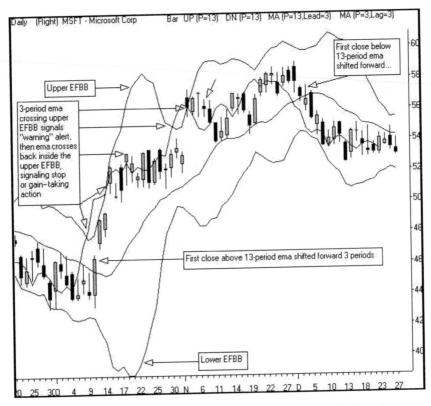

Figure 15-1 Daily price chart for MSFT showing the extreme Fibonacci Bollinger bands, the 13-period 3-shift (forward) ema tool, and the 3-period 3-shift (backward) ema tool.

which also occurs in this illustration. Note also the convergence of methods. The crossing back below the EFBB signaled an exit in the market on the basis of *extremity* conditions in the candle-stick period in which MSFT also hit the limit-wave target. There followed several periods of consolidation. *The convergence of several methodological factors at the same price and time level is always a good set of conditions to use as an exit or gain-taking strategy.*

Note that when the market consolidates, the EFBB differential (that is, the difference between the upper and lower bands) becomes smaller, and when the market has made an extreme move, the differential becomes much larger. Figure 15-2 illustrates the value of attending to the EFBB constriction. This is a chart of the S&P 500 futures in a 13-minute time frame. As the constriction narrows with each successive period in a narrow range, the breakout/breakdown points tend to be associated with Fibonacci ordinals, 8, 13, and 21 being the most common periods of consolidation before the narrowing resolves into a sizable move. The ordinal will not in itself indicate the direction of the move, but there will often be a directional signal present as the tension of the consolidation begins to unwind. In this case, the market closed below the 13-period 3-shift (forward) ema for the first time. In addition, the downside structure registered the impulse wave down and the 13th-candle period announced the potential for a breakdown under these conditions. In this case, the market went into a persistent decline, a good example of a market going to an extreme and staying extreme for a long period.

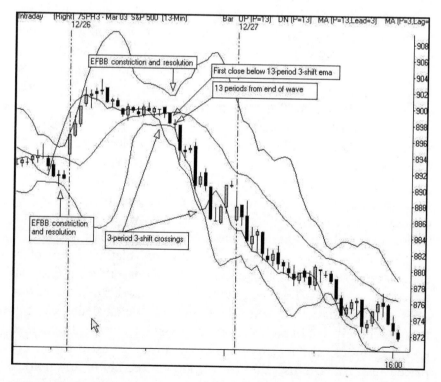

Figure 15-2   The importance of the EFBB constriction as a prelude to a major market move.

The market tends to move in extremes, and with EFBB the degree of extremity can be tracked to provide a useful contextual tool. The addition of the 13-period 3-shift (forward) tool and the 3-period 3-shift (backward) tool provides additional context to enable the trader or investor to have more confidence in trade signals and gain-taking price points. The constriction of the EFBB coupled with the Fibonacci ordinals provides leading indicators that can prepare the alert trader or investor to participate in the resulting sizable moves as the constriction unwinds and the market moves strongly, as shown in Figure 15-2.

VOLATILITY SIGNALS

Volatility is a concept that is frequently ill defined and improperly used. For example, media commentators and others often use the word *volatility* to refer to markets that are going down, but they rarely use the word in relation to markets that are going up. Since the nominal expectation for markets is for prices to increase, when prices fall it is called "volatility," and it is this kind of volatility that investors are presumably supposed to discount as long-term investors. This is a fairly useless meaning for the word.

A more useful meaning of volatility is what I call *range volatility,* where the market is oscillating back and forth within a specific range. Most periods called "consolidation" are of this type. In this case, *volatility* means that there is an increased number of trends in a relatively small period of time, trends of small degree that reverse frequently. Thus, volatility refers to a condition in which a market is not trending strongly in either direction during the period of interest.

Another, even more useful meaning of volatility is in reference to the size of a single-period reversal that is sufficient to break a trend in progress. That is, in an uptrend, how large a down day does it take to signal the end of the uptrend? We have already seen that the three-price break method provides one answer: It will take a down candle sufficient to close below three boxes in the three-price break chart. This value can be known readily in any market and any time frame as long as one has a current three-price break chart.[5] This is what happens in a three-price break of a trend—a single-period move that is so different from the behavior in other periods that it serves to break the trend.

In addition to the three-price break method, we have also used the Fibonacci series to determine this. Developing this approach often provides directional signals that will be anticipatory to three-price break changes in trend. The method is deceptively simple. Based on yesterday's close, we use certain Fibonacci ratios as percentages to project the "volatility ranges" for today's trading. For example, consider the situation in which the Dow closes at a value of 8432.61 (see Figure 15-3). To calculate the "low-volatility" range for the next day of trading, the Dow's *closing* price is multiplied by 0.00618. This yields a value of 52.11. This is added to and subtracted from the Dow's prior close, yielding a range of 8380.50 to 8484.72 as the expected "low-volatility" range for the next trading day. The "high-volatility" range is calculated by multiplying the Dow's *close* by 0.01618. This yields a range of 8296.17 to 8569.05. Suppose that the Dow is currently "long" on volatility. If the Dow trades between 8296.17 and any point higher, then the volatility trend will continue long. However, if the Dow trades a tick below 8296.17, this will be considered a reversal and the volatility trend will be "short." Once a volatility trend begins, it tends to persist.

Markets differ in their constants of multiplication for volatility signals. For example, the Dow, the S&P futures, bonds, and soybeans will provide excellent signals with the values used in this example (0.00618 and 0.01618). For the Nasdaq 100 futures, 0.01618 and 0.03618 are best. For the Japanese yen (Forex market), 0.00328 and 0.0100 are used. This method can be used with stocks as well. Determining the value to use requires proper measurement of the inherent degree of volatility in the specific market. The yen, for example, is less volatile than the Nasdaq 100.

---

[5] Software is now available for instantly determining the three-price break trend in any market in significant Fibonacci-based intraday time frames (1, 3, 5, 8, 13, and 30 minutes) as well as daily and weekly time frames. For information on this tool, see http://ralomatic.com.

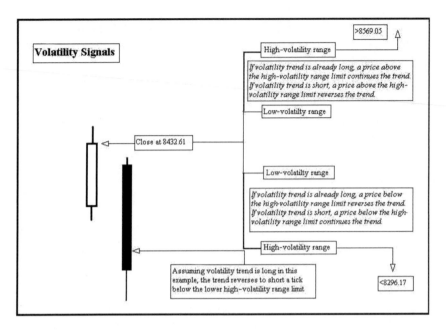

Figure 15-3   Illustration of low- and high-volatility ranges and the volatility trigger.

There are two specific uses of the volatility signal method at undergroundtrader.com. The first is as a context variable. Knowing that a specific market is "volatility short" provides a basis for being alert to short signals that develop. The second is that when a trading day (or series of days) has been in a low-volatility trading range, the likelihood of volatility expansion increases. This alerts the trader to act on *range*-based signals, such as the 3-period range method described earlier.

NATURAL SQUARES AND HARMONICS OF RANGE

Natural Squares

Two of the most important context factors are *natural squares* and *harmonics of range.* Figure 15-4 shows the monthly price history for MSFT from 1996 through 2002. In this price chart, horizontal lines are placed at *natural square* price points, that is, at the *squares* of the whole integers 3, 4, 5, 6, 7, 8, 9, 10, and 11 (plotted as 9, 16, 25, 36, 49, 64, 81, 100, and 121).[6] In the bull market rise from 1996 to the 1999 high, notice how frequently a natural square price line initially served as a resistance (marked by arrows) before a breakthrough. In the subsequent bear market, notice how frequently the natural square price lines served as support in declines and then as resistances to advances.

Combining natural squares with the *Rule of Three* provides the following "price zones" for meaningful divisions of stock prices:

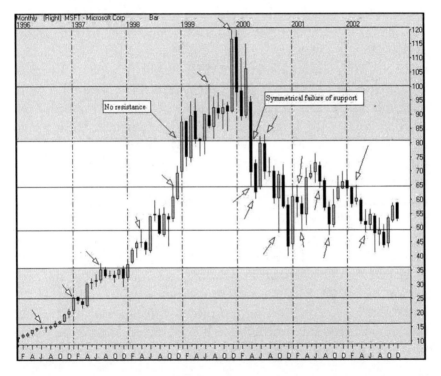

Figure 15-4   MSFT monthly price chart showing the natural squares price points and the transition in Rule-of-Three price zones.

[6] W. D. Gann was instrumental in bringing the ancient traditions of sacred geometry to bear on the financial markets. Natural squares, harmonics of range, and other methods to be described later are all representative methods that have their origins in sacred geometry. For a fine and readily available text on this essential background, see Robert Lawlor, *Sacred Geometry: Philosophy and Practice* (London: Thames and Hudson, Ltd., 1982).

low-priced stocks (0–9), medium-priced stocks (9.01–36), high-priced stocks (36.01–81), and mega-priced stocks (81.01–144). These ranges are shown in Figure 15-4 for MSFT as it made the cycle through these price zones.

Most of the time, in rising markets, a close above a natural square implies that the next higher natural square will be hit *before* the next lower natural square. For example, the close above 25 in January 1997 implied that MSFT would close above 36 before it closed below 16. On the downside, if there is a close below a natural square, it carries the implication that the market will close below the next lower square before it closes in the square above. Note that the high in December 1999 failed to close above the natural square at 121. In the following month, MSFT closed below the natural square of 100. This implied that MSFT would close below 81 *before* it closed above 121. This is the *dynamic* principle of natural squares in action. As you can see, MSFT closed well below 81 in April 2000. In May 2000, MSFT closed below 64. This implied that it would close below 49 before it closed above 81. As you can see, MSFT failed to close above 81 during the rebound in the summer of 2000, and it subsequently closed at the lowest close during the bear market at 43.38 in December 2000. This essentially is an example of the principle of *alternation* in operation.[7]

One last point on the natural squares method: Note that the natural square of 81 offered no resistance to the rising market in January 1999. This sets up a *symmetry* projection. That is, the projection is that the 81 price square will not serve as support if the market falls. Note that the largest monthly decline during the bear market occurred in April 2000, when 81 failed to offer any support, and so support was not operative until the 64 square.

Harmonics of Range

Harmonics are price points in any range that are calculated by various mathematical configurations of the three primary numbers in sacred geometry: 2, 3, and 5. These numbers are the first set of three nonzero and nonunity numbers in the Fibonacci spiral.[8] Any range may be considered equal to the value representing "the whole," that is, 1. We have already seen that dividing 1 by the

Fibonacci constant of 1.618 divides any unity into the portions of 0.618 and 0.382. The reciprocals and the square roots of 2, 3, and 5 will also be found to have important implications. At undergroundtrader.com, these various mathematical expressions are part of a simple harmonics of range calculator for ease of determining relevant values of range. These harmonic points in a range (or their extensions beyond the range) will *always* be important price points that are of interest to the trader and investor. Prices will often turn at or very close to these values, and so these values serve as alerts to the trader and investor. Various patterns of relationships between waves will also form at these price points. Markets are always either trading within a meaningful range or moving beyond the range in a significant breakout or breakdown. Without knowledge of the harmonic points of range or extensions of range, the trader or investor will not know where in the subsequent price action to pay specific attention to how the market behaves.

---

[7] When the principle of alternation is violated, this generally means that the market is undergoing a "change of character." When MSFT closed at 43.38, the natural squares method implied that MSFT would close below 36 before it closed above 64. This did not happen, and for this reason it can be said that MSFT began to change character (e.g., it did not make new lows while the Nasdaq 100 made new lows through October 2002). It had led the market lower from the earlier highs. Instead of making a lower low, it now made a higher high in terms of natural squares. Note that the close above the 64 square implied that MSFT would close above 81 before it closed below 49. This also did not happen, as MSFT closed below 49 in July 2002. Thus, the principle of alternation was violated again. The principle of symmetry suggests that these violations are balanced and equalized, and that MSFT will now return to the typical operation of the squares. This suggests that MSFT will close below 36 before it closes above 64. As with any methodological projection, it must be understood that this is a conjecture. The important point from the perspective of method is that the conjecture is specific, testable, and useful. Note for example, the last two candles in the chart. These are forming a dark cloud cover candle pattern, which is bearish. A far month option position at or near the target (July 2003 puts at 35) is a reasonable position given this setup. The natural initial stop is at the high of the dark cloud candle. (Note: The projection based on the initial close in a new price square must be resolved before additional projections take effect.)

[8] While sacred geometry may seem esoteric, the value of the mathematical formulas based on these simple integers for relating to and understanding the underlying principles of the financial markets cannot be underestimated.

While harmonics of range may be based on any range in any time frame, I recommend that harmonic analysis begin with the monthly chart of the market being traded. Figure 15-5 plots the monthly price data for MSFT from 1997 through 2002. By convention, we look for market extremes within the last 89 periods. This is a time frame of nearly $6^1/_2$ years on the monthly chart. In this case, we have two points of reference: from the low in 1996 to the high in 1999, and from the high in 1999 to the low in December 2000. Generally, I begin a study of harmonics with the longest time frame, in this case, from the low in 1996 at 9.99 to the high in 1999 at 119.94. Figure 15-6 illustrates a portion of the harmonic calculator used at undergroundtrader.com. The range limits are entered into the calculator, and an array of information concerning harmonic price points is automatically calculated. The

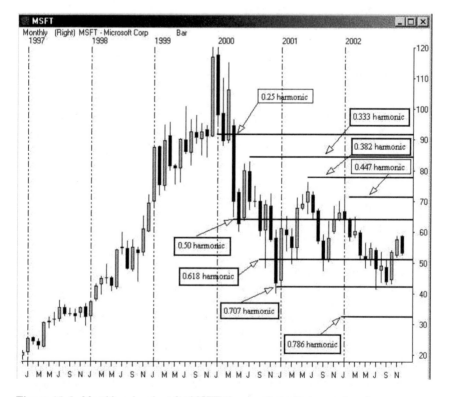

Figure 15-5 Monthly price chart for MSFT showing the major harmonics of range.

Monthly	Low	High	Range
Input-------->	9.99	119.94	109.95
Harmonic	Value	Upside	Downside
2+3	5.000	559.740	-429.81
2*2	4.000	449.790	-319.86
π	3.142	355.453	-225.52
√9	3.000	339.840	-209.91
Phi+1.00	2.618	297.839	-167.91
√5	2.236	255.846	-125.92
√4	2.000	229.890	-99.96
√3	1.732	200.429	-70.50
Phi+1.00	1.618	187.889	-57.96
√2	1.414	165.483	-35.55
√1.618	1.272	149.847	-19.92
√1.00	1.000	119.940	9.99
1/√1.618	0.786	96.428	33.50
1/√2	0.707	87.736	42.19
1/Phi	0.618	77.944	51.99
1/√3	0.577	73.470	56.46
1/2	0.500	64.965	64.97
1/√5	0.447	59.161	70.77
1/(Phi+1.00)	0.382	51.991	77.94
1/√9	0.333	46.640	83.29
1/π	0.318	44.984	84.95
1/√(2*2)	0.250	37.478	92.45
1/(2+3)	0.200	31.980	97.95

Figure 15-6   The price/time harmonic calculator.

various harmonic points that are typically of most interest are listed on the left, and the calculated values on the right.

Following the peak, the first market structure low of what would become a major bear market formed near the 0.25 harmonic; the second market structure low formed near the 0.50 harmonic, the third market structure low formed near the 0.618 harmonic; and the lowest market structure low to date formed at the 0.707 harmonic. It is not possible to predict at what harmonic the market will find support. What is important is that the trader and investor be aware of these price points and the potential for them to become reversal points. Note that the upside rallies reversed near the harmonic points of 0.333, 0.382, and 0.447.

Figure 15-7 presents the same chart, with the harmonics range now from the peak of the bull market to the lowest point of the bear market to date. In this chart, the first advance from the low could not sustain the 0.618 harmonic, nor could the second advance. The chart ends with MSFT failing to hold above the 0.786 harmonic.

It is often very useful to compare the harmonics with the natural squares. In Figures 15-5 and 15-7, it is clear that there is a relationship between the 0.50 harmonic and the natural squares of 64 and 81. What this suggests is that in MSFT, the 0.50 harmonic gains added weight. For some other markets, it will be the 0.618 or the 0.786. In any event, the trader and investor will find that knowledge of these relationships will add important context infor-

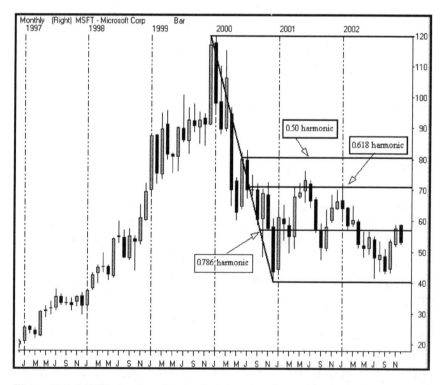

Figure 15-7 MSFT price chart showing the harmonics of range following the peak of the bull market.

mation that can be immediately useful in trading. For example, after studying the monthly chart, one should do the same for the weekly and daily charts, and then for one of the major intraday periods, such as 13 or 30 minutes. In the case of MSFT, one would want to see if the 0.50 harmonic continues to point toward the natural square price points. This would be true as well as one examines smaller ranges. For example, the last major monthly low in MSFT was at 41.41, and the December 2002 high was at 58.96. The 0.50 harmonic of this range is at 50.19, very close to the natural square of 49.

Natural squares, harmonics, and extensions of range are a rich source of contextual information for the trader and investor. Perhaps this is sufficient introduction to spark an interest in these numbers, which have fascinated the human imagination from antiquity to the present day.

THE PROJECTIVE POWER OF MARKET STRUCTURE

The contextual methods discussed thus far have emphasized price points. Market structure points may also be conceptualized as time points, and the distance between these structural points can be thought of as a "clock." If this clock were an equidistant clock (as our standard clocks are), resolving time in the markets would be relatively simple. But the market clock is not an equidistant clock, but rather is more like those clocks that have variable distances between "ticks"—for example, the human heart. While *ordinary* time-keeping devices may not work very well on the other side of the "looking glass" or in Alice's Wonderland, time is nonetheless kept after a fashion in those places as well. The market is the same. One might say that it keeps track of time in its *own* way for its own purposes. If one conceptualizes market structure points as "ticks" of the market's clock, then the relationship between market structure points may be useful in projecting the future time points of important events. Generally, what is meant by "important events" will be market structure points; significant highs, lows, or closes; wave structuring points; trend-breaking points; and other such points. The market structure clock projects these points in time far in advance of their occurrence, so the trader and investor can be alert to important characteristics of price behavior in these specific time areas.

The method is relatively simple. For example, a market structure low followed by a higher market structure low projects a *rising* line from the first low through the second low and on into the future. The market structure high *between* these lows is then projected as a *horizontal* line into the future. Where the two lines intersect is a *time point*, which may be associated with a significant price point such as a wave target. Figure 15-8 shows the daily price chart for MSFT from mid-September through December 2002. As an illustration of the method of constructing a "market structure clock," note the rising line from the bear market low through the higher market structure low that forms the anticipatory upside wave. A horizontal line is then drawn from the peak of the anticipatory wave across the price chart until it intersects with the rising bull line. From this intersection, a *vertical* line is then drawn upward and downward so that this time point will be clearly visible on the chart whether the market rises or falls. The nature of the time point cannot be predicted—only that the market's structure is projecting something important at that point in time.[9]

In the illustration, the market was in a consolidation phase following the completion of the move to the limit-wave target. On November 4, the market gapped up sharply, nearly hitting the 2.0 squared extension of the anticipatory wave and just shy of the 1.618 extension of the limit wave. These are very unusual extensions that indicate an extraordinary move. This was the third strong gap in MSFT since the reference low. It is rare for a market to gap more than three times before at least one of the gaps is "filled."

---

[9] This is a good example of using the information available in the price chart itself to project future price and/or time behavior rather than relying on sources outside the chart of prices.

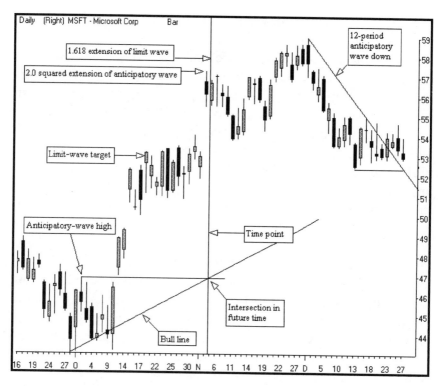

Figure 15-8   Constructing the market structure clock.

Most important, this gapping action sent prices into the "time point," which was known from a much earlier period. This trade "expected" an important event to occur in this time period. The time point marks the market structure high of the third (and usually the last) of the "island" gaps. From this point, the market fell until the third gap was closed. The achievement of a price objective (such as a wave target) does not in itself limit the further extension of the move. However, *time* seems to play a more active role in limiting price. If one attends to the time aspects (which few traders or investors do), it becomes clear that time frequently will cut price short, whereas price alone may continue if a critical time point has not yet been reached. This illustration does not prove this point, but it will serve to heighten a trader's awareness of time as important. It was Gann's observation that *time* was the most important factor of all.

In following market structure timing, it should be noted that a rising market structure clock will continue to be in effect, perhaps with multiple time points along its axis, until either prices fall *below* the price line or time points based on downside structures become active. Again this is an example of the principle of alternation. In Figure 15-8, a downside structure develops from the peak, and this cancels the further projective significance of the original bull line. The downside market structure clock projects to the completion of a market structure high that forms a bearish candle pattern that I call FOPS, for "fall-off pattern signal." This is a market structure high in which the *close* of the third candle is lower than the low of the prior two candles. (Similarly, a bullish TOPS, or "takeoff pattern signal," is a market structure low formed by a *close* in the third candle that is higher than the highs of the prior two candles.) Generally, specific candles or candle patterns associated with market structure time points gain added significance. Note, for example, that the market structure high candle is the first candle to trigger the impulse wave down.

Market structure timing is a rich and easy resource for the trader and investor. These simple illustrations are only suggestive of the power of this method to pinpoint and contextualize price behavior in relation to time.[10]

---

[10] An important point to note in terms of constructing market structure clocks is that it is best to observe the strict order of market structure points and to always construct the clock lines from sequential market structure points that are themselves significant. Thus, a reference high followed by a 5-period downside structure can serve as clock points. If there is also a market structure high after 3 periods, the former would be favored because it forms the wave structure, whereas the latter does not. Likewise, market structures that are marked as time points can be used as subsequent clock points themselves because they tend to be significant. In practice, the rules for clock construction are more precise than may be evident here. Hopefully, this is sufficient introduction to enable study of this powerful tool.

THE CONCEPT OF PRICE/TIME

Most traders and investors are heavily focused on price and pay little or no attention to time as an active factor in trading. This is unfortunate, because a better understanding of time is very likely to increase a trader's or investor's profitability in the markets. We have just seen one use of market structure *prices* to project points in *time*. There are actually several useful ways to approach the use of price behavior to become more aware of time points.

Figure 15-9 illustrates one of these methods, the use of Fibonacci projections based on distance between important market structure points. Here a 10-period anticipatory wave forms. The method involves projecting into the future three time points based on the square root of the Fibonacci growth factor (1.272), the Fibonacci growth factor (1.618), and the second-degree Fibonacci growth factor (2.618). These factors are multiplied by the distance between the candles forming the wave (10). The resulting values are then rounded up to the next whole integer. This yields values of 13, 17, and 27. These time points are then plotted from the market structure low between the two highs. In all cases, counting begins with the market structure candle as 1. The figure shows arrows drawn to the candles at those distances from the low of the anticipatory wave.

This simple timing method projects potentially important time points in the future based on the characteristics of the anticipatory wave. Knowing that time points are often associated with market structure turns enables the trader to pay close attention to market behavior at critical times. For example, the trader would be short on this anticipatory wave. As point 13 approaches, with the potential for a market structure low to form, the trader can lower the stop and be ready for a turn. If the market does not turn, no harm has been done. The time point simply focuses the trader's attention and lets that trader know what to look for.

As soon as the market drops below the low of that 13th candle, the trader knows that a market structure low is not possible, and with this knowledge is able to ride the move down. Gains

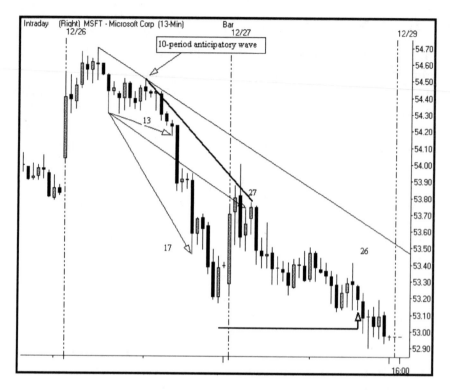

Figure 15-9   Illustration of Fibonacci-based time projections using market structures.

would be taken near the low of the large down candle as the
impulse wave reaches its target. Entry into the limit wave on a new
low trigger is made with the awareness that this candle is a time
point (17), and, as can be seen, it becomes a market structure low.

This timing tool is a *general* timing tool, meaning that the
price points used can be any price points that are "significant." For
example, the structuring point of the anticipatory wave and the
time point marked 27 are important points. These points are connected in the chart with a thick line. The low of the move between
these points is also an important point. The distance between the
two highs is 20 periods. This projects 26 periods from the low as
an important price point, and you can see that this point is com-
pleting a market structure high.

The use of the market structure clock method and the distance between market structures method is complementary. Using both provides the trader with "time windows" that generally will be the locus of important market events and can be used by the trader to manage trades more profitably. These timing methods will prove their value over and over, and the curious trader and investor will discover many ways to make use of them.

These methods illustrate an intimate relationship between price and time. While we typically consider price and time to be separate factors, the reality is that there can be no real separation between them. Prices are always operating *in and through time,* and therefore our treatment of price and time as separate is arbitrary. Figure 15-10 pictures a typical trend, in this case a downtrend. From its peak to its trough, the price value is "traveling" through time. Notice that when a box is drawn around this trend, it is clear that the trend line is the hypotenuse of a right triangle.[11] *This will always be true of any trend line drawn between two points.* The hypotenuse of this triangle is not price or time, but can be more properly conceptualized as *price/time.* Likewise, because it is always the hypotenuse of a right triangle, we always know the value of price/time because it is equal to the square root of the sum of price squared and time squared—the famous Pythagorean solution.

We know by the principle of alternation that a downtrend is followed by an uptrend is followed by a downtrend, and so on. The points of interest to the trader are most specifically those points in time where price will turn. We have just seen how to use market structure points to cast time projections into the future, where

---

[11] It should also be noted that any such trend is equal to the diagonal of a pentagon and that the length of the diagonal of a pentagon is always equal to the Fibonacci growth constant (1.618) multiplied by the length of the side of the pentagon. Because of this, it is possible to construct a "pentagonal" clock from any trend length, with two of the pentagon's angular points being time points in the future and one being a time point in the past. The pentagonal clock is a much-overlooked timing device. It was first applied to the financial markets by Harahus [as cited in James E. Schildgen, *Analytical Methods for Successful Speculation* (Chicago: Capital Futures Associates, Ltd., 1986), pp. 166–167].

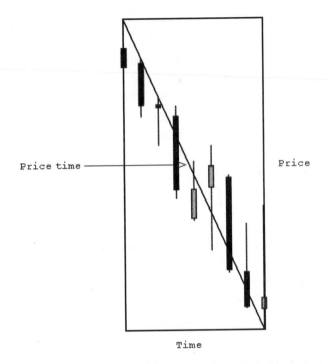

Figure 15-10   Simple downtrend illustrating the concept of *price/time* as the hypotenuse of a right triangle.

such turns may occur. The question that follows from Figure 15-10 is, does the *value* of price/time provide a method for projecting important time points into the future?

Price/Time and Symmetry

Earlier, reference was made to the principle of *symmetry*. We can make use of that principle here by suggesting that when a trend with a specific price/time value is followed by another trend (typically in the opposite direction), crucial time points will be marked at Fibonacci ratios and extensions of the *price/time* of the original trend. For example, the trend in Figure 15-10 is 9 periods long. Let's say that it covers 18 points in price. This tells us that the price/time value is equal to the square root of 9 squared plus 18 squared, or 20.12. We can then anticipate that when the subsequent trend reaches a price/time value of 20.12, this will mark an important point in both time and price.

The trader will also want to be attentive to those points that represent important Fibonacci ratios (0.382, 0.618) and Fibonacci extensions (1.27, 1.618, 2.618). It is astonishing how frequently, for example, a market that is languishing in a narrow consolidation period after a sizable move will make a major breakout or breakdown at the point of symmetry (or extension) of the price/time value of the initial trend.[12]

To keep track of the symmetry effects of price/time, we have developed a useful calculator that can be easily used in active trading. The range and time period values of an initial trend are placed in the calculator, and price/time is calculated. Once the trend is complete, the new trend values for both price and time are added for each passing period. The calculator then provides the trader with an assessment of the new trend's price/time symmetry in relation to the prior trend. The equality of price/time is a particularly important point in time.

THE OWL METHOD: CONSISTENT SQUARING OF PRICE AND TIME

In the previous section, we saw that any trend between two chart points is the hypotenuse of a right triangle. Of course, the momentum of the trend will create angles of trend that vary considerably from one trend to another. The symmetry calculator is one device for determining potentially important symmetry points in trends with different angular momentum. A different approach to the comparison of price/time trends was suggested by W. D. Gann.

---

[12] For example, if the consolidation range is 3 points, it will take about 20 periods for price/time to reach symmetry. This will bring the market near the Fibonacci ordinal of 21, where the probability of a breakout or breakdown from the consolidation increases.

This approach essentially "squares" price and time—that is, one unit of time becomes equal to one unit of price. A "squared trend" will of course be a triangle with an angular momentum of 45 degrees. This was Gann's "basic" trend angle, and all other trends were assessed in relation to this angle.

All charting programs are based on equidistant time periods and variable price ranges. Unless special considerations are brought to bear on price charting, price and time are *not* square. The author's solution to this is to force the relationship between price and time for any selected price range *or* any selected time range to become 45 degrees. A price/time *box* is then available for *any* such range selected.[13]

An example of *the Owl's* price/time box drawn to encompass a trend is shown in Figure 15-11. The geometric features of this price/time box will then have implications for subsequent price and time behavior. For example, the price/time trend line of this box will inscribe an arc. The point in time where this arc reaches maximum inflection is almost always a critical time point. Figure 15-11 shows this time point as being convergent with the end of a sharp downtrend. "Arc expiration" serves as an alert to the trader or investor to prepare to act on the next market structure signal— in this case, an upside structure that began to develop from the point of arc expiration. Likewise, the upward and downward limits of the arcs will mark price limits that are typically limiting of price behavior.

The Owl also marks the major Gann angles. In addition, marking the angles from both the upper and lower origins of the price/time box will inscribe background "diamond" shapes (the dashed lines in the illustration). I refer to these as Gann "diamonds." They are important because of their boundary effects (that is, these boundaries often serve as resistance or supporting

---

[13] I call this tool *the Owl*. It is available in Investor/RT from Linn Software, Inc., http://www.linnsoft.com. The author wishes to express his thanks to Dr. William E. Linn and Chad L. Payne for programming the Owl tools and making them a part of the Investor/RT family of tools.

price points), as well as their time-marking effects—especially the *apex* points of the diamonds. Note the low at the apex of the diamond shortly after arc expiration.

The Owl price/time box can be used in many general ways. For example, the box can be used in any time period. Squaring the first 13 minutes of the trading day, for example, sets up important Owl projections in the price/time space that can be especially useful to the trader focusing on the first hour of trading. Squaring 34 periods of a price/time box on a weekly chart sets up Owl projections in the weekly price/time space that are of value to the intermediate-term trader. Squaring yesterday's trading range for the 13-minute trading periods sets up Owl projections for today's trading. For example, the time point of arc expiration under such a construction is a constant, and that time point is always an important time point. Many aspects of the Owl tool are used constantly at undergroundtrader.com to alert traders to these contextual geometric time and price points that are of importance in real-time trading.

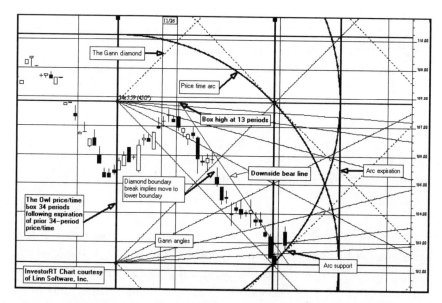

Figure 15-11   Illustration of *the Owl* price/time box on the daily chart, showing price and time squared at 45 degrees for the 34-period price/time box in the US$ Index.

EXTERNAL MARKET CLOCKS

An enormous amount of effort has been expended over the years on attempts to find determinant recurrent patterns that are "responsible" for the apparent cyclicality of the financial markets. These efforts range from "obvious" potential patterns (e.g., a "presidential" 4-year cycle) through less obvious patterns (e.g., the 11-year sunspot cycle) to esoteric patterns (e.g., astrological cycles of varying types). The research methodology in these studies may begin with market cycles (obvious highs and lows of major degree), followed by an effort to see if there is any obvious correlation between these cycles and "anything else." Or, the analysis may begin with the cycle itself—say, the 4-year presidential cycle—to see how this correlates with the highs and lows in the market.

The overall results of these efforts tend to be disappointing in that they do *not* add incrementally to the actual trading results achievable with regular methods. Because external clocks (of whatever sort) do not appear in the chart of prices, trading exclusively on external clock signals violates the rule of trading only on what occurs in the chart of prices and therefore is not recommended to the trader or investor as a trading method.

Clearly, however, cycles are fundamental to life and to the behavior of all things. For this reason, the consideration of cycles as *contextual* information is very much a part of the regular trading approach at undergroundtrader.com. Here we take an *empirical* rather than a dogmatic approach. That is, cycles from any perspective are considered in terms of their actual relevance to trading. Two examples may suffice to provide a flavor of this approach.

The principle of *alternation* suggests a strong criterion for cycles: namely, strict alternation. For example, if there is a 4-year cycle, we would expect the pattern UDUDUDUDUDUD, where U = up and D = down and the cycle is 4 years in length. The problem, of course, is the exceptions. There is clearly some kind of 4-year pattern that more or less corresponds with the presidential election cycle. But the number of exceptions and the disruptions in the order of peaks and troughs renders the cycle of no particular value in actual trading.

A study of "strong alternation" actually reveals that the *only* cycle that is nonrandom and fully alternating over a period of nearly 200 years is a 13-year cycle—a fundamental Fibonacci cycle that is of considerable importance. The results of this study by Michael Alexander are shown in Figure 15-12.[14] A robust 13-year cycle is a useful cycle to know about in relation to signals developing in the *monthly* price chart. The contextual knowledge of this cycle encourages taking long-term positions on short signals as they develop in the monthly chart over the next several years.

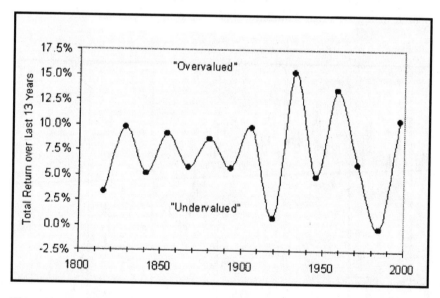

Figure 15-12 Illustration of the strict "alternation" cycle of 13 years showing the market cycling from undervaluation to overvaluation.

---

[14] Michael A. Alexander, *Stock Cycles:Why Stocks Won't Beat Money Markets over the Next Twenty Years* (Lincoln, Neb.: Writers Club Press, 2000). This is an exceptionally fine treatise on stock cycles that was written before the bear market began in 2000. Of particular interest is the idea that the alternating 13-year cycle may also account for the long-period cycle of Kondratiev. Four cycles of 13 would complete one long wave of 52 years, just as 4 cycles of 13 weeks completes a year and 13 moon cycles complete a year as well.

At undergroundtrader.com, we make considerable use of what I call the *lunar clock*. In the equity markets, there is a fairly pronounced tendency for the *full* moon time point to be associated with important market structure lows, and for the *new* moon to be associated with important market structure highs. These highs and lows may *not* be the market extremes.[15] Moreover, when a violation of alternation occurs, it is typically followed by a *major* market move that may extend over several cycles. As indicated earlier, when *alternation* is violated, the market is in the process of changing *character*, and this, of course, can lead to extreme volatility, as seen in major trend breaks. Figure 15-13 illustrates how the *lunar clock* has been used in trading the US$ Index. The simplest rule is to take the first market structure signal to complete and trigger *following* the

Figure 15-13   Trading the US$ Index in relation to the lunar clock cycle.

[15] An important error in many studies of lunar correlation is that these studies are seeking correlation of moon phases with market extremes. Of more importance in trading is the "leading" indicator quality of lunar time points in terms of directional market structure signals.

lunar time point. This is a good example of an extended move lower following the alternation violation.

GENERALIZING THE THREE-PRICE BREAK

The basic *three-price break* method, as described by Shemizu and by Nison and as discussed earlier, is one of the essential trend-determining and trend analysis tools used at undergroundtrader.com. In addition to the regular method, I have generalized this tool in three ways: by method, by time, and by variable.

Three-Price Break Methods

Three-price break charts are kept on a continuous basis. Because time does not enter into the basic chart, there is no indication of sessions or periods. This makes the three-price break method difficult to use on an intraday basis because the break price is often very far away—particularly on days with large gaps. In an effort to render the three-price break more useful for intraday traders, I have developed two additional methods: *carryforward* and *fresh start*.

The carryforward method begins each day without regard to prior three-price break data except for the prior day's closing price. In this method, the prior close is carried forward to be the *start* price for the next day's trading. This method is particularly useful when the market's opening is near the prior close or when any gaps are fairly small. It allows one to take a position on the first *close* of the new session in whatever time period one is trading in. In the fresh-start method, the opening tick sets the start price for the day, so that the resulting chart is completely independent of prior session history. This method is especially useful on larger gap openings. The use of the carryforward and fresh-start methods often enables the trader to trade significant price movements before there is any change in the continuous data.

Another general method that I utilize is what I call the *internal* three-price break method. This method can be used within any of the methods just described. At any point where a new trend price does not occur (as, for example, when a market goes into a consolidation period of many "skips" without a break or a new trend price), the extreme of that trend to date may be taken as an "internal" start point and a countertrend three-price break sub-chart in the same time period can be initiated. These countertrend charts are extremely useful for assessing the strength of a countertrend before the regular method provides any break signals or a new trend price.

Three-Price Break and Time

Because the three-price break method relies solely on the period *close*, time is effectively eliminated from the three-price break chart. One way to generalize the three-price break method in relation to time, however, is to have available a constant three-price break analysis of trend in meaningful time periods. The standard time periods used at undergroundtrader.com for this purpose are the Fibonacci-based intraday time periods of 1, 3, 5, 8, 13, and 30 minutes. With three-price break information constantly available in all these time periods at once (see footnote 5 for details on the software that has been developed for this purpose), plus daily and weekly time periods, it is typical, for example, to be entering a trade on 13-minute signals and to be able to manage that trade based on three-price break trends in the 1-minute or 3-minute data.

The market is *always* trending, although such trends may not be visible in the time period that one is trading. Being able to open trend analysis to sub-time periods is of enormous benefit, particularly to the active intraday trader. Having these data available makes possible several new contextual methods that were not readily available before. For example, in what I call *trend weight,* the time periods are weighted according to their duration (1 minute = 1 point, 8 minutes = 8 points, etc.). The sum of the trends in the different time periods becomes a useful measure of extremity. For example, when the trend is short in all periods from 1 minute through weekly, *trend weight* has reached a maximum, and the trader begins to look for signs of reversal. Reversal will typically begin in the shorter time periods. One can see the trend begin to break across the different time periods, and this becomes visually compelling for the trader who is short, for example. This knowledge enables the trader to improve transaction timing in terms of entries as well as gain taking.

Another important feature of access to trend in different time periods involves *body weight*. Little attention has been paid to the use of body weight in the candlestick literature, but it is one of the most important characteristics of candles and one of the reasons that they are so useful. Body weight is simply the price differential between the open and the close of the candle. If the close is above the open, the body weight is positive. If the close is below the open, the body weight is negative. Tracking the sums of body weights in the different time periods provides unique information for the trader. For example, at any one point in trading, one of the time periods will have the largest total body weight. I describe this time period as "the heavy." The significance is that trading in that time period is likely to be most productive because it is that time period that will "lead" the market. Without knowledge of trend state and body weight in the different time periods, the trader will have no way of knowing what time period to focus on. Most traders become habituated to specific time periods. However, different time periods will lead the market, and this leadership may change during different sectors of the trading day.

Three-Price Break and Variables Other than the Close

While three-price break methods have traditionally employed the *close* as a basis for charting, there is no need to restrict the method in this way. There is no end to the creative possibilities that generalizing the three-price break methods makes possible. For example, one of the major alternatives to the three-price break based on closing price is the three-price break based on *body midpoint*. This method is exceptionally useful in managing impulse trends, as the body-midpoint trend will frequently break before the closing price breaks as the trend peaks out with smaller candles.

The important point to realize is that the three-price break method is a *general* method. As such, it does not "care" what it tracks—whether it is closes, body midpoints, range midpoints, body weight, or any other meaningful variable. This generalized use of the three-price break method throws new light on candle methods that can prove of significant value to both traders and investors.

THE MARKET'S INTERNAL SENTIMENT INDICATORS

Market sentiment indicators are popular with traders, who are ever alert for indicators of trend change. When sentiment reaches extremes, the market is very likely to turn simply because too many traders are on one side of the boat. When sentiment becomes extremely bullish, no one wants to sell, but the number of new buyers reaches a null point. Under these conditions, the market is subject to vicious reversals as it stalls or begins to decline. Suddenly, all the bulls want to sell, but there are no buyers to sell to. This is ludicrous, of course, as there are always buyers to sell to and sellers to buy from. But it is the *intensity* of desire that is the issue. When too many people want to sell at the same time, prices must fall, and they often do so rapidly. The same is true in reverse when market sentiment reaches deep despair.

Most measures of sentiment take place outside of the price chart. The percentage disparity between bullish and bearish newsletters and the relative disparity in premiums paid for call and put options are good examples. Then there are measures of sentiment that are based on prices, such as various measurements of disparity from central tendency (such as the extreme Fibonacci Bollinger bands described earlier). Figure 15-14 illustrates a sentiment measure derived from basic price elements. This is easiest to see in relation to candlesticks. By definition, the "wicks" are prices that could not be sustained. This means that for every candle, there will be a certain degree of bullish and bearish *failure*, that is, a measure of the degree to which prices were attained but failed to hold. When prices open near the low of the day, move lower, and then move strongly higher, closing near the high of the day, the degree of bearish failure will be many times the degree of bullish failure. Computing these values for each candle in each period and keeping a cumulative "score" provides a direct measure of market sentiment.

When such sentiment values are tracked by three-price break methods, one has available Fibonacci-based points of reference of "extremity," such as 21 or 34 new highs (or lows) in the sentiment indicator. Charting the sentiment indicator provides data that can be treated as waves similar to those for price data. Sentiment typically peaks out at a limit wave, which can be computed using wave targets in the manner described for prices. This *bull-bear failure index* is utilized at undergroundtrader.com to indicate when *contrarian* moves are imminent. Best of all, this measure comes from the price chart itself and requires no reference to anything outside the chart. It is, moreover, applicable to any market and in all time frames.

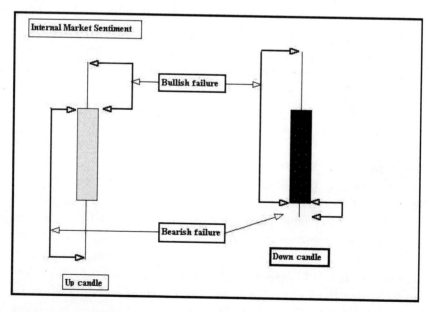

Figure 15-14   Measuring bullish and bearish "failure" as a chart-based measure of sentiment.

THE TRADE FILTER

The basic idea of a trade filter is to apply a *global* rule or rule set as the final arbiter of trade action (entry, gain taking, or stop). Generally, trade filters will follow from detailed knowledge of context variables as well as trader-specified reward-risk parameters and money management requirements. The setting of trade filter conditions is part of what makes trading an art, as it is not possible to establish a "one size fits all" set of filter conditions. One trader may wish, for example, to trade only impulse-wave signals on a daily time frame basis, and only when one of the major intraday time periods (e.g., 13 or 30 minutes) indicates that the three-price trend is long and the three-period trend is long. Or, a hyperactive trader may wish to trade impulse-wave structures in 5-minute data with 1-minute three-price break trend data as the basic management method.

Whatever set of conditions is chosen, traders and investors should realize that *trading results will improve with the disciplined use of trade filters.* The filters can be simple (e.g., take trading signals only in the first 89 minutes of the trading day) or very complex, such as requiring an entire specified set of context conditions to be satisfied before permitting a trade signal to be acted upon (e.g., in order to go long on a 13-minute market structure low, one might require that the trigger be above an active bear line, the 3-minute three-price break trend be long, and the reward-risk ratio exceed 2.0, meaning that the gain from trade entry to the target must be twice the projected loss from trade entry to the indicated stop loss).

Personality characteristics will often determine the trade filters even if the trader is unaware of using filters. For example, a risk-prone trader may pull the trigger only when the market is moving sharply and excitement is in the air, while throwing up his hands and becoming angry when the market is slow and consolidating. A detailed analysis of trades made and the conditions under which the trades were made will always reveal the active set of trade filters that is at work. Because these are generally unconscious, the trader's reward-risk ratio plummets, and while his or her trading may satisfy a need for excitement and risk, the trader starts incurring increasing losses without a clue as to how to change this.

Invariably, every trader and investor is faced with the task of learning the set of trade filters that not only is most effective, but also fits her or his style. The trader or investor may need to *change* her or his style of trading in order to become successful, as well as change the set of filters under which trading takes place. These are unavoidable tasks if trading is to become a successful venture. Instrumental in accomplishing these tasks is the trading journal.

THE IMPORTANCE OF THE TRADING JOURNAL

If there is a single factor that is common to those who *fail* in trading, it is the failure to keep and make use of an adequate trade journal. Many traders have the idea that the purpose of a trade journal is accounting or bookkeeping, and given this notion, they quickly become bored and abandon the trade journal completely. Of course, this is *not* the purpose of a trade journal. The primary purpose of the trade journal is one of *discovery*: discovery about oneself and discovery in relation to the market.

Self-deception is an ever-present factor in trader psychology. Part of this stems from a common operating belief that "things go wrong" not because of one's own actions, but because of the actions of others. In addition to this factor, problems of selective memory are so rampant, particularly in relation to emotion-based trades, that the *only* cure is accurate and precise use of the trade journal. Many traders lose partly because the factors they are trading on amount to a *desire* to lose. Traders become inhibited in writing out precisely what is operating because, in their experience, these factors operate best when they are hidden, even when the trader is engaged in hiding them from her- or himself. Self-delusion is a major occupational hazard in the business of trading and investing.

In general, the first step toward the alleviation of trading problems is the revelation of "secrets." Any trader will profit from a daily "telling" of the results of the day's activities. There are two parts to this. The first is to tell oneself. Here, in addition to making the trade journal entries, one must always know the state of one's performance. This should always be current, and one should know it without fail. The second is to tell someone else how you did today—someone who is important to you. It is astonishing how frequently traders refuse to track their performance and fall into secrecy. This is the beginning of many levels of self-defeating activity that finally lead to a common plight: not only the *risk* of ruin, but the *reality* of ruin as well.

Trading journal entries must include the price and basis for each *entry, target,* and *stop.* In addition, context variables should be noted, and the trade should be tracked as it unfolds. The more focused on the chart one can be, the more focused will be the important observations that will prove beneficial. The most difficult part of the journal entry is recording what happens once one is in the trade. Being *in* a trade always produces experience factors that are not present otherwise. It is always a challenge to record these factors honestly and accurately. This is where most traders begin to fail: by refusing to write down the contents of one's actual experience—the fantasies, the fears, the wishes, the upsets, the enthusiasms, and so on. The "outer" context factors must be recorded as well: listening to the news, or the commentator, or the play caller in the chat room, or others of any kind or description.

This sounds like a terrible chore, and indeed it is a chore, but the potential for learning about oneself and about the market that comes from this is available *nowhere else.* Only in your own experience can you find *your* interface with the financial markets. That is your individual space that no one else knows. Your obligation as a trader and investor is to know that space as well as you are able to and to become as responsible as you can be for what takes place there. The trading journal is instrumental in accomplishing this. Consider it an essential and *never-ending* tool in your education as a trader.

THE IMPORTANCE OF MULTIPLE TIME FRAMES

In an earlier chapter, reference was made to the studies by Hurst showing that improved transaction timing coupled with the compounding of gains produced larger gains as a function of *decreased* time between transactions. While these studies were based on the comparison of periods of time that were *weeks* in duration, following the principle to its logical conclusion points toward intraday trading periods as potentially the most productive of all time periods for the purpose of compounding gains.

This factor places a premium on the study of intraday time periods. What time period is best? Is such a time period consistent across large periods of time, or does it change with the character of the market? Do different markets have "time signatures"— for example, might one find that trading the Nasdaq 100 futures is best done in an 8-minute time frame, whereas trading soybeans is best done in a 30-minute time frame? Or, do the differences between time periods "wash out" over time, so that no time period dominates? Are time periods different for different days of the week or different segments of the day? And why should the gains be larger in 13-minute trading than in 5-minute trading?

I raise these questions not so much to provide answers (although answers will be forthcoming from research that is underway), but to emphasize that the question of *time* is generally an undervalued and underresearched area of study in relation to the financial markets, where price is the dominant focus. Just one example of this type of knowledge mentioned previously (the "heavy" time period "leading" the market) illustrates the value that knowledge of temporal factors may bring to the trader or investor.

ASSESSING RISK, SELF-PERFORMANCE, AND MARKET BEHAVIOR

No trade should be undertaken at any time or under any conditions without the trader's specifying the best estimate of the known risk that he or she is *willing* to take on the trade. Ignoring this *absolute* condition is typically first on the list of bad habits that failing traders invariably develop. As noted earlier, wherever possible, the trader should seek a *market behavior* basis for assessing risk rather than setting a constant dollar or constant point value. While the latter approaches are certainly better than nothing, they do *not* tend to encourage sharp and penetrating analysis of the market's behavior.

As soon as a trade is entered, the trader or investor will be well served by placing an order to liquidate the trade at the indicated risk point (stop). Having the order in the market lessens the likelihood of the "rationalizations of belief" that begin to plague traders when the market moves contrary to their expectations. The trader will actually find that once trade entry is signaled, orders placed at the risk point and the target area will enable the trader to focus on the dynamics of the trade itself and to gather those observations for the trading journal that will build success.

Each day (no matter what the trading period and with no exceptions), the trader or investor *must* assess her or his performance. This is a second area that failing traders begin to ignore—partly because it is often painful, even humiliating. If the trader or investor has had a position in a stock, let's say, for several days and has failed to put in an order at the risk point, and now the price is below that point, the reality of this failure must be attended to each day and, as noted earlier, *told* to someone else. Generally, this will be sufficient to induce better trading and investing habits.

If a trader fails to undertake risk assessment and analysis of trading performance, the probability of failure increases dramatically. This situation represents not so much problems in trading as general psychological issues that require not better methods, or even better mentors, but psychological treatment. Most failing traders and investors are attempting to resolve psychological problems through the market, and this is the leading cause of failure on the part of so many. The market will not "cure" these conditions; it will only ensure that these problems will increase the *risk of ruin*, not only financial ruin but ruin in many other areas of the trader's or investor's life.

There is no one standard for assessing one's performance, but a good rule of thumb is provided by the Fibonacci ratios. Try to aim for 61.8 percent winning trades, and try to keep your winning trades 1.618 times larger than your losing trades. Keep this up for any length of time and you will be pleased with the results. If you can achieve this result, your net profit ratio will be 2.618.

THE VALUE OF REAL-TIME ANALYSIS AND EDUCATION

Looking at almost any static price chart is something akin to examining a dead butterfly that has been pinned in a fixed position. There is a kind of objectivity that prevails, with the luxury of time permitting close examination and studied conclusions and projections. Looking at a *real-time* chart is quite another matter. The butterfly is no longer pinned but free, and the trader's experience is something akin to trying to catch hold of it without a net. One is dealing with something that moves this way and that and is most definitely *alive*. Trading sometimes seems as difficult as trying to anticipate where the butterfly is *going to be* a few minutes from now.

Longer-term traders and investors whose primary experience of the market is limited to reports of closing prices for the trading day and static charts have little or no appreciation for the value of experiencing the markets in real time. When the Nasdaq 100 lost nearly 90 percent of its value from March 2000 through October 2002, many investors rode this slide all the way down. It is this slow, gradual deterioration that lulls the longer-term investor. Dramatic declines in real time, however, have something to teach us, namely, the *urgency* of action.

Even traders who are paralyzed into inaction experience the powerful sense of drama inherent in the real-time move. Reading about declines, seeing the reports on the news, and looking at the decline in a chart fails entirely to teach the value of the *real-time* drama and its psychological impact. This is one reason why I always recommend that any investor or trader, no matter what her or his time perspective may be, sit through a few days of watching the drama of the real-time market. Only in this way can the longer-term investor or trader experience the *fractal* nature of the living organism that we call the market. One can then experience in a few minutes *exactly* what can happen in a few years. What this teaches, at least potentially, is the *necessity* of action. One may know this *consciously*. But it is experiencing the drama of it in *real time* that teaches the reality of it. One does not have to become a day trader to profit from this lesson.

At undergroundtrader.com, we are committed to the *education* of the trader. In this respect, educating in real time is of enormous value. The reason for this is that one can begin to clearly see the market structures develop and unfold into wave patterns; one can see the same structures in the 1-minute chart as in the 30-minute chart and begin to incorporate the fractal nature of market behavior into one's bones. One can project the bear and bull lines into the future and watch the market react to the "live-wire" qualities of contextual price and time points.

Knowing what the market is doing and seeing it unfold, seeing it succeed and seeing it fail, begins to teach one about risk and reward, gains and losses, and what the *real* business of trading is all about: how to manage *risk* in order to achieve *consistent gains* for the purpose of *compounding*. These lessons are certainly possible in longer time frames, but only in real time does one begin to relate to the animal that is *alive* in the market. That animal is the human *crowd*, and it is very much alive. The financial markets are one of the places where one can not only experience and learn the deep functioning of the collective, but profit from doing so as well.

SELF-AWARENESS METHODS

There is no certainty in the markets. Past results do not guarantee future results. No one *knows* where the market is going. Everyone has opinions, claims, and predictions, and many of these are offered with a certainty that can be compelling and demanding and is *always* seductive. Just check the latest market mailing in your mailbox, the latest system offered on the Web, the last issue of

Barron's, the cover of *Fortune,* or the next commentator on CNBC. The future is by its nature *uncertain,* and this applies to the financial markets, the economy, and everything else related to trading and investment. And because of this uncertainty, anxiety and fear underlie all efforts to make it seem *as if* we know the future.

There is only one meaningful certainty: *what to do if and when.*

The trader or investor should seek to develop an approach to the financial markets such that he or she will know what to do if and when such and such happens in the markets. This is the meaningful certainty that will underlie successful trading and investment.

Nonetheless, almost everything the trader is exposed to will conspire against this simple truth. The emotional crosscurrents of fear and greed are always ready to engulf the trader and lead to a forgetting of the method and a failure of resolve. *No trader or investor is immune to these effects.* This reality makes it essential that the trader or investor seek out ways to remain self-aware or to recover self-awareness at the earliest possible moment.

I have found two methods that are especially effective in *recovering* self-awareness. When one is watching the market, whether in real time or not, it is the *visual* aspect that commands attention. This is similar to the way the visual component stands out in dreams—it is even the movement of the eyes that is associated with dreaming sleep. However, it is often the *auditory* dream that reaches one's awareness more profoundly.[16] The auditory channel can become an effective inducement to consciousness.

One simple way for the trader to take advantage of this is to use the computer to record a set of statements that can function as punctuating reminders: *Follow the method . . . What is your stop? . . .*

---

[16] See Julian Jaynes, *The Origin of Consciousness in the Breakdown of the Bicameral Mind* (Boston: Houghton Mifflin, 1976). Jaynes argues that "by carefully analyzing consciousness into its component features and modes . . . it will then be seen that consciousness is based on language, in particular its ability to form metaphors and analogies. The result is that consciousness is not a biological genetic given, but a linguistic skill learned in human history. Previous to that transitional period, human volition consisted of hearing voices called gods, a relationship I am calling the bicameral mind."

What is the next entry setting up? . . . What is your target? . . . Did you enter that in the trade journal? . . . Where's the bear line? . . . What is the three-period trend? . . . What is the wave structure? and so on. It will help if you have these sound bites recorded in the voice of someone you care about. Have these played at *random* times throughout the trading day. This works against the secretiveness that serves that forgetfulness of mind under the weight of the *emotions* that often sets the trader on the spiral of defeat.

A second method is very simple and very effective. In addition to the formally defined bull and bear lines that underlie the current wave structure in the chart being traded, *always* keep an active period-by-period bull and bear line even before structures form. This forces the trader to pay attention to what the market is actually doing and overcomes the *lull* that can interfere with active observation of the market's behavior. If you are in a trade, and that trade suggests that the market should be going down, pay attention if it is staying above any 2-period bull line! This forces you to be interactive with the chart and more observant concerning what the market is actually doing. These simple devices, in conjunction with close study of the trading journal, should facilitate keeping one's self-awareness in good form. The trader or investor may also wish to make good use of certain books that explore this territory in unusually effective ways.[17]

THE MARKET CANDLE BY CANDLE

Neither the static chart of prices nor the emotional tensions of interacting with the live market provides the best conditions for *learning* to trade. The best conditions for learning to trade involve close analysis of a market candle by candle in a situation where one

---

[17] In particular, every trader and investor should read and reread Mark Douglas, *The Disciplined Trader: Developing Winning Attitudes* (New York: New York Institute of Finance, 1980) and *Trading in the Zone: Master the Market with Confidence, Discipline and a Winning Attitude* (New York: New York Institute of Finance, 2000).

can begin to bring all the contextual and signal conditions to bear on the developing picture. This is difficult to do in the real-time situation, although it is what one aims for. It is difficult to do on a static chart because what has already been pictured determines much of the impact of the chart.

In real-time analysis at undergroundtrader.com, I will frequently do a candle-by-candle analysis of what is unfolding. Most traders find this extremely helpful in learning what to pay attention to. But it is not the same as the trader's doing this on a candle-by-candle basis. Unfortunately, there is little in the way of software support for learning markets in this way. Ideally, outside of market hours, without the pressure of trading, the trader needs to be presented with the market as it unfolds, candle by candle—whatever the time period chosen.[18] This is not just the realm of the day trader. Playing back the market (whatever market) in the longer time frames (daily, weekly, or monthly) on a candle-by-candle basis presses home the *sensibility* of what constitutes correct and necessary action.

Consider Figure 15-15. This shows the results of the first 8-minute period for the S&P futures. Let's imagine that we do not have any idea of what has happened before this open, and clearly there is the blank canvas of the future price/time space. The only information we have is that in the chart. Given the methods considered, what is the trade setup?

There are no waves and no market structure with only one candle. Before there can be a trade setup using those methods, more time must pass. The *fresh-start* three-price break tells us that this candle sets a *long* trend in motion and that at the close of the candle, one should go long (at 888.20 close). So clearly, after only one candle, we have an *entry* point. What is the stop? One possible stop would be a close below the open (886.80), because such a close would reverse the trend. But at this point we don't know where the close is going to be. We can't specify a price for the stop.

---

[18] See footnote 5 for software that makes full use of this feature for any market in the important Fibonacci intraday time periods.

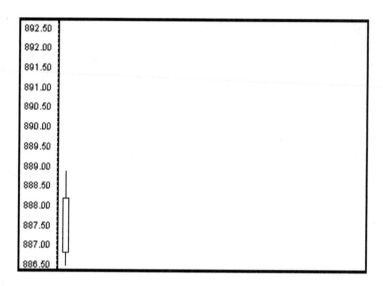

Figure 15-15 First 8-minute candle of the day for the S&P 500 futures, showing the "blank" future price/time space. Before playing back the second candle, the trader or investor must specify the trade parameters from only the information in the chart.

If we can't specify a price, we can't specify the risk. If we can't specify the risk, we can't make the trade.

Is there a target? One target might be *three* highs on the fresh-start three-price break. That's a clear target, but at this point we cannot know what price it represents. Earlier, it was pointed out that volatility ranges can be calculated for today's trading. So, one target might be a volatility range limit. In this case, we have only this one candle. Still, we can use the volatility calculator to calculate an upside target from the *low* of the first candle. This will be the low × 0.0068. The low here is at 886.50. This yields a "low-volatility" target at 891.98.

OK, so now we have an entry price and a target. What can we use as a stop without being arbitrary in terms of points or dollars? The one piece of information we have at the moment that we could use for a stop would be a tick lower than the low of this first candle, or 886.40. Now we have the relevant information for calculating the reward-risk ratio for this trade. The reward is 891.98 − 888.20 = 3.78 points. The risk is 1.70. The ratio of 3.78/1.70 is

2.22, so this meets the requirement for a good reward-risk ratio of 2.0 or greater.

Seeing only this first candle and not being pressured to trade allows us the luxury of being able to fully think through the conditions and reasons for the trade, to set up the parameters (entry, target, stop) of the trade, and to bring any other context variables into relationship with the trade. Of course, as one practices and learns, this will become second nature and can be done very fast, and it can then be done in real time. But it is very difficult to do this in real time without initial grounding in the candle-by-candle approach.

Figure 15-16 shows the visual plot with the addition of the entry, target, and stop. This visual setup of the trade parameters is very important, and most traders and investors neglect this simple procedure to their detriment. Now that the trade parameters are known, it is useful to look at the 1-minute data. The reason for this is that after 8 minutes of trading, even though we have only one 8-minute candle, we will have eight 1-minute candles and a possible structure in place.

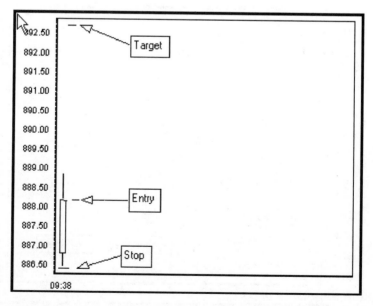

Figure 15-16   First 8-minute candle of the day with the entry, stop, and target prices clearly marked on the chart.

Figure 15-17 shows the 1-minute data for this first 8-minute candlestick. An upside structure has formed, and the anticipatory wave has formed. Its trigger is just above the entry price. Its limit-wave target is 892.78. In addition to the volatility target at 891.98, we now have a 1-minute limit-wave target at 892.78 as well. There is no set rule on which target to use. What we have is an initial target *zone*. When the targets are less than 1 point apart, we generally use the larger value. If this were real-time trading, an order would be placed to sell at 892.70 (rounded down).

Figure 15-18 includes the second 8-minute candle. As can be seen, the second 8-minute candle hit the target and went a bit beyond, triggering the closing sell trade for a gain of 4.50. It is important in the education of the trader that even when one is using a "step-through" approach in the candle-by-candle training of oneself, one should keep a trading journal just as one would do in real time. One thing that should be recorded here is the final result of the trade, not only in terms of the actual gain, but in terms of the risk that was involved.

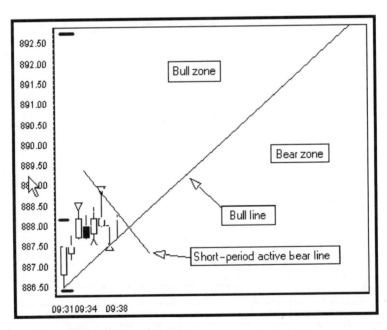

Figure 15-17   The first 8 minutes of data from the 1-minute chart.

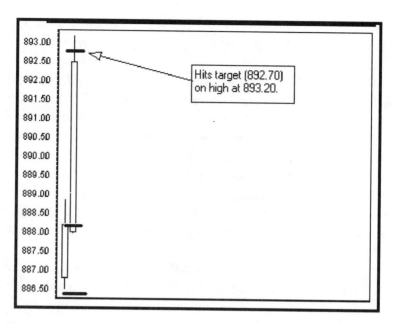

Figure 15-18   The second 8-minute candle hits the target.

Now that one has taken a setup trade with a known reward-risk ratio and has taken a respectable gain by selling at the target, the question that will haunt the trader is, *what now?* This question is much easier to deal with when one has gains in one's pocket than when one has to deal with emotional worry about the trade. What are the conditions of entry now? The fresh-start trend is long 2 at 892.50 with break price 886.80. There still is no market structure, and no waves have formed. The only bullish failure so far has been a minor pullback from the high at 893.20. A new high trigger is in order as long as the trade meets the required reward-risk conditions. So entry will be on a print of 893.30. What is the target?

The next Fibonacci-based value from the target calculator based on the low would be at 0.01618 × 886.50, or 14.34 points, which when added to the low at 886.50 equals 900.84. This is the "high-volatility" target. If the new high entry is triggered, where should the stop be? We know that with a large move, as occurred in the second candle, the body midpoint of that candle is an important price. So that is one candidate for a stop (890.25).

Using these trade parameters, the reward-risk value is 7.54/3.05 = 2.47. The trade is placed on this basis, with the stop and target placed as well.

Figure 15-19 shows this setup and the third 8-minute candle. Note that the candle opened lower than the prior high, came down below the prior close, did not reach the body midpoint stop, and then made a move up, triggering the entry. We know that at some point, the market is going to reach a "top," form a market structure high, and then move lower to form (perhaps) a higher low. So at present, we are expecting the market to form the top of an anticipatory wave. This means that with each successive candle, the stop must be raised. The next stop point is at the low of the just-concluding candle, or 892.20.

Notice the upper wicks on the bullish candles—they are increasing. This means that the degree of bullish failure is increasing. We do

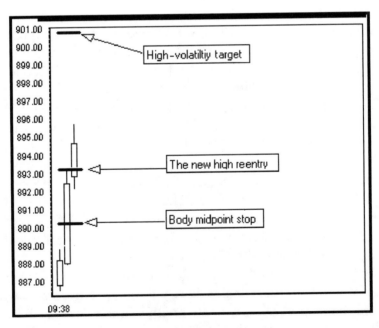

Figure 15-19   The third 8-minute candle, showing the reentry price, the new stop, and the new target.

not know whether the market will reach the target, but we do know that gain preservation will become increasingly important as time passes and the likelihood of a top approaches. For all the trader knows at the moment, the top may already be in place. The trader can, of course, just sell at 898 and take the gain. There's no harm in that. But that is not a method. That's an emotional reaction. What we want is a method-based stop.

On the 8-minute chart, we could raise the stop to the body midpoint of the just-completed candle at 896.50. That would be a method-based stop. Another method would be to go to the 1-minute data and see what structures are forming. These data are shown in Figure 15-20. Here we see that the market has formed a market structure high. This gives us an excellent basis for a stop—that is, the triggering of this market structure high. This requires a stop at a tick less than 898.00. On that basis, the order is entered

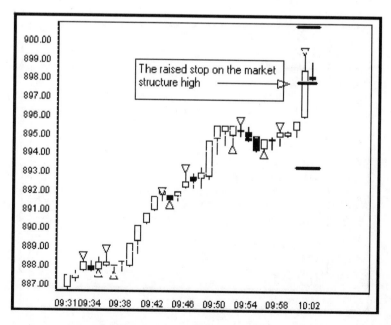

Figure 15-20   The 1-minute chart showing the market structure high that prompts the raising of the stop.

on a one-cancels-the-other basis. Figure 15-21 shows the 5th 8-minute candle triggering the stop. And we are out at 897.90 for a gain of 4.60.

Now the market has formed the first market structure high of the day—always an important time and price point. With this formation in the 8-minute data, there is clearly a market structure high trigger at a tick less than 896.20 to go short. The stop is a tick above the market structure high at 899.50, a risk of 3.30 points. This suggests the possibility of a downside structure in the 1-minute data. Figure 15-22 shows this to be the case. The 1-minute downside structure has in fact just triggered short.

Analysis of the anticipatory down wave indicates a limit-wave target at 891.12. If our initial stop is based on the reference high, under these conditions the reward-risk ratio based on the 1-minute limit wave is less than 2. The trader then has two choices: to forgo the trade and wait for the next setup that meets the reward-risk

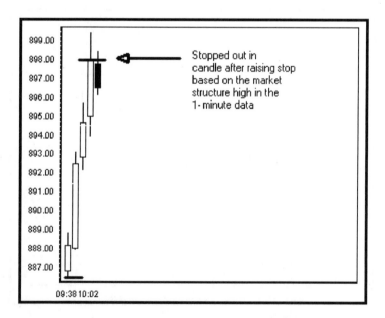

Figure 15-21   Stopped out in the 5th candle after the stop is raised based on the market structure high in the 1-minute data.

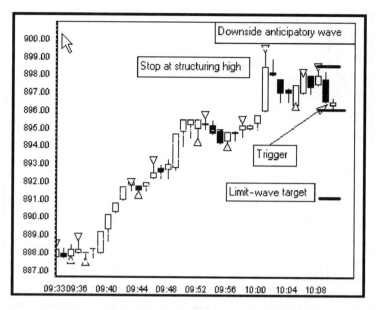

Figure 15-22 The downside structure setup in the 1-minute chart used for entry on the short side.

ratio, or to lower the stop to a meaningful market-based point that brings the reward-risk ratio into the acceptable range. Here, the figure shows the stop lowered to the lower market structure high. The trader chooses to keep the 8-minute trigger for trade entry.

Figure 15-23 shows the 8-minute data for the next several periods. Note that as the market fell, it formed a market structure low. The stop would have been lowered to the triggering point of that market structure. As can be seen, however, this market structure did not trigger, and the market fell further into and through the target area. Taking the gain at the target yields an additional 5.00 points.

In this example, selected at random, there were three clear setup trades indicated by the methods, and both a basic trading interval (8 minutes) and a "microscopic" trading interval (1 minute) were used as a way of peering into and refining trade entry points, target setting, and stop setting. A total of 14.10 points was produced by these very straightforward methods-based trades

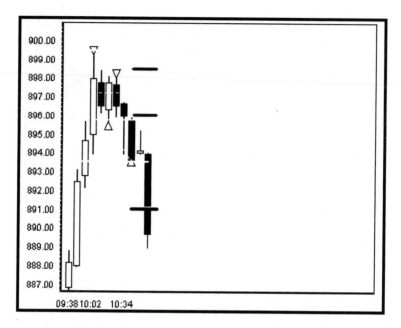

Figure 15-23   The 8-minute data in the several periods following the downside entry.

in the first 90 minutes of trading. Working with the methods this way using a candle-by-candle "step-through" approach is the ideal way of training oneself to trade in real time.

While this illustration showed the interaction between an 8-minute period and the 1-minute period in relation to entry, stops, and targets, the fractal nature of markets is such that these could be any time periods, and therefore the illustration is useful for the general question of trade setup and execution, regardless of time period.

WHAT'S IN STORE FOR THE FUTURE?

As computer access becomes available to the global markets and to an ever-greater density of market participants, everyone will be subject to several inevitable features of trading in the twenty-first century. The first of these features we can call the principle of *instantaneity.* Market movements, news events, and other driving factors of price change will increasingly have an instantaneous effect in the markets. As global markets head toward continuous trading (perhaps 24 hours a day, 7 days a week), there will be no time at which market positions will be without exposure to risk—perhaps uncontrollable risk. This principle of instantaneity has, I believe, played a large part in the increase in shorter-term trading on the part of market participants at all levels. This is a fundamental shift, and it is likely to play an increasing role in undermining the popularity of "buy-and-hold" strategies.

The increasing globalization of markets will inevitably lead to an increase in the principle of *instability,* as money at all levels of the financial spectrum seeks the greatest opportunities in terms of reward-risk ratios. The loyalty factor will diminish, as traders and investors will no longer stay in their own local markets, but will trade and invest on a more global scale. The combination of these factors will inevitably lead to an ever-greater degree of short-term capital movement, and hence the instability of any particular market as the reward-risk premium fluctuates around the globe.

In this regard, an ever-increasing degree of computer power will be brought to bear on reward-risk assessment on a global basis, and computers will inevitably be at the forefront of methods to take advantage of these disparities *instantly.* It seems clear that chaos theory, complexity theory, and new developments in the broad-scale "artificial" intelligent use of advanced concepts will begin to dominate capital flows.[19] How will the individual trader and investor fare in this environment?

While the computing power of the little box that is on everyone's desk today far exceeds that of the earliest machines, which required rooms of large-scale equipment, it is also true that "big money" will always have access to a greater level of computing

---

[19] For a glimmer of what this might look like in the future, see Thomas A. Bass, *The Predictors: How a Band of Maverick Physicists Used Chaos Theory to Trade Their Way to a Fortune on Wall Street* (New York: Henry Holt and Company, 1999).

power than the small participants in the markets. In this sense, it will probably always be the "same old story." Large-scale money, whether in the hands of individual participants or in the hands of institutions, will continue to dominate the financial landscape, largely at the expense of the smaller participants. The principle of constant positive multiplicative compounding will continue to drain the resources of the large majority of traders and investors.

Is there an equalizer? Yes. The equalizer is that the trader or investor *must* learn to be responsible for the exposure of her or his own capital to risk and *must* learn to take advantage of the *nature* of market movements. The former follows from the dawning realization (hopefully encouraged by the bear market of 2000 and all that followed in its wake) that when one's money is being managed by others, it is not necessarily being managed for one's own welfare. The latter follows from the realization that when capital leaves a market, the market will *fall*, and when capital enters a market, the market will *rise*. These are natural and inevitable processes. Only by taking advantage of this natural character of markets will the individual trader and investor be able to equalize the disadvantage that large-scale capital engenders in the markets.

In short, no matter what the "new" developments may be, the fundamental principles of market dynamics will remain the same: Markets will rise, and they will fall. The time frames will become shorter at all levels in the financial world. This creates an enormous *opportunity* for the small investor and trader—the opportunity to compound realized gains with greater frequency. As Hurst described, improved transaction timing is worth all the effort we can bring to it. I believe that the principles and methods outlined in these chapters will serve traders and investors as well in the coming time as they did in the past. In this sense, the methods and principles are related to fundamentals of crowd behavior, and, as Goethe said, changes at this level occur with "glacial slowness." Changes in markets are inevitable, and one must learn to adapt to them. The methods and principles outlined here will help both the trader and the investor to do just that.

DIRECTIONS FOR FURTHER STUDY

Any market in any time frame can be fully described in terms of the relatively simple mathematics of the numbers 2, 3, and 5, the principal numbers in the tradition of *sacred geometry*. This is not in itself surprising, as much of human form and function is also describable in this way. The problem, of course, is how to *anticipate* effectively which of these numeric principles will be operative in the *next* wave or trend of market movement. An enormous amount of work has been done in this area with regard to prices and price patterns, and the trader and investor is encouraged to study these efforts, particularly in the works of Gann, Elliott, Prechter, Jensen, Pesavento, Miner, and Fischer, among many others. Progress with regard to *time* factors in general and market-generated time factors in particular has been considerably less. This area has been the focus of these same technicians, but much more remains to be discovered here.

At undergroundtrader.com, we are working diligently to develop the necessary new tools and techniques that are related to price and time, and especially to the concept of price/time. As Gann observed, *time* is the most important factor, and it is this factor that most traders and investors overlook and undervalue. Therefore, the trader or investor who takes up *time* as an area of study is likely to be well rewarded.

Good luck and good trading!

E-minis: Taking Advantage of the New Markets

Luke of Undergroundtrader

Today's markets are very different from the markets of the past. While some fundamental things will never change, such as the war between fear and greed, the day-to-day market fluctuations operate under a new paradigm. This change is *not* simply a product of the current bear market. Much of it is due to the Internet revolution. The Internet has speeded up the flow of information tremendously. This, in turn, has caused an extreme shift in the way the markets flow.

Many traders are lost in this new trading environment. Trading techniques that have worked in the past are not holding up under these new conditions. Even those who are seeking low risk and low returns are struggling to find proper investments. Lately, many people have come to feel that they are lucky if their losses aren't as bad as their neighbors'. Because of the speed with which the markets move now and the extreme trading conditions, many have chosen to step aside.

Mutual funds, Wall Street analysts, and the television finance fallacy perpetuators have offered very little in the way of help. Many funds offer only stagnant, passive, dinosaurlike buy-and-hold strategies. The Wall Street analysts, the people who are supposed to know more than the average investor, have offered only mostly bogus stock recommendations with ulterior motives. With such a bombardment of misinformation and unfounded hype, most traders today never even get a legitimate shot at generating a consistent profitable return.

However, some positive changes have taken place thanks to this new paradigm shift in the markets. For those who are willing to embrace these changes, there are several new advantages. One in particular is the fact that new instruments to trade have been created to meet the demands of the newly empowered online trader. Markets that were once difficult to access are now only a mouse click away. Markets that were once traded only in the open outcry pits can now be traded by anyone with access to a computer. The S&P 500, the Nasdaq 100, the Dow Jones, the bond markets, currencies, and many other markets have become easily accessible electronically through what are called the "e-minis" futures markets.

E-MINI BASICS

These new e-mini markets allow a trader to participate in market moves without having to select individual issues. These instruments closely follow the price movement of their underlying index. They are easily accessible, and they have tremendous liquidity.

The two most popular e-mini stock index futures are the S&P 500 e-mini, or "ES" contract, and the Nasdaq 100 e-mini, or "NQ" contract. These two contracts are traded electronically on the Chicago Mercantile Exchange (CME). There are numerous advantages to trading these new instruments. And even though there are similar stock-related instruments that follow the indexes, such as exchange-traded funds (ETFs) like the SPYs and QQQs, I feel that there are several key features that make the e-minis a better use of one's trading capital.

These contracts are smaller in size, basically representing one-fifth of the underlying "full" contract. This allows for lower margin requirements and the ability to play these markets on a smaller scale. For example, the full S&P 500 contract currently requires an initial margin of $17,800, whereas you can trade one ES e-mini contract for an initial margin of $3500. Also, for every point the full S&P 500 contract fluctuates, your account will go up or down by $250. On the ES e-mini, each point move is worth $50. On the Nasdaq 100, each point move on the full-size contract is worth $100, whereas on the smaller NQ e-mini each point is worth $20. Keep in mind that each point has its own minimum "tick" value as well. On the ES this is 0.25. So each point has 4 ticks, worth $12.50 each. A move of 1 tick from 1000.00 to 1000.25 is a $12.50 move on 1 e-mini contract. On the NQs, the minimum tick value is 0.50. These relatively lower dollar moves allow smaller players to participate without the large amounts of capital required to trade the bigger contracts. It also allows one to put positions on without having to take on as much risk per point move.

The basic formula for calculating a contract's value is the index value times the contract's multiplier value. You can go to the CME's Web site (www.cme.com) to find out the multiplier. For example, if the index value of the NQs were 1250, you would multiply 1250 times the NQ contract multiplier value ($20) to get the value: $1250 \times \$20 = \$25,000$. Given that one can trade one of these contracts for a small initial margin requirement, the leverage is tremendous. If you know how to use this leverage properly, it is a *huge* advantage. But, as with all futures trading, caution is warranted. Since you can control a sizable amount of money with a small initial outlay, if you are not careful, you can lose more than your initial investment. For more details, make sure you read the Commodities and Futures Trading Commission's (CFTC) material on the risks of trading futures. Its Web site is www.cftc.gov.

Another advantage of the e-minis is the fact that they are very liquid. The first day the ES was open for trading was September 9, 1997. That day, there were 7494 contracts traded. Volume has been increasing steadily ever since. In fact, on July 24, 2002, the ES hit a single-day record of 975,985 contracts traded. The NQ's opening day was June 21, 1999, and 2136 contracts traded that day. In just 3 years its volume has increased tremendously, with 376,120 contracts traded on July 24, 2002. This means that under most circumstances it is easy to get in and out of the market without some of the problems that occur when trading illiquid markets. Problems such as extreme slippage, fill report delays, moving the market with size, and so on are for the most part rectified on these highly liquid instruments.

Since everything is done electronically via the GLOBEX system, most of the time fills are instantaneous. This makes trades very easy to execute. Also, these e-mini markets are open for trading almost 24 hours a day. This allows one to get into or out of the market quickly and to capitalize on potential market-moving events such as overseas news and economic reports even when most other U.S. markets are closed.

Since you are trading an index-type instrument, some of the dangers of trading stocks will also be muted. You will not have the danger that the NQ or ES will be cut in half overnight because of one company's negative news, whereas this is always a risk when holding an individual stock. Another advantage of e-minis over stocks is the fact that it is just as easy to sell short as it is to go long on the e-minis. Unlike the situation with stocks, there is no downtick rule.

One final benefit of trading futures is the 60/40 tax treatment. With e-minis, 60 percent of your gains are taxed at long-term capital gains rates and 40 percent at your ordinary income rate. This can result in a tremendous savings when compared to the tax consequences of comparable stock gains. Please consult your own tax professional for more details.

THREE MUST-HAVE PILLARS FOR PROFITABLE TRADING

It is my belief that profitable trading is mainly the result of playing mathematical probabilities, keeping one's emotions in check, and applying sound money management to geometrically grow equity while minimizing risk. Those three pillars are the backbone of any sound trading methodology.

To generate a respectable return on equity, the trader needs to take an active approach. One needs to go short just as easily as one goes long. One needs to play the oscillations of the market, not just "sit" waiting in a position with capital tied up. I believe that capital should constantly be looking for opportunity, not sitting idle. An investment position should be viewed like an employee. If it is not generating profits in a small amount of time, one should "fire" it—exit the position and look for a new one. This is not to say that I am against initiating long-term positions when they are warranted. But I think it is very naïve to take that buy-and-hold approach if the investment is not showing signs of producing returns.

To facilitate this active approach, one must work at mastering the three areas mentioned previously. First, one needs a technical entry and exit method that is based on probabilities to give one a winning edge. Second, and most important, in my opinion, one needs rules or aids to help one combat the psychological obstacles to trading. And third, one needs a systematic money management plan to exploit the entry/exit edge through sizing of positions.

TECHNICAL METHODS TO EXPLOIT PROBABILITIES

As I indicated earlier, I believe that the psychological aspect of trading is more important than entry techniques. All too often we get hung up on the latest indicator or method to predict market direction. The fact of the matter is that profitable trading is mostly simple mathematics, devoid of emotions. It should be viewed from a probabilities standpoint. We need to find an edge and exploit it with mathematics. That being said, here are some simple methods that I feel will give one an entry/exit edge in the markets.

I believe that technical analysis should supersede fundamental analysis. An axiom I believe in is, "It's all in the charts." I have found this to be very true. Contrary to popular belief, our markets are not particularly "free." They are heavily manipulated by insiders with the deepest pockets in the world. To compete with this big money, I believe technical analysis of charts is our best tool. The charts do not lie.

I have studied the works of the most renowned market technicians, as well as an army of lesser-known self-proclaimed gurus. I have come across some great teachers with very enlightening material. But none of these traders or instructors has the Holy Grail for trading. In fact, the Holy Grail does not exist.

The closest we can come to the Holy Grail is the realization that there isn't one. That is a very liberating notion indeed. It allows us to focus on the real deal—probabilities and money management.

To slant the probabilities in your favor, I would recommend studying Fibonacci methods and Japanese candlestick patterns. Then watch the markets to begin to get a feel for how the methods play out in real time. By watching and trading the market in real time, you will develop a trading intuition that you cannot learn from instructors, at universities, through books, or at seminars. This style of intuitive trading is the highest level one can attain. It has been compared to the state that professional athletes get into when they are said to be "in the zone." This state will come only through much practice and live experience.

Learn to combine this intuition with cutting-edge technical analysis techniques. You want a method of entry such that the market will tell you quickly if the entry is incorrect, so that you can exit with a stop loss that is small in comparison to the potential profit that was initially targeted. Most important, the method *must* be in harmony with your psyche. If it is not, you will not stick with it, and your trading will be overrun with errors. I also recommend that you make only trades with a very high reward-risk ratio—a minimum of 2 to 1.

Space will not allow an in-depth look at how Fibonacci and candlestick analysis can give you an edge in the markets. However, there is no lack of valuable information available in the many books and Web sites on these subjects.

However, I will outline two simple tools that anyone can use to help with trade entry decisions. These do not require intense study, as candlesticks or Fibonacci methods do, but they will give you an edge that you can exploit. Also, I believe that the two methods I chose are based on technical indicators that most charting programs have built in. I am not a big fan of linear technical indicators, as most have an inherent lag built in, but these two entry techniques use the indicators in an innovative way that excludes many of the problems associated with lagging indicators.

The 20-Period EMA Retracement Technique

The first of these techniques is the 20-period exponential moving average (ema) retracement entry technique. I am not the originator of this tool. However, I have watched it in real time for so long that I feel I can contribute some added usefulness to it. In the past, many technicians have taught that if the ADX (average directional movement indicator) is greater than some preset threshold, you then buy or sell retracements to the 20-period ema. The problem with this is that today's intraday markets move too fast and often have large morning gaps (the open price is far away from yesterday's close). This causes bogus ADX readings, and it takes too long for the ADX to catch up to the current trend. What I focus on is the slope of the 20-period ema. Basically, for intraday trading, I watch for a nice slope on the 5-minute 20-period ema—roughly between a 40 and a 70 degree angle. If the slope is much less than this, there is barely any trend, and if it is much more than this, it is parabolic in nature, and a more than normal retrace is very possible.

The 20-period ema retracement rules are as follows:

- Find a 20-period ema on a 5-minute chart with a slope that is roughly between 40 and 70 degrees.
- If prices are above this slope, buy a pullback to the 5-minute 20-period ema.
- Put your stop on the other side of the ema. (Do not stop out with just a flash of prices on the other side; require there to be a significant break before you stop.)

- Set a profit target of at least a 2-to-1 reward-risk ratio. If you are risking 1.5 points on the ES, target at least 3 points. You can also set a trailing stop using the 5-minute 20-period ema.

- If the slope on the 5-minute 20-period ema is flat or flattening, be very careful about initiating trades.

- You want price to move into the ema. You do not want the ema to move into price. For example, the latter will happen if prices drop and do not bounce. The ema will "pull into" the price because of the time lapse. This is what you do not want. You want prices to bounce or fall into the ema.

- Reverse these rules for sells.

  Figure A-1 gives an example.

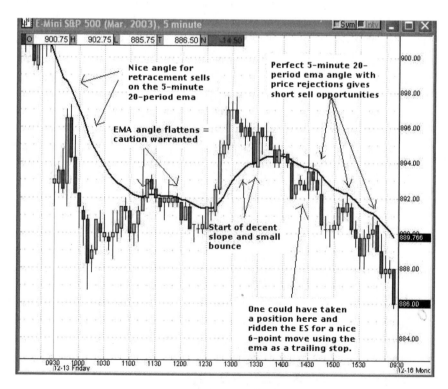

Figure A-1   20-period retracement technique.

Stochastic Divergence Trades

Another useful technique that will give you an entry or exit edge in the markets is the stochastic divergence setup. Divergence is one of the best technical tools I know of to aid in spotting potential reversal points in the market. Although we are going to look at stochastic divergence, I would recommend that you study other techniques in the same vein as well. MACD, CCI, RSI, and %R are other indicators that traders use to spot divergence.

Divergence is a situation in which the stock or an index is moving in one direction, while the indicator is doing the opposite. When this occurs, a high-probability trade is present.

The stochastic divergence rules are as follows:

- Settings for the slow stochastic are 5 for length and 3 for the smoothing. On Q charts, this is 5,3,3; on TradeStation, use 5,3,2,1.
- Set up the chart so that only the %K is visible. We are not concerned with crosses, so it is not important for us to see %D.
- Look for divergence only in the proper context. Good reasons would be support/resistance areas, such as low-of-day tests, Fibonacci values, gap fill areas, and so on.
- When divergence is suspected, wait for the bar to close. Once this occurs and divergence is confirmed, use the high or low of the confirming bar to trigger the entry.
- Place the stop above or below the nearest swing high or low and target a minimum of a 2-to-1 reward-risk ratio on the trade. For example, if divergence sets up and the required stop on the NQs is 2.5 points, target a 5-point minimum profit.

Figure A-2 shows an example using a 1-minute chart.

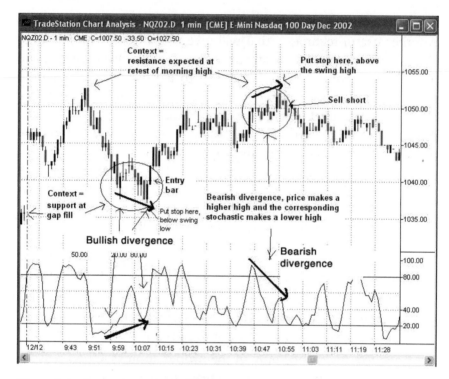

Figure A-2   Stochastics divergence technique.

PSYCHOLOGICAL OBSTACLES AND THE IMPORTANCE OF A PROPER REWARD-RISK RATIO

The second and most important pillar of profitable trading, in my opinion, is mastering the psychological aspect. If you can't get a foothold in this area, you are doomed to fail. All new traders should spend most of their time studying and preparing to handle the emotional challenges they will face when they are trading live with real money. Then they should slowly work into real trades with real money.

Of all the techniques I have studied, I have found trading with a 2-to-1 minimum reward-risk ratio to help me the most with the mental aspect of trading. It removes a lot of the performance pressure and puts the outcome in the hands of mathematics. For every dollar I risk, I want at least two dollars in profit. This is one of the absolute biggest keys to a high percentage return on equity. If one maintains this 2-to-1 minimum on all trades taken, it reduces trading to a mostly mathematical endeavor. If I have four winning trades and two losers, my equity will increase substantially. If I have two winning trades and two losing trades, my equity will still increase. If I have four losing trades and two winning trades, I lose nothing. These are the kinds of numbers that produce both a monetary and a psychological edge in the markets.

A solid psychological pillar is required for trading success. And trading with a 2-to-1 minimum reward-risk ratio gives one a mental edge that will help to combat every profitable trader's enemy—fear and greed.

Basically, even at a 50 percent win rate, I will produce a very nice return using this 2-to-1 minimum ratio. *(In reality, I would never settle for a 50 percent win rate. But, if that were to result, the mathematics of it would still produce a nice return.)* Many people talk of this, but few of them take it to heart and put it into practice. Lately, I have finally begun to place more importance on this aspect than I do on entry techniques or direction picking. I feel that entry techniques are of secondary importance compared to the importance of controlling one's emotions and trading with discipline.

MONEY MANAGEMENT

Finally, the third important pillar of profitable trading is the application of sound money management. To truly manage capital correctly, one needs to engage the multiplying effects of compounding gains. There are many different techniques for doing this. The one that makes the most sense to me is fixed ratio.

Basically, fixed ratio will help you analyze a potential trading system or method and determine a "delta" value. This delta value then becomes part of a formula that is recalculated after each trade. The formula analyzes many variables and will tell you how much size (number of shares or contracts) to trade on the next trade.

Fixed ratio is very powerful. It exploits the equity curve and makes it very efficient. It increases gains geometrically at a very significant rate while minimizing the drawdown when a method goes through a downturn. The best way to see its effect is through graphs. Here are a couple of examples.

Figure A-3 is a graph of a system that I designed and back-tested from January 2, 2001 to April 30, 2002. Without the application of fixed ratio, it produced a nice return of about $32,000 (a 106 percent return) on 1 e-mini—a huge return, considering that one would have needed only approximately $3500 in initial capital to begin trading this system.

However, in the graph, you can see that the equity curve without money management applied (the lower line) is dwarfed by the equity curve line with fixed ratio money management position sizing applied (the upper line). Keep in mind that the same exact trades are

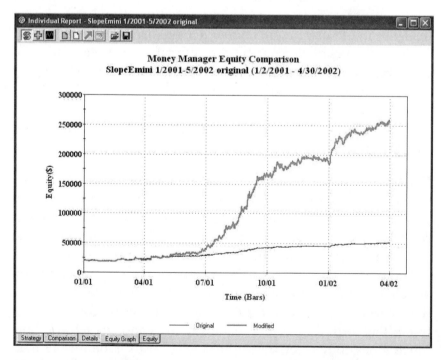

Figure A-3   Money management equity comparison with and without fixed ratio.

executed for each equity curve. The only difference is in the fluctuation of position size as dictated by the fixed-ratio formula.

Drawdown periods were kept in check by money management, while growth periods were enhanced tremendously. Net profit went from $32,000 (a 106 percent return) to $237,000 (a 593 percent return), while the worst maximum drawdown increased only 8 percent (see Figure A-4). That is how you compound gains.

CONCLUSION

In summary, I think it is important to put emphasis on three all-important areas:

- Trading mathematical probabilities

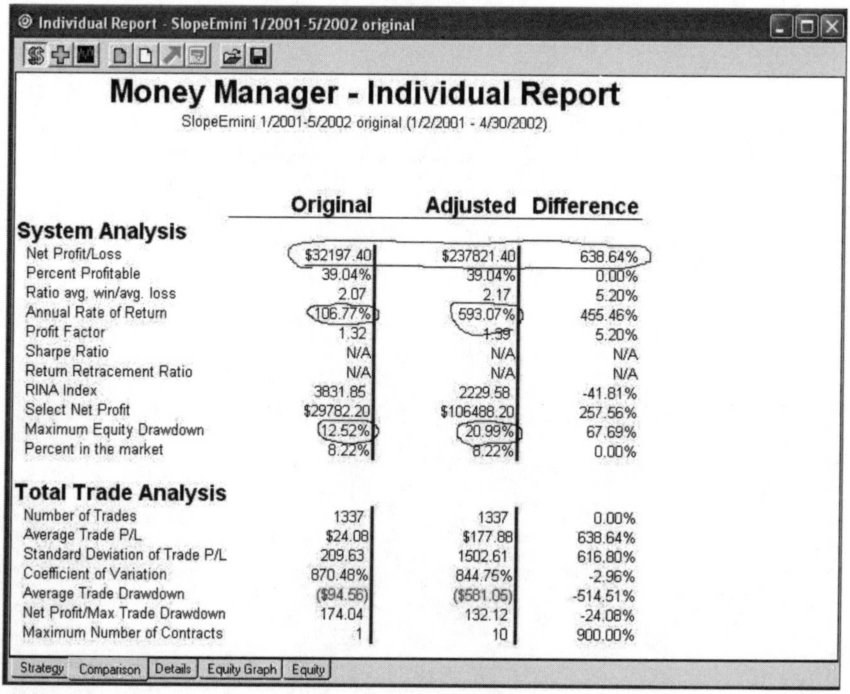

Individual Report - SlopeEmini 1/2001-5/2002 original

Money Manager - Individual Report

SlopeEmini 1/2001-5/2002 original (1/2/2001 - 4/30/2002)

	Original	Adjusted	Difference
System Analysis			
Net Profit/Loss	$32197.40	$237821.40	638.64%
Percent Profitable	39.04%	39.04%	0.00%
Ratio avg. win/avg. loss	2.07	2.17	5.20%
Annual Rate of Return	106.77%	593.07%	455.46%
Profit Factor	1.32	1.39	5.20%
Sharpe Ratio	N/A	N/A	N/A
Return Retracement Ratio	N/A	N/A	N/A
RINA Index	3831.85	2229.58	-41.81%
Select Net Profit	$29782.20	$106488.20	257.56%
Maximum Equity Drawdown	12.52%	20.99%	67.69%
Percent in the market	8.22%	8.22%	0.00%
Total Trade Analysis			
Number of Trades	1337	1337	0.00%
Average Trade P/L	$24.08	$177.88	638.64%
Standard Deviation of Trade P/L	209.63	1502.61	616.80%
Coefficient of Variation	870.48%	844.75%	-2.96%
Average Trade Drawdown	($94.56)	($581.05)	-514.51%
Net Profit/Max Trade Drawdown	174.04	132.12	-24.08%
Maximum Number of Contracts	1	10	900.00%

Strategy | Comparison | Details | Equity Graph | Equity

Figure A-4 Further comparison of management techniques.

- Using proper reward-risk ratios to maintain psychological sharpness
- Applying sound money management that geometrically compounds gains

By focusing on these areas, one can become a profitable trader. And because of the aforementioned advantages, I feel that the e-minis are a perfect vehicle for putting these three pillars of trading into action.

To get more information on trading the e-minis, be sure to visit the CME's Web site, www.cme.com.

Trading the Soybean Markets

John Allen

INTRODUCTION TO SETTING UP THE CHART FOR DAY TRADING

The instrument discussed in this chapter is the CBOT soybeans contract, particularly on the date July 25, 2002. This contract has low liquidity compared to the S&P 500 futures contract. In addition, the price movements on a daily basis often contain large gaps, which may or may not be in the direction of major indicators. This second characteristic makes it somewhat undesirable to hold positions overnight. In particular, a failed evening star pattern (if entered according to signals in a daily or weekly chart) can prove expensive. Therefore, it was decided to trade on an intraday basis only, without holding any positions overnight.

Before deciding on the chart interval to be used, one needs to consider the types of orders that are allowed for the instrument to be traded. The Chicago Board of Trade (CBOT) periodically changes the types of orders that are accepted. For the soybeans contract, the CBOT will usually accept stop orders, stop-on-open-only orders, market orders, limit orders, market-on-close orders, and fill or kill orders. At times, however, stop orders are not accepted. When that happens, the trader must wait by the computer and enter a market order when the stop is hit. This limits the speed of execution and makes it preferable to avoid using very short chart intervals.

Beyond the consideration of acceptable types of orders, liquidity constraints limit the speed of order executions. In cases where the order is continuously marketable, trade executions in soybeans frequently take place in 1 to 3 minutes, but some executions take place in 5 to 7 minutes, with a rare case taking as long as 10 minutes. This rules out scalping from a 1-minute chart. However, if a 30-minute chart is used, the major part of a day's price move may take place within a single chart interval. Experience has shown that the basic 13-minute chart is most useful for intraday trading.

Actually, the choice of the 13-minute trading interval was made for two reasons: (1) This is the shortest time interval in which most candlestick patterns are reliable, and (2) using this interval permits trading an instrument that has poor liquidity while capturing the major portion of a price move. While candlestick patterns are reliable in the 13-minute interval, they become only marginally useful in the 8-minute interval, and they are practically useless in the 5-minute interval. The sole exception to this is the use of market structures, which remain useful even in the 1-minute interval. Using 13 minutes as the trading interval, once a candlestick trigger is seen, it often takes three to six chart intervals for a well-chosen exit target to be hit. Thus, a major portion of a potential gain on a trade can be realized in this time interval.

While trading is done strictly on an intraday basis, with an exit from every trade being taken by the close of the trading session if not earlier, the 13-minute interval is not the only chart used. Daily candlestick signals can be used effectively in intraday trading, and a daily candlestick chart is used, as shown in Figure B-1.

Figure B-1 shows an important application of the daily chart in intraday trading. Prior to the open of trading on July 25, 2002, this chart shows a piercing pattern. This pattern is bullish, provided that there is a subsequent price movement above the high of

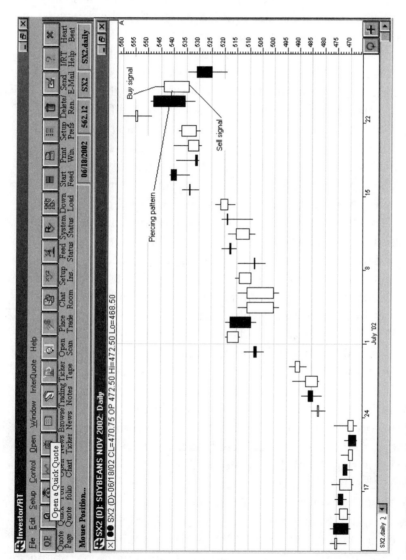

Figure B-1 Soybeans daily chart.

the piercing candle. However, this pattern can be considered to have failed if there is a downmove below the low of the piercing candle, in which case the pattern is bearish. On the day in question, the instrument opened below the low of the thrusting candle. This is a daily sell signal, and one can expect that the day will consist mostly of downmoves. There can be upward countertrend trades during the day, but they are likely to be brief and limited in price movement. This is important information to remember when examining the 13-minute chart as it develops for the day.

In intraday trading, there are two entirely different kinds of trades: (1) trading reversals in the course of intraday oscillations in price, and (2) entering and then exiting trades during a single trend that is in progress. Many traders consider only trading reversals. Others prefer to trade only single trends. Entering and exiting an ongoing trend is by far the more difficult of the two methods. When viewing a chart as it unfolds, it is often difficult to determine the intraday trend, although it will be obvious when it is seen after the fact. There are several techniques that can be used to reveal this trend, such as moving averages, point-and-figure charts, trading channels, the 13-period moving average shifted 3 periods into the future, and the three-line break chart.

Of all the available trend indicators, the Japanese three-line break chart is the finest. This indicator whipsaws somewhat less than the 13-period moving average shifted three periods to the right. In the case of a gap opening, the three-line break chart can be considered internally, using the open as the initial price. This serves to provide a reasonably close stop. When the opening gap is not large, the three-line break chart can be used on a continuous basis, using data from the preceding day.

On the three-line break chart, there is a tendency for a price move to stall or reverse near a Fibonacci number of new prices in a series, e.g., 5, 8, or 13 new highs or new lows. This can be used, at times, to modify exit targets that were originally based on natural-square eighths, 15-degree multiples, Gann angles, or Fibonacci targets. Thus, although the three-line break chart is seldom used as the sole determination of a trade, it is frequently used in combination with other technical indicators.

To expand this concept, when trading an ongoing trend with the three-line break chart, one can either enter the trade at the first new high or low and then stay in the trade until a break price is established, or enter a trade at a new high or low and exit the trade at a Fibonacci number of new highs (lows). Alternatively, one can exit the trade when the price reaches a 15-degree multiple, a Gann angle, or a natural-square eighth, because the price move will often stall or reverse at these points. Rather than trading trailing reversals, as the three-line break method was originally conceived to do, it is recommended that one exit the trade at a specific price level. Experience has shown that higher profits are realized this way.

An example of a three-line break chart is shown in Figure B-2. In this example, the continuous method is employed because the gap at the open is small.

In the context of daily signals, the candlesticks derived from the overnight trading session are useful. A daily candlestick can be used in combination with the candlestick from the overnight session. The pattern obtained from that pair can often be used as the basis of an opening trade or an intraday trade, using such patterns as piercing pattern, dark cloud cover, thrusting pattern, and many more. Also, the candlestick of the overnight trading session can be used by itself at times. Candlesticks such as the hammer, shooting star, dragonfly, or suicide doji can be used as single-candle trade entry signals, and the candlestick extremities may give useful information on support and resistance that cannot be found from any other source. Professional pit traders use this overnight information extensively, and this use affects the points where a price move can be expected to stall or reverse.

There are many useful candlestick patterns in addition to the few that are referred to here. An excellent reference for all such patterns is *Japanese Candlestick Charting Techniques,* by Steve Nison.

While the daily chart and the daily chart combined with the overnight trading data are useful for trade signals, the bulk of the

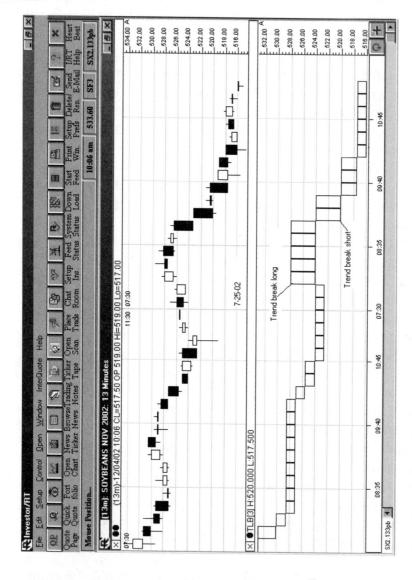

Figure B-2 Soybeans 13-minute three-line break chart.

intraday trade signals are to be found in the 13-minute candlestick chart. In addition to displaying reliable patterns, this chart shows usable wave structures that experience a low failure rate.

With some exceptions, once a price move begins, it will continue until the price encounters a barrier or impediment to further movement. It is normal for the price to oscillate in the course of this movement. These impediments to price movement may take the form of wave targets, price moves to Fibonacci targets (T3, T5, etc.), the occurrence of natural-square eighths, Gann angles (45-degree multiples), or lesser Gann angles (15-degree multiples). These impediments to price movement become excellent trade exit targets. Also, these impediments are useful for setting stops. For example, it is known that when a price move encounters a natural-square eighth and then moves to the other side of the eighth, if the candle close occurs on this other side of the eighth, then the price move is likely to continue. Thus, this becomes a useful stop for exiting a trade when the price moves against the trader and the candle closes on the opposite side of the eighth.

Gann angles, as used here, are calculated on a single-price basis with respect to the extreme high or extreme low in the entire trading history of an instrument. There are other possible methods of calculation, such as from the extreme high or low seen over a fixed number of trading days (for example, the last 89 trading days), and these also give useful results. To avoid becoming overwhelmed with more data than can be assimilated, however, the practice in use here is to limit the angles to those obtained from the extreme high or low in the entire trading history of the contract. A square-of-nine chart is used to find the range corresponding to a 360-degree rotation from the extreme, and this range is further divided into 45-degree segments, the so-called Gann angles. The 45-degree segments are further divided into three segments each, to obtain the so-called 15-degree multiples, which are also important price points.

Boxpoints are used as determined by Terry Davis a number of years ago. These are 2.2-point intervals, and they are calculated in two ways: from the settlement price, and from major intraday market structure highs and market structure lows. While boxpoints give significant points where a price movement may stall or reverse, they are somewhat less important than natural-square eighths and Gann angles.

Gann lines are obtained by squaring the price/time box and projecting straight lines from the 1:1, 1:2, 1:4, 1:8, and 1:16 points along the price axis of the box, which is the ordinate. Of particular interest is the price/time box obtained from the true range of the entire prior day's trading history. Projections are made throughout the current day's trading activity. This is shown in Figure B-3, the 13-minute chart of the current trading day.

Figure B-3 shows a number of technical indicators that have abbreviated annotations. These abbreviations are T2 and T3, the Fibonacci target prices associated with the 0.00618 and 0.01618 multipliers; EBB, the extreme Bollinger bands using 2.618 standard deviations and 13 periods; NS, the natural squares; NS8th, the natural-square eighths; GA, 45-degree Gann angles; 15-deg, 15-degree multiples; 0.382 UAE, the 0.382 up angle extension; 0.618 UAE, the 0.618 up angle extension; 0.382 DAE, the 0.382 down angle extension; 0.618 DAE, the 0.618 down angle extension; 13-shift, the 13-period ema shifted 3 periods to the right; 3-shift, the 3-period ema shifted 3 periods to the left; and 1:1 through 1:16 lines, the Gann lines associated with the price/time square.

There are times when the price activity does not follow the Gann lines defined by the true range, but instead follows the Gann lines defined simply by the prior day's range. It is the practice here to construct charts both ways. Usually, the applicable price/time box will be apparent after a few 13-minute periods. Then the non-performing chart will be discarded. More often than not, the chart based on the true range will prevail.

Once a price movement begins to follow a particular Gann line, it tends to continue following that line until an impediment such as a natural-square eighth, a Gann angle, a 15-degree multiple, a boxpoint, or an intersecting Gann line is encountered. Thus, it becomes possible to project the time required for a trade to reach its target. This is seen in Figure B-3, where, after a high-of-day trade entry trigger, the price is seen to follow the 1:2 upside Gann

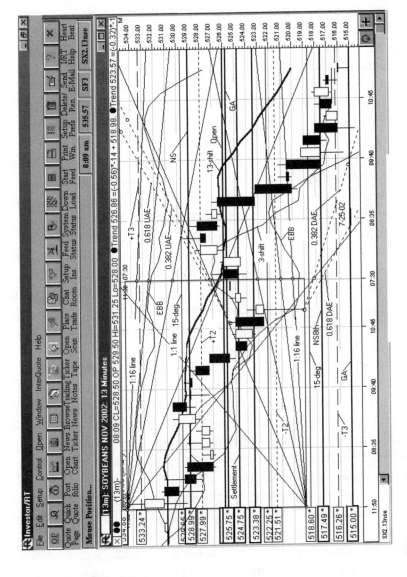

Figure B-3 Soybeans 13-minute chart.

line. The price is projected to intersect the 529.00 natural-square eighth in the 5th candle of the day. The exit target is hit during the 4th candle, which is quite close in time.

Other lines of interest, based on the price/time square, are the Fibonacci relations, which are the 0.382 and 0.618 angle extensions, projected both upward and downward. The price/time ordinate range is divided into three segments, bounded by the 0.382 and 0.618 fractions of the true range of the prior trading day. These segments are used to determine the slopes of the applicable lines. These slopes are used to extend the angles upward from the last market structure high and downward from the last market structure low. These angle extensions may be determined either mathematically or graphically, using a clear plastic overlay. The plastic overlay method, while less precise, gives adequate accuracy. Furthermore, the graphical method will reveal many computational errors and is recommended in preference to computation. These angle extensions are shown as well in Figure B-3.

The Fibonacci angle extensions are valuable trading tools. Under typical market conditions, a price move that exceeds the 0.382 angle extension, upward or downward, will not be sustained. Under extreme market conditions, a price move that exceeds the 0.618 angle extension will not be sustained. In particular, if a price move that exceeds the slope of either of these extensions also exceeds the 1:1 Gann line, the price will almost always return to that Gann line during the trading day.

A price move may follow one of the Fibonacci angle extensions, just as it may follow one of the Gann lines. When this occurs, the tendency to follow the extension will usually continue until one of the impediments to price movement is encountered. This also makes it possible to project the time to a trade exit target.

Another category of so-called impediments to price movement is the Fibonacci targets. Fibonacci targets are calculated both from the prior day's settlement price and from major intraday reversal points, as described elsewhere in this book. In intraday trading, the most important Fibonacci targets are T3 and T5, although T2 is also significant when the trend is not strong. The multipliers for T2, T3, and T5 are 0.00618, 0.01618, and 0.03618, respectively. The T3 and T5 targets are equal in importance to the natural-square eighths. The T2 targets are somewhat less important.

The problem involved in using the natural-square eighths, Gann angles, 15-degree multiples, boxpoints, and Fibonacci targets is being able to quickly assimilate an overwhelming amount of data. To accomplish this, all the previously described factors are entered into a spreadsheet and sorted by price. Then these factors are annotated on the 13-minute candlestick chart as horizontal reference lines. While the chart looks cluttered, it is unambiguous when these lines are color-coded, and it becomes easy to see what factor the price is approaching in real time. These factors will not be unambiguous when these annotated lines are viewed in a monochrome display.

A further consideration in setting up the trading chart is the price movement with respect to extreme Bollinger bands (2.618 standard deviations, 13 periods). Empirical considerations warn that once a Bollinger band that is so constructed is penetrated, the price movement may stall or reverse near this point. Of course, the price movement may continue for some distance after such penetration. A useful operational aid that can be directly applied to trading is to use the 3-period ema shifted 3 periods to the left (referred to as 3-shift in this appendix). When this ema moves outside the Bollinger band, then moves back inside, this is a useful warning to exit the trade.

THE IMPORTANCE OF THE COMPOUND FILTER

In order to reduce the incidence of losing trades, it is desirable to filter the trades. Criteria are selected that, when met, ensure that a high percentage of trades will be successful.

There are a number of criteria that can be used. One may look at the daily context variables, which include the T3 volatility signal, three-candle range limits, daily market structure, flex zone breakout or breakdown, daily three-line break trend, 233-period ema, daily wave structure, and price with respect to the bozu controller, among others. These context variables are covered elsewhere in this book.

The bulk of the author's trading is done in the basic 13-minute interval, and there is a particular leading indicator that can be used. This is the 13-period ema shifted 3 periods into the future. This indicator will be abbreviated 13-shift, in order to save space. When a long trade is triggered above the 13-shift or a short trade is triggered below that ema, there is a probability of approximately 80 percent that the trade will be successful, as long as the stop and the exit target are well chosen. When this moving average is shifted 3 periods to the right, it becomes a leading indicator, and its performance is much improved over the abysmal performance of the unshifted ema, which is a lagging indicator.

Also, it has been noted by several successful traders that the opening price can be used as an effective trade filter. When the long trigger is hit above the opening price, the trade has a much better chance of being successful than a long trade that is triggered below the opening price. The same can be said of a short trade that is triggered below the opening price. Thus, whether the current price is above or below the opening price may be considered an effective leading indicator of the probable outcome of the trade. The reliability of this filter is not as good as that of the 13-shift filter. There is a probability of approximately 70 percent that the trade thus constrained will be successful, as long as the stop and the exit target are well chosen.

The trigger used to enter a trade must be well chosen. One effective trigger is a 13-minute candle close above or below the 13-shift ema. A somewhat more effective trigger is a candle close where the body midpoint is above or below the 13-shift ema. Also, the high of day or the low of day is an effective trigger for a long or short position. When a reversal is occurring, the piercing pattern, dark cloud pattern, bullish engulfing pattern, and bearish engulfing pattern are effective when the trigger is selected to exceed the piercing or engulfing candle. When the opening price gaps significantly from the prior day's closing price, the fresh-start three-line break point at the end of the first 13-minute period often becomes an effective trigger. The market structure low buy trigger or the market structure high sell trigger associated with a wave-3 impulse move of a wave structure, described elsewhere in this book, is particularly effective. As described elsewhere, a wave-5 price movement is usually complex and difficult to trade, with many uncertainties involved. The component waves that make up the total wave-5 movement can be traded individually, however.

While either the 13-shift ema or the opening price works as an effective filter, the two indicators can be used together as an even more effective filter. To do this, one simply declines a trade at an entry trigger unless the price at that trigger is on the correct side of the 13-shift ema at the same time that a long trade trigger is above the opening price or a short trade trigger is below that price. This, then, becomes a compound filtered trade. Such a trade has a particularly high probability of success, exceeding the probability of either filter alone.

The compound filter need not be used to the exclusion of every other trade criterion. One can also often use daily market structure signals, for example, to exclude trades that do not have a high chance of success. For example, if a daily market structure low has formed, and the price has retraced to near the low of the second candle of the market structure low, and if a low-of-day trigger is seen that satisfies the compound filter, one may wish to decline the short trade unless the market structure low is violated. Otherwise, the low of the second candle of the market structure low is likely to become support, limiting the extent of the down-move.

One can also use the prior day's candle in combination with the candle from the overnight trading session to exclude potentially losing trades. For example, speaking hypothetically, yesterday's candle in combination with the overnight session may form a thrusting pattern. While this is a weak bullish pattern, many consider it a bearish pattern. It does not become a sell signal unless the intraday price subsequently falls below the low of the thrusting candle. When the thrusting pattern is in effect on a daily basis, it is good practice to decline any short intraday trade until such time as the price falls below the low of the thrusting candle, irrespective of the earlier occurrence of any other intraday trigger.

There are limitations on the effectiveness of the compound filter. Few markets are either exclusively trending or exclusively oscillating. In general, a market follows a trend while simultaneously oscillating within a channel, which may itself be of variable width. The compound filter works better in a market that is preponderantly trending than in one that is preponderantly oscillating. In a market that is oscillating, in order to trade effectively with the compound filter, one needs to select exit targets that are quite close.

In the market being traded here, the author seldom enters a trade before the close of the first 13-minute period. Although one can trade the open, using stop orders in pairs, orders will seldom be filled within a tick or two of the opening trigger points. More often than not, because of liquidity constraints, the order will be filled near the worst possible price. It is better to wait patiently until the first 13-minute period has closed, then reevaluate the market at that time to determine under what conditions the compound filter requirements will be satisfied.

In the example used here, at the end of the first 13-minute period, it is seen that a price move to either a new high of day or a new low of day will satisfy the dual requirements of the compound filter based on the opening price and the 13-period 3-shift-right exponential moving average.

IDENTIFYING THE TRIGGER, TARGET, AND STOP

With due regard for the requirements set forth in the preceding section, one needs to analyze the market in advance of entering any trade. As part of this analysis, one should recognize that two different numerical conventions apply to the soybeans contract. The tick interval is 0.25 point, but actual trades take effect in eighths of a cent per bushel. Thus, a price of 529.25 is the same as

529'2 cents per bushel, where the number to the right of the apostrophe is eighths of a cent.

The trigger to enter a trade may be a market structure low buy signal or a market structure high sell signal, a high-of-day or low-of-day price, a high-of-trend or low-of-trend (intraday basis) price, a daily market structure signal, a 13-minute three-line break new price, or a three-candle range limit violation, to name a few. Before entering the trade, however, one needs to know under what conditions he or she will exit the trade. One needs an exit target in case the trade is successful, and one needs a stop in case the trade is unsuccessful. Failure to decide the stop in advance and then to exercise that stop without fail will ultimately result in catastrophic losses. Similarly, failure to decide the exit target and then exit the trade without exception will frequently result in the vanishing of sizable gains.

In identifying the exit target, one needs to know under what conditions the market price movement is likely to stall or reverse, and then set the exit target near that point. It is also important not to get overloaded with data to such an extent that one is overwhelmed when one tries to make trade decisions. To this end, three indicators are used; in order of decreasing importance, these are natural-square eighths, 45-degree Gann angles with their 15-degree derivatives, and 2.2-point boxpoints. In addition, one needs to look at the Fibonacci T2, T3, and T5 targets, both from the settlement price and from the last intraday reversal. Only in a very strong trading market will the price advance much beyond T3 or T5 without stalling or reversing. In a weak trending market, the price movement will often stall at T2 as well.

In identifying the exit target, then, the nearest natural-square eighth is often the best choice. If the market is strong trending, intervening 15-degree multiples may often be ignored, but the more effective 45-degree Gann angles should be considered. Often, the 2.2-point boxpoints (both from the settlement price and from the last market structure point) may be ignored, although one should understand their placement and recognize that the market will often stall, at least momentarily, at these points.

Examining the 13-minute chart, one sees that no high-of-day trigger is hit in the second period, although both a buy stop and a sell stop are in place a tick beyond the range limits of the first candle. It is in the third period that the buy stop is hit. After the buy stop is hit, the price oscillates both above and below the trigger point. The order is filled at 526'4, and the 529'0 natural square is selected as the exit target. A sell stop is entered at 523'6, a tick below the 524'0 low of day. This corresponds to a market structure low violation in a time interval shorter than 13 minutes.

In the fourth period, the exit target at 529'0 was hit, and a market sell order was entered as soon as the target was hit. The price went a half point higher before starting to retrace. The order was filled at 528'4, for a 2'0 gain.

EXHAUSTION, CONSOLIDATION, AND REVERSAL

The effect of hitting the 529'0 natural square was to exhaust the upmove. The natural squares, as differentiated from the eighths between those squares, are extremely strong points of exhaustion of price movements. This happens far more frequently than not, irrespective of the placement of Fibonacci targets and Gann angles. Often there will be a consolidation about the natural square for a period of time before either the trend resumes or a reversal begins. That did not happen in this case. In one more period, a market structure high was formed, and in the following period a market structure high sell signal was hit, indicating that a reversal was underway.

In connection with the reversal of trend just described, it is important to note the difference between leading indicators, lagging indicators, and indicators that are neither leading nor lagging. Candlestick patterns are leading indicators of changes in trend, as are certain time-shifted moving averages. Unshifted moving averages are lagging indicators. Three-line break charts, on the other hand, are neither leading nor lagging. The three-line break chart makes no attempt to project a developing change in trend. This chart simply expresses the trend once it is established.

When trading reversals of trend, it is often desirable to enter a trade at the earliest indication that a trend reversal is taking place. If one does not, a sizable percentage of a price movement will have been made before the trade is entered. To this end, a leading indicator, such as a candlestick pattern, is a good choice for trade entry. A lagging indicator should not be considered. When one is trading an ongoing trend, rather than reversals, use of the three-line break chart is a good choice because the three-line break chart will often give an advance indication that a trend is about to stall or reverse as the number of new prices in a series approaches a Fibonacci ordinal, such as 5, 8, or 13 new highs or lows.

At the market structure high sell trigger, the price was still above the opening price, although it was below the 13-period 3-shift-right ema. The conditions for a compound filter were not met, so no further trade was entered at that time.

During the seventh period, the 3-candle range short trigger was hit. This was a useful entry trigger, and at this level, the dual requirements of the compound filter were met. This trigger was hit at a sell stop of 525'6, and the order was filled at 525'4. An exit target at T2 of 521.51 was decided, and a stop a tick above the 529'4 high of day was entered as a buy stop. This stop, if hit, would represent a failure of the 13-minute market structure high and would be an indication of market strength, in which case one would no longer want to be in a short position.

MODIFYING TARGETS AND STOPS

Sometimes there are valid reasons for changing the exit target or the stop or both, although the stop should never be made wider than the value chosen initially. Changing the stop to one wider than that initially chosen is usually a psychological response to an undesired price movement, and making this psychological response consistently will eventually result in large losses. During the seventh period, the market showed impressive weakness, indicating the likelihood of a further decline. With the likelihood of increasing the gain on the trade, it was also desired to protect the position. It was decided to extend the target to the 517'6 natural-square eighth and to remove the initial buy stop, replacing it with a 13-minute trailing stop. As long as the downmove continued to be impulsive in nature, the buy stop would be maintained a tick above the high of each successive 13-minute candle. Thus, the trade would be terminated either when the 517'6 natural-square eighth was hit or when the movable stop was hit, whichever occurred first.

By the tenth period, the trailing stop had not been hit. The exit target at 517'6 was hit during the tenth period, however, and a market buy order was entered while removing the buy stop from above the ninth candle. The market buy order was filled at 518'0, for a gain of 7'4.

THE IMPORTANCE OF CONTEXT AND THE ASSESSMENT OF REWARD-RISK IN TRADE FILTERING

After the second trade of the day was concluded, the market was watched for the possibility of further trades. The general downturn continued. By the eleventh period, a low-of-day trigger a tick below 515'0 would satisfy both the opening price and the 13-shift compound filter. However, there was a Gann angle at 515'0, only a half point away. If one were to take that trade, the nearest market-based stop would be 522'2, some 7 points away. The reward at that Gann angle would be minute compared to the risk. Therefore, it was decided to decline that trade. The Gann angle was hit briefly. The market was watched through the close, in the event that another potential trade would develop. No further trade signals were seen that would satisfy the dual requirements of the compound filter.

As an aid to minimizing the number of unsuccessful trades, one should consider the importance of context variables, described elsewhere in this book. There are many possible context variables. A few of the more important ones are the T3 volatility signal, the daily 13-shift indicator, the daily 233-period ema, the daily wave structure, the last daily 3-period breakout or break-down, the price with respect to the daily bozu controller, the price with respect to the daily flex range, and the price with respect to the daily extreme Bollinger band indicator. For simplicity, each variable can be assigned one of the ordinals −1, 0, and +1, and the arithmetic sum taken. This can be used as a rough guide to favor either short or long trades.

Of course, there are exceptions to slavishly taking either short or long trades to the exclusion of all others. For example, when a wave structure of 5 to 13 periods has been formed in the intraday chart, it is often advisable to take the market structure trigger that signals the start of wave 3, irrespective of the sum of the context variables. However, one would be well advised to take such a trade only when the Rule of Three is satisfied, i.e., when there are at least three context variables in the desired direction.

ASSESSMENT OF THE TRADING DAY AND REVIEW OF PERSONAL PERFORMANCE

There were two trades. In the first trade, a trigger was hit that vio-lated the high of the first 13-minute candle. The buy stop was filled at 526'4, and after the natural square was hit, the trade was exited at 528'4, for a 2'0 gain. In the second trade, at a 3-period range breakdown, the sell stop was filled at 525'4. The modified exit tar-get at the natural-square eighth was hit, and the trade was exited at 518'0, for a 7'4 gain. On a per-contract basis, this represents a gain of $475 while requiring a margin of $810, a before-commission return of 58.6 percent.

It should be noted that in each of these trades, the stop was ini-tially wider than the potential gain. This happens often when mar-ket-based stops are used and when market data are used to derive exit targets. If, instead of trading, one were gambling, as in rolling the dice, and one had a 50/50 chance of a successful trade, then over time one would be guaranteed to lose money. However, when one is using well-chosen market-based targets and stops, one is speculating rather than gambling. This tilts the odds heavily in the trader's favor, and with a greater than 80 percent chance of success in a trade, one can afford to have stops wider than the targets.

Different traders have different trading styles. For example, there are traders who expect to be successful no more than 40 percent of the time. In order to be profitable, those traders must select stops much closer than the exit targets. Unfortunately, when this is done, either the stops or the targets often are not market-based. Too often, a price movement will stall well short of the selected target, or a stop will be hit, only to have the undesired price movement stall nearby, when a wider market-based stop would have sufficed to permit a profitable trade. All too often, the goal of having a few successful trades with very large gains is not realized. The remedy is to trade in harmony with the market, using market-based triggers and targets and stops, with the attendant high success rate. This technique is not amenable to the setting of daily profit goals. Instead, one simply takes whatever profits the market gives. Over a period of days, this technique is highly profitable if it is used in a disciplined manner.

Index

363

ABOUT THE AUTHORS

Jea Yu is cofounder and managing partner of undergroundtrader.com, considered one of today's dominant swing trading websites. A popular speaker at trading conferences nationwide, Yu has written articles for industry journals including *Active Trader* and *Online Investor* and also created two top-selling trading videos, *Level 2 Trading Warfare* and *Beating the Bear.*

Russell Lockhart, Ph.D. is primary instructor and technical analyst at undergroundtrader.com. A Jungian psychoanalyst in private practice for nearly 30 years, Dr. Lockhart has held faculty positions at UC Santa Barbara, UCLA Neuropshychiatric Institute, UC Berkeley, and other institutions. He is author of the online Hints & Helps for the Active Trader, *The Owl* newsletter, and trading articles such as "New Light On Candles" in Chartpoint.